THE U.S.-MEXICAN
BORDER TODAY

Latin American Silhouettes
Series Editors: William H. Beezley and Judith Ewell

LATIN AMERICAN SILHOUETTES

Recent Titles in the Series

For a complete listing of titles, visit https://rowman.com/Action/ SERIES/_/LTA.

THE U.S.-MEXICAN BORDER TODAY

Conflict and Cooperation in Historical Perspective

Third Edition

PAUL GANSTER

with David E. Lorey

ROWMAN & LITTLEFIELD
Lanham • Boulder • New York • London

Published by Rowman & Littlefield
A wholly owned subsidiary of The Rowman & Littlefield Publishing Group, Inc.
4501 Forbes Boulevard, Suite 200, Lanham, Maryland 20706
www.rowman.com

Unit A, Whitacre Mews, 26-34 Stannary Street, London SE11 4AB,
United Kingdom

Copyright © 2016 by Rowman & Littlefield
First edition 1999. Second edition 2007.

All photographs by Paul Ganster unless otherwise noted.
All maps prepared by Harry Johnson.

British Library Cataloguing in Publication Information Available

Library of Congress Cataloging-in-Publication Data

Ganster, Paul, author.
  [U.S.-Mexican border into the twenty-first century]
  The U.S.-Mexican border today : conflict and cooperation in historical perspective
/ Paul Ganster with David E. Lorey. — Third edition.
      pages cm. — (Latin American silhouettes)
  Includes bibliographical references and index.
  ISBN 978-1-4422-3110-8 (cloth : alk. paper) — ISBN 978-1-4422-3111-5 (pbk. :
alk. paper) — ISBN 978-1-4422-3112-2 (electronic) 1. Mexican-American Border
Region—History—21st century. 2. Mexican-American Border Region—History—
20th century. 3. United States—Relations—Mexico. 4. Mexico—Relations—
United States. I. Lorey, David E. II. Title.
  F787.G36 2016
  972'.1—dc23
                                                                    2015014338

∞™ The paper used in this publication meets the minimum requirements of
American National Standard for Information Sciences—Permanence of Paper
for Printed Library Materials, ANSI/NISO Z39.48-1992.

Printed in the United States of America

CONTENTS

ILLUSTRATIONS

MAPS

FIGURES

PHOTOGRAPHS

TABLES

ACKNOWLEDGMENTS

We extend our appreciation to those who contributed to this work in one way or another. Harry Johnson prepared the maps. Jan Thurman helped update a number of the tables. Bertha Hernández provided helpful comments on editorial and content issues. Elizabeth Eklund provided useful suggestions for the revisions. Bill Beasley and Judy Ewell were very helpful in providing guidance and suggestions for this new edition, as were two anonymous reviewers. Discussions with colleagues in Mexico helped clarify many issues related to the complex history and development of this dynamic border region. These experts include David Piñera, Antonio Padilla, José Luis Castro, Carlos de la Parra, Laurie Silvan, Andre Williams, Juan José Cabuto, Carlos Graizbord, Gabriela Muñoz, Margarito Quintero, and Walter Zúñiga. Likewise, U.S. colleagues Kimberly Collins, Christopher Brown, Steve Mumme, Dave Fege, Doug Liden, Héctor Vanegas, Elsa Saxod, Francisco Lara, Rick Van Schoik, Jim Peach, Oscar Martínez, Andy Carey, Mike Wilken, Jenny Quintana, Al Sweedler, Héctor Vanegas, Margaret Wilder, and Ricardo Martínez freely shared their thoughts and observations. Finally, scholars from different regions of the world who visited the California–Baja California border region and elsewhere along the U.S.-Mexican border have provided us with new insights. These include David Newman from Israel, Akihiro Iwashita from Japan, Martin van der Velde and Freerk Boedeltje from the Netherlands, Ana Marleny Bustamante from Venezuela, Pertti Joenneimi and Jussi Laine from Finland, and Anne-Laure Amilhat-Szary from France.

PREFACE

The U.S.-Mexican Border in Global Context

As we note in our collection of readings published in 2004, *Borders and Border Politics in a Globalizing World*, the continued importance and divisiveness of borders throughout the world present an intriguing paradox for the twenty-first century. Globalization is proceeding everywhere at an astounding pace, merging economies and cultures through world trade, regional economic integration, new forms of mass media carried into hundreds of millions of homes by cable, satellite, and the Internet, and ever more mobile populations. And yet, at the same time, political borders separating peoples remain pervasive and problematic. Rather than being purposefully erased by humans or dissolving of their own accord as other boundaries between economies and cultures are weakened, borders between nations, cultures, and ethnicities appear to be as strong as ever—and are perhaps growing stronger.

We have become convinced that, in the twenty-first century, humankind will face mounting challenges at both international borders and at subnational boundaries where human populations meet in conflict, challenges that will demand responses from regional, national, and multilateral governments and authorities. Challenges will range from resolving political conflict and managing migrant flows to dealing with transboundary environmental issues such as toxic-waste disposal, air pollution, and the overuse and pollution of freshwater resources. The varied effects of global climate change will likewise have ramifications for border regions and the interface of adjacent political and social systems. The most serious of these many border-related issues will be those that have the potential to lead to deadly conflict within regions, war between nation-states or ethnic groups, public health crises, and irreversible decline of natural ecosystems.

We can begin to prepare for these challenges, which will affect people far from borders as well as those who live in close proximity, by seeking to better understand the complexities of border regions—how they function, how they can become dysfunctional, how they create tensions, and why they demand cooperation. In this volume, we present a survey of the historical development, current politics, and daily life of the U.S.-Mexican border region. In this preface, we seek to place the U.S.-Mexican border, briefly, in the wider global context in order to provide a broader perspective for the themes and issues we cover. As the single best documented and most thoroughly studied case of a border region, the U.S.-Mexican border is the best-known illustration of the paradoxical continued importance of borders in our globalizing world.

There are many ways in which the U.S.-Mexican border provides a paradigmatic case of global border development. We will proceed here by very briefly sketching a list of what we see as ten of the most significant characteristics that are shared by the vast majority of borders and border regions. The following chapters on the long-term historical development of the U.S.-Mexican border flesh out these and other unique and important border characteristics.

First, even if borders occasionally appear to follow the natural features of a landscape, they are fundamentally human constructs. This fact is most obvious in the case of walls, both ancient and modern. Hadrian's Wall, for example, was constructed in the early centuries of the Common Era by the Romans across one of the narrowest points of Great Britain in order to control the marauding tribes to the north and thereby provide stability for the Roman province of Britannia to the south. The Great Wall of China, another defensive structure designed to protect the Chinese Empire from neighbors to the north, extended more than thirteen thousand miles and took centuries to complete. The Berlin Wall, built beginning in 1961 to separate the Soviet-controlled portion of Berlin from that controlled by the United States and its allies, symbolized the division of Europe into two spheres during the Cold War (1945–1989); its destruction in 1989 symbolized the end of the Cold War and the fall of Soviet socialism. More recently, Israel and the United States have installed formidable structures along parts of their borders to deter unauthorized immigrants, smuggling, and terrorist activities. Water boundaries perhaps best highlight the negative impacts and insensitive nature of human-made borders. Rivers, although frequently used to demarcate boundaries between people, represent the approximate middle of vast watersheds that are, in fact, best managed as single entities.

Second, given the arbitrary nature that stems from their human construction, borders rarely make clear and simple divisions between or among peoples. Goods, services, and people flow across borders in spite of the division they imply. Interestingly, the people who live at and along borders

The port of entry from Tijuana to San Diego at San Ysidro, where most pedestrian and passenger vehicle crossings take place. On a typical weekday in 2005, more than two hundred cars were in line waiting to cross, with delay times of an hour or more. By early 2015, new lanes and other infrastructure significantly reduced pedestrian and vehicle wait times for northbound crossings. 2005.

tend to ignore them when that serves their interests and to take advantage of their existence when that is more convenient. The most obvious example of this is transboundary trading, where both merchants and consumers become extremely savvy about short-term and short-distance variations in prices created by a border.[1] Similarly, regular and customary transboundary population movements also show people taking advantage of, and thriving in, situations of created boundaries. At the U.S.-Mexican border, for example, only a tiny percentage of the people crossing the border on a regular basis do so without proper authorization; yet this percentage frequently constitutes the only border story deemed worth reporting in the mass media of both Mexico and the United States. Compared to the dozens or hundreds who may cross illegally every night, approximately forty thousand people cross from Tijuana to San Diego to work every day, and another eighty thousand cross to shop, visit friends and family, or enjoy the many attractions of the San Diego and Southern California region. There were more than 170 million legal crossings each way in 2014.[2] Ironically, then, borders generally bring people together at the same time that they separate them.

Third, borders and the border regions they define tend to be very diverse along their length and from one region to another, with different areas showing different realities.[3] Border scholar Oscar Martínez has identified four "ideal types" of borderlands. First, we can identify *alienated borderlands*, border regions in which transboundary exchange is either nonexistent or very modest, principally due to animosity between peoples on both sides of a border. The second ideal type is what Martínez terms *coexistent borderlands*. Here, relations between peoples on either side of a border are characterized by regular contact and generally friendly relations between two polities. In the third type that Martínez describes, *interdependent borderlands*, peoples on both sides of the border are involved in a symbiotic relationship characterized by significant flow of goods, services, and people across the boundary. In Martínez's fourth ideal type, *integrated borderlands*, practically all barriers to trade and human movement have been eliminated.[4] One of the great advantages of Martínez's typology is that it can be applied to both international borders and various other sorts of borders, including those between ethnicities and religious groups. The typology works well, for instance, in comparing and contrasting the very different kinds of borders between the French and English (across a so-called natural water boundary), between the English and the Scots or Welsh, and between English-speaking Protestants and Catholics in Northern Ireland.

Fourth, borders are hardly ever static for long. Borders have distinct histories, emerging and becoming more rigid over time and then eventually disappearing or even reemerging through a process of rebordering. Borders made by humans existed before the emergence of nation-states and, apparently, can exist just fine when nation-states are suppressed. The European Union is an excellent example of this latter point: a unified western Europe now struggles not so much over internal boundaries as with the incorporation of new members—eastern European and other countries beyond the borders of the present union. However, even within the European Union, new borders have emerged, as in the case of the blue line separating the northern Turkish and southern Greek portions of the island nation of Cyprus. Although borders are established for distinct purposes, their creation and development frequently have unexpected and unintended consequences. As we will see, the U.S.-Mexican border region is an excellent example of how the historical process of border development can unfold and how, in a relatively short period, major transformations can take place.

Generalizing—and there are many exceptions—we can identify a three-part chronology shared by many borders. First, a frontier period, or a period of multiple, interpenetrating frontiers, lasts from first contact between peoples to the point where contact becomes a mixing process. Second, a borderlands era, during which peoples intermix and interact without attention to or from national powers, develops. Third, there is a period during which a distinct border region is formed with clearly demarcated boundaries and definable social and political responses to the boundary. In addition to these three periods of border development, we might add a fourth stage of dissolution. In the long run, many borders are erased or dissolved. Although we tend to think of borders as being immutably fixed in time, in fact the most common ultimate outcome for an individual border is its eventual dissolution.[5]

Fifth, border regions are diverse within. Economic, social, political, and cultural borders frequently fall in different places. As a result, there are generally subregions within a given border area that only relate loosely to international or interethnic boundaries. U.S.-Mexican border phenomena are now experienced as far from the international boundary as Chicago, New York, and Atlanta.[6] To deal with this complexity, Michiel Baud and Willem Van Schendel have identified three essential regional units of analysis for border study. One is the *border heartland*, which abuts the border and is dominated by its existence and where social networks are shared directly by the border. A second category is that of the *intermediate borderland*, a region that feels the influence of the border but in intensities ranging from moderate to weak. Finally, there is an *outer borderland*, which only under specific circumstances feels the effects of an international or interethnic border.[7] The long-term trend favors border regions that continue to expand in social, cultural, and psychological senses. Social networks are created and cultural patterns established that constantly shift the boundaries of the border world outward.

Sixth, borders everywhere are characterized by amazing social complexity. In *Border People* Oscar Martínez has developed a schema for understanding the complex social landscape of the U.S.-Mexican border world that is also useful for understanding other borders, both national and subnational. Martínez includes in his typology the following groups: transient migrants (people residing only briefly in the border region), newcomers (people newly arrived in the border region), nationalists (long-term residents of the border who purposefully do not partake of the culture of the other side of the international boundary), uniculturalists (people who live wholly in the culture of one side or the other of the border), binational consumers (persons whose main experience of the other side of the border is commercial), settler migrants (people who move to the border region and remain for a long time), commuters (people who move back and forth across the border on a regular—frequently daily—basis to work), biculturalists (persons, generally bilingual, who have roots and live adult lives on both sides of the border), binationalists (people, frequently businesspeople and professionals, who live and do business on both sides of the border, operating at a very high level of transboundary social integration), and permanent residents (people, frequently retirees, who live permanently on the other side of the border).

Seventh, border politics are easily as complex as border social realities. Baud and Van Schendel provide a useful typology of border politics. The *quiet borderland* is one in which nations, regional elites, and local populations are combined into a coherent power structure with relatively low tension. Territorial control by either state does not lead to major confrontations in the borderlands. The Dutch-Belgian borderland since 1830 can be termed harmonious, while the border between North and South Korea since 1953 is an enforced version of the quiet borderland. An *unruly borderland* exists when power structures are less coherent and neither the state nor the regional elite has established a commanding position over local border populations. Local people resist the new social and territorial boundaries and the rules that come with them. The authority of the regional elite is sometimes weakened because it serves as an agent of the national state rather than a protector of local rights and concerns. Northern Ireland is a classic case of an unruly borderland, where in the late 1960s a Protestant elite backed by the British state lost its ability to control a local population. Finally, we can speak of *rebellious borderlands*, where regional elites side with local populations against national states that seek to impose authority on the border. Rebellions can be regionalist, separatist, or irredentist in their objectives. An example of a rebellious borderland is the golden triangle straddling the borders of China, Laos, Thailand, and Burma, where various guerrilla groups have been fighting state armies and each other for decades in attempts to establish separate states. Complicating this typology is the fact that different sides of the border can fall into different categories: for example, one side of the border can be quiet while the other is rebellious—for instance, the Yugoslav (Kosovo)/Albanian borderland in the 1980s.[8]

Eighth, borders are the central flashpoint for social and political conflicts over migration, immigration policy, and migrant rights throughout the world. Migration across borders is occurring everywhere at an unprecedented pace. Political unrest, famines and drought, the effects of climate change, economic disparities, shifting labor markets, demographic trends, improved communications and transportation, and globalization of the economy have all contributed to increasing flows of people from poor areas to less poor areas. Nations with expanding populations and little economic opportunity see tens of thousands of their citizens cross borders in search of better lives in more developed countries. Every highly developed country is faced with significant flows of legal and undocumented, or unauthorized, immigrants that are exacerbated by regional political unrest, pandemics, and natural disasters. No country has developed completely adequate or uncontroversial policies for coping with this flow of humanity that impacts both the sending and the receiving nations and is most clearly evident in border areas.

Ninth, border regions are frequently found far from the center of the nations. They are divided, created, administered, and maintained by outsiders in places distant from the borders. National institutions, indeed institutions in general, are often weak in border regions, and border peoples are frequently economically and politically marginalized from the life of the nations of which they are citizens. Border people feel that central authorities impose arbitrary policies without consulting local opinion and that national priorities are not always borderland priorities. Moreover, imposed national policies often have unintended consequences for border residents. This factor impedes finding solutions for problems that develop along borders and also hampers the implementation of policy designed at a distance.

Tenth, negative stereotypes are frequently held about border regions, stereotypes that often linger long after reality has changed. The U.S.-Mexican border, for example, has long been the subject of negative stereotypes by both the United States and Mexico. The 1920s saw the border depicted as a haven for gambling, prostitution, and vice, an image that has continued while other layers have been added. In the 1980s and 1990s, the border was frequently decried as a center of worker exploitation in assembly plants (maquiladoras), serious environmental problems, and out-of-control urban growth. The flow of illicit drugs across the border to consumers in the United States has produced the perception of a region characterized by drug wars and corruption. These stereotypes have been widely disseminated by Mexican cinema as well as by Hollywood. After the September 11, 2001, terrorist attacks on New York and Washington, D.C., the perception that the U.S.-Mexican border was porous and a threat to U.S. national security was transformed into a widely held stereotype. This occurred despite the fact that there is no specific evidence to support the theory that the southern border is a security threat.

As practical and political issues related to globalization and borders have grown and evolved over the first decade and a half of the twenty-first century, the formal study of borders has expanded remarkably. Modern border studies emerged beginning in the 1970s in a systematic and multidisciplinary fashion addressing the characteristics of the border between the United States and Mexico. Centered in a number of universities in the Midwest and scattered along the border and at emerging research centers in Mexico, the new discipline of border studies was organized in the Association for Borderlands Studies (ABS) and its annual professional meetings and research publication, *Journal of Borderland Studies.*[9] Initially largely devoted to research from many

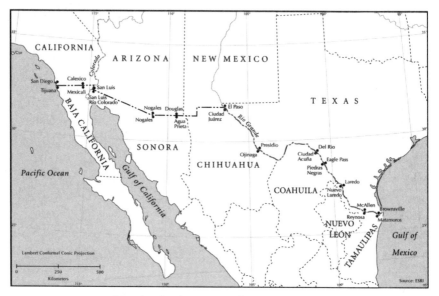

Map 1.   Border states and major twin cities.

disciplines on the U.S.-Mexican border, the ABS annual meetings, especially from the 1990s, began to include more participation from Mexico, Canada, Africa, and Europe, a shift in geographical focus that is also reflected in pages of the journal. By 2014, the ABS president was from the Netherlands, the president elect was from Japan, the vice president was from Mexico, the past president was from Canada, and the secretariat was located in Finland. The first ABS world conference was held in the spring of 2014 in the Finnish-Russian borderlands and had strong participation from North America, Africa, Asia, and Europe. Networks of border researchers are emerging in Africa, Asia, and Latin America.

The inclusion of new geographical regions and more disciplines has significantly enriched the study of borderlands, which can be noted by an explosion of publications on world border regions. The engagement of new institutions and scholars has significantly enriched the disciplinary, method-ological, and theoretical approaches to border studies. It has also stimulated comparative border studies and efforts to develop general and specific theories on borders and border regions.

It is an inescapable fact of twenty-first-century life that our global village is characterized by walls that one cannot climb and by streets that one had better not cross. Readers of this book in their teens, twenties, and thirties are very likely to be directly affected by the continued prominence of borders. As noted at the beginning of this preface, we hope that this volume will raise awareness and inform readers that we may better resolve the challenges posed by borders of the future. Humans will face tremendous challenges along the borders that unite and divide them in the twenty-first century, and the solutions will not be obvious or easy. We present this survey of the historical context of the contemporary U.S.-Mexican border to shed light both on how border conflicts arise and how they can be creatively and productively addressed.

NOTES

1. Michiel Baud and Willem Van Schendel, "Toward a Comparative History of Borderlands," *Journal of World History* 8, no. 2 (fall 1997): 211–42. Much of the discussion that follows here draws heavily on this important article. See also Norris Clement, "International Transboundary Collaboration: A Policy-Oriented Conceptual Framework," in *Cooperation, Environment, and Sustainability in Border Regions*, ed. Paul Ganster (San Diego, CA: San Diego State University Press, 2001), 17–31.

2. "Border Crossing/Entry Data: Query Detailed Statistics," Bureau of Transportation Statistics, http://transborder.bts.gov/programs/international/transborder/TBDR_BC/TBDR_BCQ.html.

3. See the December 2014 special issue of the *Journal of Borderlands Studies* (29, no. 4), titled "The Multiple US-Mexico Borders," which addresses many of the regional differences encountered along the length of the border.

4. Oscar J. Martínez, *Border People: Life and Society in the U.S.-Mexico Borderlands* (Tucson: University of Arizona Press, 1994), 5–10.

5. See Ellwyn R. Stoddard, "Frontiers, Borders, and Border Segmentation: Toward a Conceptual Clarification," *Journal of Borderlands Studies* 6, no. 1 (spring 1990): 1–22. See also the five stages of growth identified by Baud and Van Schendel, "Toward a Comparative History of Borderlands," 223–25.

6. The fastest growth of Mexico-origin population in the 1990s was experienced in the nonborder states of Oregon (55 percent growth between 1990 and 1996), Nevada (77 percent), Nebraska (70 percent), Iowa (52 percent), Arkansas (104 percent), Tennessee (58 percent), Georgia (70 percent), North Carolina (73 percent), and Vermont (55 percent). See Edwin Garcia and Ben Stocking, "Latinos on the Move to a New Promised Land," *San Jose Mercury News*, August 16, 1998. Also see Rakesh Kochhar, Roberto Suro, and Sonya Tafoya, "The New Latino South: The Context and Consequences of Rapid Population Growth," Pew Hispanic Center Report, July 28, 2005, www.pewhispanic.org.

7. Baud and Van Schendel, "Toward a Comparative History of Borderlands," 221–22.

8. Baud and Van Schendel, "Toward a Comparative History of Borderlands," 227–29.

9. Information about the ABS and the journal can be found at the association's website (http://www. absborderlands.org).

INTRODUCTION

Defining the Region, Objectives, and Approaches

The two-thousand-mile international boundary between the United States and Mexico gives shape to a unique economic, social, and cultural entity. The U.S.-Mexican border region has the distinction of being the only place in the world where a highly developed country and a developing nation meet and interact. The complex history of the economy and society of this border makes it a fascinating region to study.

At the end of the nineteenth century, the U.S.-Mexican border region was a vaguely defined territory in which sparse populations, separated by an international boundary, came into uncertain contact. With a few exceptions, the border neither attracted much notice nor caused much alarm. Undefined for most of its length, the boundary presented little inconvenience to residents of the states that abutted it. More than a century later, however, the demarcating line defines a region in which "two different civilizations face each other and overlap."[1] During a century of rapid and dramatic change in both the United States and Mexico, the border has come to unite as well as divide the two countries and their historical experiences. By the second decade of the twenty-first century, the boundary was, paradoxically, both more and less intrusive than it had been at the beginning of the twentieth century.

The border region emerged over the course of the twentieth century and the first years of the twenty-first century as a place of pressing concern for local, regional, and national leaders. In particular, after the United States and Mexico implemented the North American Free Trade Agreement (NAFTA) beginning in 1994 to confront the economic blocs of Europe and the Far East, the area became a central stage in the international politico-economic theater. Integration, which has tended to express itself most dramatically along the international boundary, brings with it a wide array of economic, social, and political challenges for border residents, scholars and students, and poli-

1

cymakers. Most recently, the issue of U.S. national security has brought more challenges for border residents, as policies imposed by the federal government have generated significant inconveniences such as excessive delays crossing the border and economic costs borne by local border communities. Deportation of large numbers of unauthorized migrants by U.S. authorities to Mexican border towns has produced severe social and economic impacts mainly on the south side of the border.

The border region is characterized by a binational economy of astounding complexity. It has seen rapid transformation in a short span of time, changing from a cattle ranching and mining area that attracted U.S., Mexican, and European capitalists in the late nineteenth century to the center of a lucrative vice- and pleasure-based tourist industry, to a region that, after World War II, attracted an extraordinary amount of international capital to its manufacturing and services sector. To complicate matters further, the border economy has always been characterized by convulsive booms and busts.

After World War II, the U.S. border states emerged as international leaders in aerospace, defense-related, and high-tech innovations. On the Mexican side of the boundary, assembly plants, generally known as *maquilas* or maquiladoras and established beginning in the mid-1960s, accounted for as much as 55 percent of Mexico's manufactured exports and 45 percent of all exports by 2006. In several subregions along the international boundary, the border economy is the only economy. People crossing from Tijuana to the San Diego region spend $3 billion each year on products and services, while economic leaders from the two communities team up to jointly market the "Cali Baja Bi-National Mega-Region" and to organize trade missions to invite global production facilities to the border region of California and Baja California.[2] Likewise, business leaders and the El Paso city government have ambitiously branded the El Paso–Ciudad Juárez region as the "world's largest international border metroplex" and vigorously tout its advantages for investment and trade.[3]

The border region, also socially complex, is characterized by a tremendous movement of people, both short term and permanent, within and between Mexico and the United States. It is useful to reiterate that, of all persons who cross the border from the South to the North, only a tiny percentage do so illegally, mass media reports notwithstanding. In 2005, more than 235 million legal entrants crossed across the land border into the United States from Mexico, and many were Mexican shoppers whose expenditures are important for U.S. border communities. These shoppers in 2005 had a total impact of $8.8 billion, with over $1 billion generated in the form of taxes. These expenditures by Mexican shoppers help support more than 150,000 jobs in U.S.

border communities. These Mexican visitors mostly do not use U.S. public services.[4] *The U.S.-Mexican Border Today* focuses primarily on the large numbers of people who live on both sides of the border, move back and forth legally, and constitute the great majority of border residents.

Although the number of illegal Mexican crossers was small, the cumulative effect was large. During the 1990s onward, the combination of insufficient job creation in the Mexican economy and increased border enforcement meant that fewer Mexican undocumented workers returned to Mexico each year as seasonal migrants, and more brought their families to live with them in the United States. Thus, the population of unauthorized Mexican immigrants living in the United States mushroomed. By 2002, one in every two Mexican immigrants was undocumented; 5.3 million unauthorized immigrants from Mexico were living in the United States, and most had arrived since 1990. By March 2005, that figure had increased to 6.2 million, and it peaked at 6.9 million in 2007.[5] By 2010, the number of unauthorized Mexicans in the United States had fallen, due to the U.S. recession and other factors, to 6.2 million, where it remained or declined slightly through 2011.[6] By 2014, for the first time, more non–Mexicans than Mexicans were apprehended trying to enter the United States along the southern border.[7]

The border society that has emerged over time as a result of massive population relocations is distinct from that of either the United States or Mexico; it is both an amalgam of the two and something entirely different from either. The border's social matrix is perhaps best perceived in its cities, large and small, which dot the landscape of the region. According to the 2010 Mexican census, Ciudad Juárez was the fifth-largest urban conglomeration in Mexico; Tijuana was the seventh largest. The Paso del Norte region (Juárez municipality and counties of El Paso, Texas, and Otero and Doña Ana, New Mexico) had a 2013 population of 2.5 million divided into two moieties by the international boundary. The greater binational metropolitan area of the Tijuana municipality and San Diego County had 4.9 million residents by 2013. In towns all along the border, binational Rotary clubs meet weekly, alternating countries. Calexico and Mexicali cooperate on firefighting and providing emergency medical services; El Paso and Ciudad Juárez cooperate on policing the drug trade. San Diego and Tijuana now cooperate on transportation and land use planning. Given the size and complexity of these binational urbanized areas, it is surprising that transborder cooperation is not more institutionalized in order to address growing problems and opportunities.

The culture of contemporary border peoples is extraordinarily rich. Originally inhabited by a great diversity of indigenous populations, the area was later populated by Europeans, people of African origin, Native American

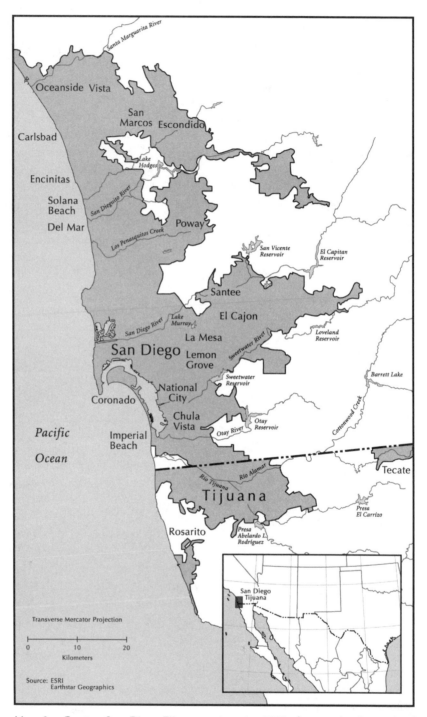

Map 2. Greater San Diego–Tijuana region. In 2005 the transborder regional population of San Diego County and the municipalities of Tijuana, Rosarito, and Tecate was 4.5 million.

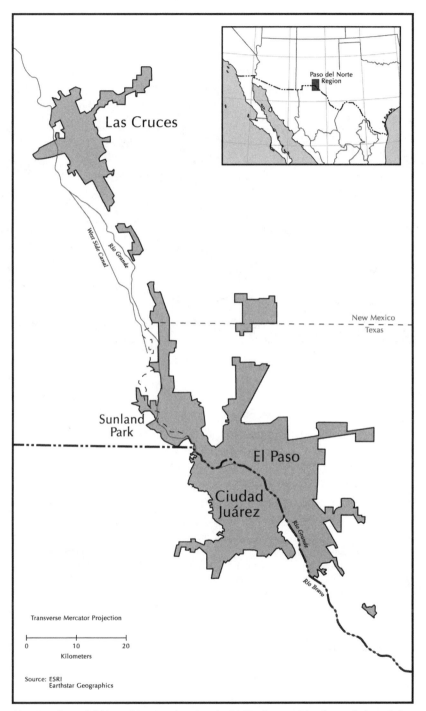

Map 3. Paso del Norte binational region. In 2005, the combined population of the municipality of Juárez and the counties of El Paso and Doña Ana was 2.2 million people.

The border fence enters the Pacific Ocean at the border between San Diego and Tijuana. Border Field State Park and the Tijuana Estuary are on the U.S. side; the Playas de Tijuana bullring is on the Mexican side. 2005.

migrants from central Mexico, Asians, and persons of mixed ethnicity. The culture that developed from the experience of these various border peoples (and the progeny resulting from their interaction in the region) is unique. The international boundary is a place where the English and Spanish languages are increasingly blended, bilingualism flourishes, and multiculturalism is a fact of daily life. In 2002, 31 percent of the residents of San Diego County spoke Spanish, and 24 percent of the residents of the greater Tijuana region spoke English.[8] Elsewhere along the international boundary, the majority of inhabitants in the U.S. part of the twin city speak Spanish.

The region hosts a dizzying array of transborder cultural phenomena. Television and radio stations, whether broadcasting in English or Spanish, draw advertising revenue from businesses on both sides of the border; flags are raised on both sides on September 16, Mexico's Independence Day; and, on Thanksgiving Day, relatives travel from the U.S. side to eat turkey dinners with their families across the boundary. Distinct border styles of music, literature, and painting have emerged. Border phenomena have spread farther than most people realize: Mexican-style salsa, for example, has replaced ketchup

The border to the east of the San Ysidro (San Diego)–Tijuana border crossing. The single fence or steel wall has now been replaced in the San Diego region and other dense urban border areas with multiple fences, several access roads for the Border Patrol, stadium lighting, and video cameras and other technology to detect illicit crossings. 2006.

as the most popular table condiment in the United States; Corona beer has become the leading imported brew in the United States (ahead of Heineken); and Mexican piñatas are ritually demolished at children's birthday parties throughout North America.

Perhaps at least partly because of this great diversity and complexity, many myths about the region exist, and mythmaking continues. Often U.S. citizens, even those who live in the border region, perceive the area in terms of undocumented migration, drug trafficking, and decaying cities. Some feel they have lost control of "their" border. One observer summarizes the popular images as follows: "The border is drowning in the filth of a putrescent Rio Grande aglow with toxic wastes; it is terminally ill with the rampant pox of poverty known as *colonias* [illegal and irregular settlements on the U.S. side of the border]; it is a land of social injustice where evil foreign *maquiladoras* unmercifully exploit downtrodden workers for their cheap labor; swarms of huddling illegals poise nightly to pour northward across the border to overwhelm American social services and steal jobs from honest workers while free-loading on the largess of hard-pressed American taxpayers."[9]

Frequently accompanying such conceptions are stereotyped, monochromatic characterizations of Mexicans, Texans, Californians, and border society in general. During the NAFTA debate in 1992, presidential candidate Ross Perot summed up the perceptions of many observers when he portrayed the border region as "one large slum." The area, with its long history of vice-based tourism, continues to be seen as a den of sin and iniquity, catering to prostitution, drinking, corruption, drugs, and gambling for both Mexicans and U.S. citizens. The border has also come to be closely identified with its economic boom; the maquiladora assembly plants and sophisticated manufacturing facilities have taken the place of casinos and brothels in the litany of abuses allegedly perpetrated upon border people. Some observers have come to see the larger boundary-development model—relocation of production in line with global trends, freer trade—as the epitome of all that can go wrong in the new global economy. Negative stereotypes of the border held throughout the United States were reinforced by the national security preoccupation after September 11, 2001, and by the rising violence in Mexican border cities during the last decade largely linked to drug trafficking to meet the insatiable demand in the United States.

Without denying poverty, corruption, drugs, decay, pollution, or unequal distribution of wealth, this study endeavors to demonstrate that such characterizations of the region obscure more than they reveal. Recognizing that there is some basis for the images that predominate in public discourse about the border, this volume explores the complex causes and consequences of such phenomena. The reality is far more interesting than popular myths and stereotypes suggest.

Part of the challenge of studying the border region stems from the difficulty of defining the scope of the geographical and temporal area to be covered. Where and what is the U.S.-Mexican border region? Why does it merit attention as a separate entity? In contrast to most regions, its defining boundary runs through it rather than around it. And that boundary was not determined by geography; it was invented by two warring nation-states, which established it a century and a half ago in a region that neither ever completely dominated. It is administered today by outsiders in distant Mexico City and Washington, D.C.

The border region can be defined in two basic ways. From the Mexican viewpoint it is that area of the Spanish and Mexican far-northern frontier where Europeans and Mexicans of mixed ethnicity encountered and settled among indigenous Americans, a region stretching from the Gulf of Mexico to the Pacific Ocean. From the U.S. perspective it is the contiguous section of the continent acquired by the United States, beginning with the Louisiana

A monument marks the international border near Lochiel, Arizona, east of Nogales. A simple cattle fence delineated the boundary in this rural area of the border in 2005. It has now been replaced with a Normandy-style vehicle barrier to prevent vehicle crossing. 2005.

Purchase in 1803; continuing with the acquisition of Texas, the Oregon Territory, and the Mexican cession of 1848; and ending with the 1853 Gadsden Purchase of the lands between the Gila River and the present Mexican boundary. With much justice, the region is sometimes called MexAmerica. The moniker is appealing because it is accurate: the border region is perhaps best defined in general terms as the area—economic, social, and cultural—where Mexico and the United States have overlapped and interacted for more than 150 years.

Because of the vague limits of the territory and the shifting boundary, we define the region, when necessary, using the simple, if anachronistic, concept of traditional political and administrative units. The statistical data in the following chapters generally refer to the ten border states in the United States and Mexico: California, Arizona, New Mexico, and Texas; Baja California, Sonora, Chihuahua, Coahuila, Nuevo León, and Tamaulipas.[10] The area included in this definition—covering 960,000 square miles—is considerably larger than western Europe. In addition, some of the data refer to those U.S. counties and Mexican municipalities that are on or very near the international

Border fence in east San Diego County, near the rural community of Jacumba, serves mainly to prevent vehicles from crossing the border. This construction also enables floodwaters produced by winter rains to flow across the border unimpeded. 2004.

boundary. These data sets include the fourteen U.S. and Mexican border twin cities that lie within the border counties and municipalities.

It is also necessary to make a temporal division. Drawing on the long and complex history of the region, we make the following chronological distinctions: (1) a frontier period, or a period of multiple, interpenetrating frontiers, lasting from contact between Europeans and Native Americans to the end of the colonial years; (2) a borderlands era from 1803 through Mexican independence in 1821 to the end of the U.S.-Mexican war in 1848; and (3) the years since 1848, for which a distinct U.S.-Mexican border region can be clearly identified. This third period is divided into two parts: 1848 to the 1880s (after which the railroad linked the area to world markets for border products) and the 1880s to the present (from the first major economic boom along the boundary to the regulated integration accelerated by NAFTA a century later). The bulk of this book focuses on the last stretch, from the 1880s to the time of publication. Chapter 1 briefly reviews the previous epochs.[11]

In both geographical and temporal terms, however, the definition of the region must remain flexible. Economic, social, political, and cultural borders fall in different places; there are subregions of the border world that relate only loosely to state boundaries. For example, border phenomena are experienced as far from the international boundary as the cities of Chicago and New York and the states of Washington, Oregon, and Colorado in the United States and Sinaloa, Durango, Jalisco, and Yucatán in Mexico, where maquiladora production has pulled people into the border world.[12] The long-term trend is that the region continues to grow socially, culturally, and psychologically. Social networks are created and cultural patterns established that constantly shift the boundaries of the border world outward. This book does not attempt to force the history of the border region to conform to what have become the standard periodizations for U.S. and Mexican history, for that history does not easily fall into these divisions. Instead, the focus on major economic and social currents in border history brings to light unusual and sometimes overlapping time frames.

In the region so defined, there is much to study that is unique to it and directly attributable to the existence of the international boundary. The economies of the region and its inhabitants share a common history of boom-and-bust cycles, migration within and between nation-states, and intense sociocultural blending and assimilation. In the sense that border phenomena are increasingly prevalent and increasingly shared, these aspects of the area, which are endlessly fascinating to scholars and students, become more and more relevant to all of us who live in North America.

A major challenge in writing a primer on the modern border is the legacy of past treatments of the area. Until recently, historians have not focused on the unique characteristics of the U.S.-Mexican border region's evolution. Following a traditional, national approach, they have given separate treatment to the histories of the northern states of Mexico and the southwestern portion of the United States, or the U.S. West. Only during the last two decades of the twentieth century did the field of border history come into its own. Now, in addition to their own work in archives and local collections, historians of the international boundary are being influenced by the work of border scholars in a diverse array of natural and social sciences, as they uncover a wealth of new sources and approach them with new methodologies to shed light on the complex past and present of the transboundary area.

A certain quantity of ideological baggage also has shaped the field. Scholars and other observers have tended to view the border region alternately as a model for U.S.-Mexican economic integration and for U.S.-Mexican relations and as an example of all the negative aspects of unchecked economic

Three Ways to Define the Extent of the U.S.-Mexican Border

Maps 4 through 6 show three different ways to think of the border region, reflecting different criteria used by government officials and researchers to define the border. Map 4 depicts the border as defined in the 1983 U.S.-Mexican La Paz border environmental agreement that establishes an arbitrary zone of one hundred kilometers (approximately sixty miles) on each side of the international boundary. Map 5 employs a definition of the border based on the boundaries of natural systems—in this case the watersheds and subwatersheds—that cross the border. Map 6 shows the administrative boundaries of the U.S. border counties and Mexican border municipalities that abut the international boundary. Since many of the basic statistics on the border region are collected on the basis of these local administrative units, including data for all of the border's twin cities, Map 6 can be thought of as the most common official view of the border.

Other options for defining the border include employing the boundaries of the ten border states, a definition used for

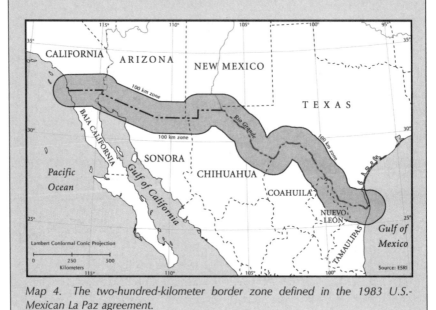

Map 4. The two-hundred-kilometer border zone defined in the 1983 U.S.-Mexican La Paz agreement.

much of the analysis in this work, or the transnational urban areas constituted by border twin cities, as seen in Map 1. A definition based on the presence of Mexican-origin populations or Spanish-language usage would encompass most areas of both Mexico and the United States.

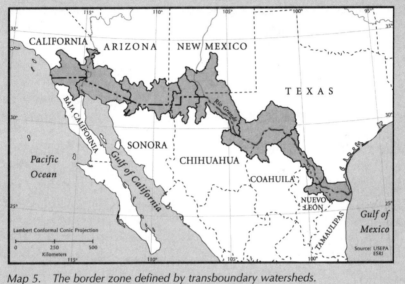

Map 5.   The border zone defined by transboundary watersheds.

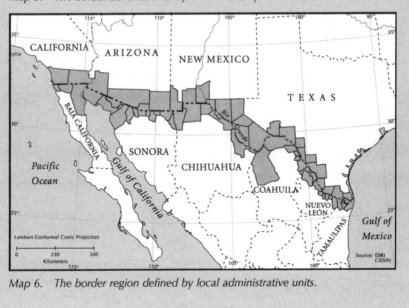

Map 6.   The border region defined by local administrative units.

growth and U.S.-Mexican interaction. Such normative judgments have colored their analyses. We suggest that the border be approached as a laboratory for the study of transboundary economic, social, and cultural phenomena in the new global economy. While the world economy has become more global in nature, it also has become more regional: the U.S.-Mexican boundary offers a unique window on this apparent paradox. To prejudge the trajectory or meaning of border history is to risk the loss of this valuable vantage point.

Drawing on the approaches and findings of recent historical research, this text focuses on social, economic, and cultural themes in the history of the border region from the last quarter of the nineteenth century to the early twenty-first century. Despite the importance of the ten border states to both the United States and Mexico, and for all the fascinating history of their interaction, we know very little about the most pressing dimensions of life and livelihood along the international boundary throughout the twentieth century and up to the present. *The U.S.-Mexican Border Today*, therefore, has three basic objectives: First, it seeks to treat the area as historically coherent. The chapters that follow adopt a region-centered focus, emphasizing crossboundary society, culture, and economic ties. Second, the book surveys the historical evolution of the region with an eye to the relationship between social and economic change, seeking to understand, for example, how booms and busts shaped border society. Third, this study considers historical change in the region as much as possible from the inside—that is, from the perspective of people who lived through and prompted the changes.

The overall approach adopted here is somewhat unusual. Topics are discussed sometimes narratively and sometimes analytically. Multiple perspectives are emphasized in order to explore the complexity of the region's past. No single ideological approach is forced on the reader because no single approach can adequately explain the evolution of border reality, and no magic paradigm can unlock the mysteries of the border's past and present. Instead, we draw on and combine diverse perspectives in an effort to contribute to an understanding of the boundary area.

This study uses macro-level approaches to explore the way in which the evolution of the border region has been shaped by outside phenomena and trends. The discussion includes world economic cycles, which have greatly affected the area. It is also sometimes useful to consider the border as an extension of nation-states, to see it as a focus of struggles between nations, and to view regional conflict and border policy issues accordingly. At another extreme, the book takes a micro-level approach to the exploration of border evolutions. The area has been characterized throughout its long history by an active and vibrant society that emerged despite the strong influence of external forces. Understanding local and subregional developments—particularly those that involve individuals and communities spanning the boundary—is as important as understanding external factors in explaining this history. Symbiotic and interdependent relationships in the region are also examined in order to analyze the developing links between the two societies and economies. Interconnectedness is a major aspect of the area's development. In particular, the historical experiences of U.S. and Mexican border towns illustrate how local border societies and economies developed over time. Through this approach it becomes evident that the historical interplay of exogenous and endogenous forces has given shape to the U.S.-Mexican boundary region and its social realities.

It is important to clarify what a book is not in addition to what it is. This study does not emphasize political issues or consider the national policymaking processes of Mexico or the United States in any direct way. Although it surveys the experiences of Mexican-origin populations in the border region, it is intended neither as a book about Mexican-origin peoples in the United States nor as a study of documented or undocumented migration. This is not a book about NAFTA or U.S.-Mexican relations at the strategic level, and it does not pretend to present histories of either the United States or Mexico more broadly during the period at hand. Each of these topics, though treated in the chapters that follow, is considered in the context of questions of major historical significance for the evolution of the U.S.-Mexican border region.

Perhaps the most general goal of this book is to advance the notion that the pressing issues facing North America must be addressed in a new regional context, a context that includes Mexico, the United States, and the boundary area that unites them. With their destinies now explicitly linked under NAFTA, the United States and Mexico will certainly face problems that the border region has struggled with since its creation. The fundamental challenge for the North American community is to develop multilateral and collaborative solutions to common difficulties; in fact, the long-term objective of thinking (on a personal level) and policymaking (on a social level) should be to overcome the U.S.-Mexican border. An understanding of the border region is essential to an understanding of the current shape of North America, the problems it faces, and the best way to meet future challenges.

NOTES

1. Stanley Robert Ross, *Views across the Border* (Albuquerque: University of New Mexico Press, 1978), xii.

2. San Diego Association of Governments, "Estimating Economic Impacts of Border Wait Times at the San Diego–Baja California Border Region," San Diego, 2004, www.sandag.org; Suad Ghaddar and Cynthia J. Brown, "The Economic Impact of Mexican Visitors along the U.S.-Mexico Border: A Research Synthesis" (working paper series, Center for Border Economic Studies, University of Texas–Pan America, December 2005); for information on the Cali Baja region, see "About the Region," San Diego Regional Economic Development Corporation, http://www.sandiego-business.org/region.

3. "International Bridges," City of El Paso, http://www.elpasotexas.gov/international-bridges.

4. Ghaddar and Brown, "The Economic Impact of Mexican Visitors."

5. In 1996 only 1.1 percent of the U.S. population comprised undocumented Mexican migrants; only 15 percent of the Mexican-origin population of the United States was in the country without authorization. See Frank D. Bean et al., "The Quantification of Migration between Mexico and the United States," *Binational Study of Migration between Mexico and the United States*, July 1997, 61. For more recent figures, see Jeffrey S. Passel, *Mexican Immigration to the US: The Latest Estimates* (Washington, D.C.: Migration Policy Institute, 2004); Jeffrey S. Passel, *The Size and Characteristics of the Unauthorized Migrant Population in the U.S.: Estimates Based on the March 2005 Current Population Survey* (Washington, D.C.: Pew Hispanic Center, March 7, 2006), http://www.pewhispanic.org.

6. Jeffrey S. Passel, D'Vera Cohn, and Ana Gonzalez-Barrera, "Population Decline of Unauthorized Immigrants Stalls, May Have Reversed," Pew Hispanic Center Report, September 23, 2013, http://www.pewhispanic.org.

7. Jens Manuel Krogstad and Jeffrey S. Passel, "U.S. Border Apprehensions of Mexicans Fall to Historic Lows," Fact Tank, Pew Research Center, December 30, 2014, http://pewrsr.ch/13HbZbn.

8. Institute for Regional Studies of the Californias, "Quality of Life in the Greater San Diego–Tijuana–Tecate–Playas de Rosarito Region" (unpublished report, San Diego, San Diego State University, 2002).

9. Timothy C. Brown, "The Fourth Member of NAFTA: The U.S.-Mexico Border," *Annals of the American Academy of Political and Social Science* 550 (March 1997): 107. For an example of the continuing media and popular fascination with negative images, see Robert D. Kaplan, "Travels into America's Future," *Atlantic Monthly* 282, no. 2 (July 1998): 47–68.

10. Unless otherwise noted, data for the period from 1900 to the 1990s are from David Lorey, *U.S.-Mexican Border Statistics since 1900* (Los Angeles: University of California, Los Angeles [UCLA], Latin American Center Publications, 1990), and David Lorey, *U.S.-Mexican Border Statistics since 1900: 1990 Update* (Los Angeles: UCLA Latin American Center Publications, 1993). Data for earlier periods are drawn from the sources cited in the chapter notes and from those listed in the suggested readings at the end of the volume. More recent data are mainly from the U.S. census and from the Instituto Nacional de Estadística y Geografía, Mexico's national statistical agency.

11. See Ellwyn R. Stoddard, "Frontiers, Borders, and Border Segmentation: Toward a Conceptual Clarification," *Journal of Borderlands Studies* 6, no. 1 (spring 1990): 1–22.

12. The areas experiencing the fastest growth in Mexican-origin population between 1990 and 1996 were the nonborder states of Oregon (55 percent), Nevada (77 percent), Nebraska (70 percent), Iowa (52 percent), Arkansas (104 percent), Tennessee (58 percent), Georgia (70 percent), North Carolina (73 percent), and Vermont (55 percent); Edwin Garcia and Ben Stocking, "Latinos on the Move to a New Promised Land," *San Jose Mercury News*, August 16, 1998. This trend of rapid growth in nonborder states continued into the new century: Jeffrey S. Passel, "Estimates of the Size and Characteristics of the Undocumented Population," Pew Hispanic Center Report, March 21, 2005, http://www.pewhispanic.org.

1

DISTINGUISHING CHARACTERISTICS AND EARLY HISTORY

Frontier, Borderlands, and Border Region

Three geographical factors have shaped the border region from the time of earliest human settlement, through its period as frontier and borderlands, to the present. First, the region is vast in size. The area through which the international boundary passes is as large as Europe, stretching across North America from the Pacific coast to the Gulf of Mexico and from the southern Rocky Mountains to the beginning of Mexico's Central Plateau.

Second, the region is mountainous, crisscrossed by a maze of inhospitable ranges that divide the area into isolated subregions. From Arizona southward the Sierra Madre Occidental—one hundred miles wide and twelve hundred miles long—cuts off the Central Plateau from the Pacific coast. Along the eastern edge of the plateau the Sierra Madre separates the coast from the central regions for nearly one thousand miles. From west Texas to California, high mountain ranges alternate with extensive basins. In an area this size and this mountainous, transportation and communication present major challenges. Only a few paved roads pierce the Mexican Sierra Madre Occidental from the interior to the coast.

Third, and perhaps most important, the border region is unremittingly arid: rainfall is inadequate for agriculture; it is also unpredictable, sporadic, and occasionally destructive. Aridity has "indelibly stamped [border] society, affecting architecture, diet, attire, leisure, socialization, and travel."[1] Although the introduction of railroads, highways, and air travel improved accessibility to this vast and rugged terrain, the lack of both water and dependable rainfall remains a major obstacle to human settlement throughout the area. Only at great federal expense was it possible to cross this geographical hurdle to create the U.S. West's stupendous late-twentieth-century wealth in agriculture and industry. The development of the Mexican border states was also undergirded by successful control of the environment.

The region now encompassing the U.S.-Mexican border has a human history that stretches back approximately twelve thousand years. The Americas in 1492 are estimated to have had a population of about 60 million; 21 million, or 35 percent, of this total are thought to have lived in Mexico. The area that today comprises the six Mexican and four U.S. border states was home to approximately 1 million people at the end of the fifteenth century. The aridity and ruggedness of much of the terrain meant that, in contrast to the inhabitants of central Mexico, most of the people of the region were nomadic hunters and gatherers, following a way of life that supported only relatively small populations. With one or two possible exceptions, the area did not generate major political structures such as those of the Aztec Empire. Instead, it was characterized by small, autonomous, local communities that were economically and politically independent of one another.[2]

The culture of this aboriginal population was extremely heterogeneous. European settlers identified and named at least forty-five different groups. In the area of modern Chihuahua and Sonora, for example, there were six major languages—Tarahumara, Concho, Opata, Pima, Cahita, and Seri—each of which had several mutually unintelligible dialects. In New Mexico and Arizona, Spaniards identified at least fourteen distinct languages. In addition to ancient inhabitants there were Athabaskan groups, which had crossed the Rocky Mountains to settle their own frontier in more recent times: the Kiowa-Apache in central-western Texas; the Lipan-Apache in southwestern Texas; and the Jicarilla, Mescalero, Tonto Apache, and Navajo in parts of present-day Arizona, New Mexico, Sonora, and Chihuahua. Yuman groups were to be found in the area of the California border region. The Kumeyaay occupied the area from the Pacific Ocean, over the coastal mountain range, and into the Colorado Desert. There, desert tribes, mainly scattered along the banks of the Colorado River, included the Quechan and Cocopah, among others.

The majority of the inhabitants in the region were what early Spanish explorers termed *ranchería* people, those who lived in small hamlets with populations of only a few hundred each. Such settlements, often scattered over large surrounding territories, relied on wild foods as much as on planted crops. Where favorable agricultural conditions permitted, larger villages and more densely settled subregions existed. Along the banks of Sonora's important rivers, for example, relatively abundant supplies of water supported the villages of the Yaqui and Mayo. From 300 BC to 500 AD, agriculturists cultivated maize, beans, and squash in the Salt and Gila river valleys in what is today Arizona. In northern Arizona and New Mexico, the ancestors of the present Hopi people and the Tanoan Puebloans of the Rio Grande Valley created complex societies. Along the Rio Grande an estimated forty thousand people, practicing intensive agriculture, lived in highly organized villages.

These people's lives would be radically altered by contact with Europeans. Resistance to the changes introduced by outsiders through the centuries was substantial. Remarkably, three-quarters of the indigenous groups would survive to maintain some portion of their identities. This staying power resulted in a border society that is not simply a European transplant. In the early twenty-first century, twenty-six indigenous groups with distinct cultures, although greatly reduced in numbers, still survive throughout the border region. These peoples represented more than one-half of the groups found in the area in the early 1500s.

THE COLONIAL PERIOD:
LIFE ON A NEW WORLD FRONTIER

The inhabitants of central Mexico—both natives and European settlers—perceived many obstacles to settling the Far North. Both the geographical landscape and the social setting made the area unattractive. Mountains and desert wastes combined with hostile indigenous populations to keep central Mexicans at bay for hundreds of years. The region was termed the Gran Chichimeca, a land of barbarous peoples. Desultory exploration by Spaniards turned up little to justify settlement. Moving north along the coastlines, explorers surveyed unknown areas in search of cultures matching the civilization of central Mexico. In the five decades after Columbus, the Spanish made a series of expeditions: Juan Ponce de León's 1513 expedition to Florida; Alonso Álvarez de Pineda's 1519 voyage around the Gulf of Mexico; Estevão de Gomes's 1524–1525 *recorrido* (trip) up the northeastern seaboard; Pedro de Quejo's 1525 voyage from Española to Delaware; Hernando de Soto's 1539–1543 visit to what is today Florida and the Atlantic Southeast; and João Rodrigues Cabrilho's 1542–1543 expedition along the California coast. Although these initial *recorridos* by sea did not turn up much in the way of liquid wealth or concentrated, sedentary populations, subsequent myths of fabulous cities and Aztec-like civilizations fueled further exploration by land.

To the continued disappointment of explorers, land expeditions likewise discovered little to sustain the attention of European settlers. Alvar Núñez Cabeza de Vaca, who had been shipwrecked in Florida and wandered through the South as far west as Texas from 1528 to 1536, met many Native Americans, exchanged goods, and heard tales of the golden cities of Cíbola. He retold the stories to believing ears, including those of the Spanish viceroy of the Kingdom of New Spain in Mexico City. From 1540 to 1542, Francisco Vásquez de Coronado mounted a search for Cíbola, moving as far north as the modern-day state of Kansas. As the first large and carefully prepared Spanish expedition into the frontier, the *entrada* (entry) of Vásquez de Coronado contributed greatly to the cultural map of the aboriginal frontier. But explorers found no cities of fabulous wealth or any other compelling reason to settle the area.

The discovery of major veins of silver proved to be the stimulus for northern expansion during the colonial period. Mining became the motor of change throughout Mexico's Far North. Mining spurred migration and led to the development of a vibrant internal economy. Silver was discovered near Zacatecas in 1546 and at Guanajuato in 1550. In the following years, prospectors struck silver in San Luis Potosí, Pachuca, and Parral. The discovery of precious ore in the North resulted in a steady influx of settlers from central Mexico. As the silver boom continued, both Europeans and Native Americans moved north. The location of mining towns was a result of serendipity rather than planning. Because silver often was found in areas where other resources were lacking, mining towns developed complex social and economic structures to meet the need for water, food, and fuel. The industry required large supplies of labor, wood, chemicals, staple foods, work animals, meat, iron, cloth, and leather. Large estates and smaller farms emerged to provision the mines; long-distance and local commerce developed to supply goods and credit. Along the major north-south road and its branch roads, thousands of mules carried commodities to the North and silver to the South.

A good example of this process of consolidation was the district of Nueva Vizcaya (now Chihuahua and Durango states). When silver was discovered in Parral in 1629, it quickly became one of the most important new settlements of the region, growing to three hundred families by 1632 and to eight hundred by 1640. The town not only produced wealth for those directly involved in the mining industry but also stimulated commerce, agriculture, and livestock raising in the surrounding region. By 1768, 149 occupations existed in the Parral region: although 40 percent of the population consisted of workers directly connected with mining, 10 percent of the population consisted of merchants and 33 percent consisted of artisans, including shoemakers, blacksmiths, tailors, and barbers. The town had one teacher and one surgeon.

The agricultural units that supported mining in the North ranged from small, intensive, irrigated plots near urban and mining centers, to small, family-owned farms and ranches, to great estates that often included many different properties managed as an integrated enterprise. The sixteenth century witnessed the rise of immense rural estates—haciendas—in some areas of the Far

North as an outgrowth of mining operations. Miners, government officials, and military men acquired large holdings through land grants, purchase, and marriage. These units produced horses and mules, sheep for meat and wool, wheat, fruits and vegetables, oil, and wine. One of the largest estates in the eighteenth century was that of the Marqués de Aguayo, which comprised 15 million acres or about half the total land of Coahuila.[3] In many regions of the North the most common unit of agrarian production was the rancho. Throughout northern New Spain this small or medium holding of land was owned or leased by a family that also supplied most of the labor for the enterprise. In the most arid regions, livestock raising prevailed; in areas with precipitation or irrigation, crop and orchard production was common.

As other European powers became interested in the region and Spain's interest in protecting its empire grew, the Far North was increasingly the focus of attempts to impede intrusions. Defense against the spreading influence of the French, English, and Russians became one of the main foundations of settlement. The Spanish Crown and viceregal government in Mexico City devised several strategies to encourage settlement in the region. In order to pacify and populate the area at minimal cost, the Crown came to rely on two institutions with funds and personnel of their own: the military and the religious orders. This approach gave rise to the classic duo of European settlement in the North: the presidio and the mission. In an attempt to protect the silver trade, the viceregal government also organized armed convoys and established towns along the road from Mexico City to the mines.

The key to defense was the presidio, a walled enclosure with a warehouse, dwellings for soldiers and officers and their families, a stable, an armory, and sometimes a chapel. The presidio was always located near a dependable water supply and was surrounded by grazing and agricultural lands. Often a mission was located nearby to take advantage of the protection offered by the garrison. Presidial soldiers possessed the secrets of European technology and know-how; many of them worked as masons, carpenters, cowboys, ranchers, farmers, and artisans. Presidios often developed into permanent towns. Gradually, warfare against raiding natives gave way to campaigns by new settlers and the government to distribute food and supplies to indigenous populations.

Missions run by the regular orders (Franciscans and Jesuits) were expected to help pacify and incorporate Native Americans; they reduced into settled units the diverse and complex populations, particularly those that were semisedentary or nomadic. Missionaries introduced indigenous people to European ways of life. Within a century a string of missions stretched from east to west, across the frontier and up the Pacific coast from Sinaloa to California.

San Xavier del Bac mission church near Tucson, Arizona, on the reservation lands of the Tohono O'odham. Founded in 1700 by Spanish Jesuit missionaries, the present church was constructed from 1783 to 1797 and still functions as a parish church. 2003.

Contrary to the classic conception of Spanish frontier society as mainly composed of missionaries and soldiers with their families, civilian settlers were greater in number and contributed in more lasting ways to the region. Initially, civilian immigrants came from Spain and central Mexico; gradually, however, immigrants were drawn from adjacent provinces. Sinaloa supplied colonists for Sonora and Baja California, and these in turn supplied settlers for Alta California. The nonindigenous working population grew rapidly and experienced some social mobility. Frontier towns attracted shopkeepers, notaries, craftsmen, artisans, and merchants, and rural areas soon had ranchers and truck gardeners who supplied the towns with staple goods.

Two characteristics made the frontier population unique. The inhabitants were of varied and mixed ethnicities, including Native Americans from all over the North and from central Mexico, as well as African Americans. Frontier society was also characterized by the prevalence of wage labor, which spread from the mines and urban settlements to agricultural areas, as a result of the high return on investment in the region, the need for skilled labor, and the location of the mining towns in areas of sparse indigenous population.

Frontier populations transformed the indigenous societies with which they came into contact. Changes rippling outward in concentric circles from European settlements, particularly missions, reached the region before the Europeans did. In many areas, Spanish material culture, like metal goods and livestock, preceded the arrival of the Europeans. These introductions greatly disrupted the lifestyles of indigenous groups. Intergroup raiding and warfare increased over the course of the eighteenth century.

The principal disruption was disease, introduced unintentionally by European settlers as they spread into the region. Although population decline on the frontier was not as great as it had been in central areas, the death toll from disease was nevertheless astounding. In the California missions, for example, Native American recruits generally survived mission life for ten years at most. In the region stretching from San Diego to San Francisco, the coastal indigenous population fell from 60,000 in 1769 to 35,000 in 1800, as the overall population of California fell from 300,000 in 1769 to 200,000 by the end of the colonial era in 1821. Within a century the native population of the frontier was cut to a little less than half its precontact size.

Spaniards tried various overt ways of reshaping indigenous life. The nonreligious impacts were probably more significant than religious impacts in and around the mission. Although legally closed to civilian settlers, the missions attracted people to adjacent areas. Because settlers demanded access to native labor, missions often developed into labor-recruitment institutions. They were surrounded by flourishing agricultural establishments and indigenous people who passed time among both nonreligious settlers and friars. In those mission areas that were near mines, population movement was particularly pronounced, and conflict between civilian employers and the mission fathers for control of natives was constant.

Because the Spaniards came from urban environments and felt that city life was part of being civilized, they encouraged Native Americans to live in or near missions. Indigenous people were taught to husband European domesticated animals (horses, sheep, goats, pigs, and chickens); cultivate European crops; use such iron tools as wheels, saws, chisels, planes, nails, and spikes; and practice those arts and crafts that Spaniards regarded as essential for civilization. Missionaries attempted to instill European ideas of discipline in several realms, and they introduced clocks and bells, thus imparting to the native population European notions of time.

The movement of Europeans—missionaries, soldiers, landowners, merchants, workers—into the North did not take the form of a constantly advancing frontier. Nomadic natives of the region reacted fiercely against the occupation of their territory and the increased competition for its meager resources.

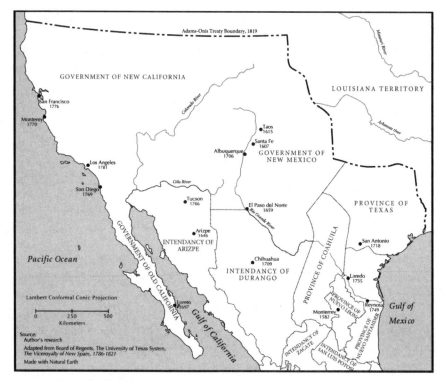

Map 7.   Spanish administrative units in the North and claimed territory, 1810.

Most threatening were raids of the Apache and Comanche, displaced from their ancient homelands by the influx of French and British settlers from the north and east. The opening of the North during the second half of the sixteenth century produced fifty years of conflict known as the War of the Gran Chichimeca. Neither the strictly military approach nor the missions and the provision of food pacified the region. Native Americans who lived in close proximity to European settlers resisted the steady change to their lives in a number of other ways. They fled missions, organized local rebellions that addressed specific grievances, and engaged in some remarkably successful larger revolts.

Resistance and rebellion meant that by the mid-eighteenth century the Spanish settlers could claim to have made only limited inroads into the region. They were besieged by powerful and confident nomadic groups on horseback. Time and again revolts forced the Spaniards to retreat and abandon their

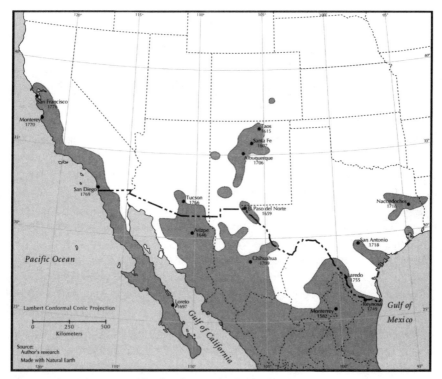

Map 8.   Spanish-occupied land in the North of New Spain, 1810.

positions. By 1700 it was clear that the northward expansion of New Spain had failed to reach the almost unlimited horizons of the early years. Practical frontiers had to be drawn, as the imperial emphasis shifted from northward expansion to defense and consolidation.

Throughout the long colonial period, frontier life, which took on processes and structures all its own, was increasingly characterized by a unique, defining culture. Settlers to the region modified Spanish customs, language, religion, and work habits in the new environment. Farming methods, labor, architecture, and local celebrations were all affected by changed circumstances. Isolation from the earlier settled regions of New Spain and from each other forced frontier dwellers to adapt to local conditions, often producing in them social and personal characteristics that differed markedly from those of the residents of central Mexico. A pride in the ability to overcome frontier challenges fostered a sense of distinction from the populations of other areas of Mexico.

FROM FRONTIER TO BORDERLANDS

During the relatively brief span from Mexican independence in 1821 to the end of the war between the United States and Mexico in 1848, Spain's far-northern frontier territories became borderlands—the relatively undefined and frequently contested terrains between Mexico and the United States. Many patterns and processes that first appeared during this twenty-seven-year period would shape border society for the following century. Mexico sought to integrate the area into the national mainstream by building political and economic ties. But attempts to make the region part of the nation fell short of success. The era culminated in the acquisition of a great portion of the Mexican North by the United States.

Following independence, the two key frontier institutions—the presidio and the mission—fell into irreversible decline. The presidio lost its imperial purpose, and resident soldiers focused their energies on nondefensive activities. The missions came under sharp attack from Mexican liberals, who denounced them for oppressing the native populations, accumulating nonproductive wealth and property, and interfering in affairs of state. Local pressure to secularize the missions, which would turn them into parish churches and pueblos, fundamentally resulted from nonreligious settlers' desire for land. By the mid-1830s, secularization was a fact in Texas, Arizona, California, and New Mexico.

Mexico's inability to integrate its northern frontier into the country's core reflected, above all, the difficulties of establishing political stability after independence. A complete collapse of effective administration in the North doomed the borderlands to remain on the periphery economically and politically. Although Mexicans understood the challenges of incorporating the region into national life, efforts to do so were overshadowed by the exigencies of nation building. Fewer than fifteen thousand Mexicans lived in the area, and frontier and central regions did not identify with one another. Independence encouraged a return to local autonomy rather than a strengthening of ties between the North and the center.

Several additional factors pulled central Mexico and the borderlands apart. In 1824 the first national constitution created a federal republic of states and territories in which states achieved considerable autonomy in decision making, but territories came under the direct control of the Mexican Congress. Under the 1824 constitution, California and New Mexico were territories, but Congress never enacted regulations for their internal governance. Texans reacted bitterly to the loss of their voice when the Mexican constitution joined them to the more powerful and populous neighboring Coahuila as the state of Coahuila y Texas. In 1836, President Antonio López de Santa Anna introduced a new centralist constitution that converted the states into military departments, a status they would retain until 1847. In the North, the result of these actions was a growing sense of separation from central authority. Relations between periphery and center became increasingly strained.

Another force that tended to move the North out of the central Mexican sphere of influence was commerce. Illegal trade with French, English, and U.S. citizens had existed under Spain, but commerce with foreigners increased dramatically after the young nation officially authorized such trade in 1821. The bulk of business was with the United States and Europe rather than with central Mexico. American farm products and British manufactured goods were exchanged for a variety of Mexican frontier products: hides from California; mules from New Mexico; and wheat, salt, silver, tallow, and other items from throughout the borderlands area. North American and European merchants established themselves in ports and cities, providing both capital and trade goods to the local population. These commercial links strengthened the economic independence of the North and tied it ever more closely to the United States.

Border society underwent several important changes during the early national period. The most notable was the decline in sedentary and nomadic native populations and the increase in the numbers of Europeans and mestizos. Under Mexican rule after 1821, the natives of the borderlands became citizens, gaining an equal legal footing with European Americans. In practice, however, they were subject to the whims of local governments, they were compelled to pay special taxes, and their movements were sometimes restricted. They were relentlessly forced off the land into towns and onto ranches as laborers. In addition to typhus, smallpox, and measles, which were prevalent in the colonial period, malaria and cholera took heavy tolls. The exodus from traditional villages also caused fewer persons to be considered Native Americans, as ethnic mixing and acculturation blended identities and categories.

The impact of immigration and colonization from the U.S. Midwest, Southeast, and eastern seaboard became clear by the 1830s. U.S. citizens sought new wealth in the mining zones of Sonora and Chihuahua and in livestock raising and commercial agriculture in Coahuila y Texas, New Mexico, and Alta California. The United States established wagon roads and subsidized stagecoach lines. The U.S. government rapidly turned public lands over to private holders throughout the West. Mexico actively encouraged U.S. migration to the frontier after 1821, hoping that an increased population would serve as a buffer between Mexico and the territorial interests of the United States. Mexican policymakers generally considered the immigration of national and foreign colonists to the sparsely populated North to be the best way to defend settled lands against the Apache and Comanche and to hold the North within the boundaries of Mexico's territory. They offered colonists land on much more generous terms than those of the U.S. government. Mexico allocated large, inexpensive tracts to settlers from other countries, including the United States, on the condition that they become Mexican citizens.

In Texas, Mexican colonization policy proved to be a mistake. The earlier U.S. purchase of Louisiana in 1803 and continued expansionist sentiment and claims caused Spain to become concerned that even prior to Mexican independence, colonists from the United States had begun moving into the region. Local Spanish military commandants, however, welcomed the newcomers as a defense against raiding indigenous groups. U.S. citizens, many of whom came with slaves, spread into the river valleys around Nacogdoches, Brazos, and Béjar. Following the Adams-Onís Treaty of 1819, which established a boundary between Spain and the United States, colonization by the United States became more purposeful. In the early 1820s, Moses Austin received permission from Spanish military authorities in Coahuila to settle colonists in Texas. His contract allowed him to bring three hundred families to settle on land near the Brazos River. Passage of Mexico's colonization law of 1824 and complementary legislation by the state of Coahuila y Texas in 1825 permitted Stephen Austin to take over his father's colony. The younger Austin brought twelve hundred families to homestead land along the Brazos River. Many more settlers from the east followed, both legally and illegally. European colonists, African American slaves and freemen, and people from the eastern United States swelled the population of Texas. From 1821 to 1836 the number of Mexican settlers increased by about one-third, but that of other colonists grew much faster. By 1830, U.S. immigrants outnumbered Mexican settlers.

In contrast to the situation in Texas, U.S. citizens who migrated to New Mexico, Sonora, Sinaloa, and the Californias went initially as trappers and traders rather than as farmers and permanent settlers. The few who stayed frequently entered into commerce, mining, lumbering, crafts, and manufacturing; later they turned to farming and ranching. And the western borderlands, again unlike Texas, presented incoming U.S. citizens with an established civilian population of Spanish-speaking landholders, merchants, and craftsmen, as well as mission and the Pueblo indigenous peoples who maintained the traditional practices of Mexico's colonial economy. Many newcomer merchants married into local families, thereby gaining access to local networks and economies.

During the brief borderlands interlude, there were three important changes in landholding patterns. First, there was a transition from the informal holding and use of land to formal, legal, written rights. Second, the period witnessed a shift from small family-run plots to large concentrations of land. Third, there was a virtual end to indigenous village possession of cropland, pasturage, and water, as title shifted to nonnative owners.

In the colonial province of Nuevo México, Governor Manuel Armijo granted large tracts of public land to private entrepreneurs in an effort to extend settlement to the upper Pecos, Canadian, and Arkansas rivers. Long-time residents of New Mexico towns and the Pueblo people contested these grants, defending the rights of communal ownership and protesting the sale of land to foreigners. In California, secularization of the missions released prime agricultural land and created a pool of cheap labor, both attractive resources for ambitious settlers. Between 1834 and 1846 the Mexican governors of California awarded seven hundred private land grants, over 90 percent of all grants issued during the combined Spanish and Mexican periods. Through marriage and business arrangements, U.S. entrepreneurs allied themselves with the local merchant and landholding elite and began to purchase land for investment and speculation.

In the Mexican North, too, the period saw the emergence of vast landholdings. In the northeastern states, extended families came to control huge estates. The combined property of the Sánchez Navarro family in Coahuila constituted the largest landed estate of the borderlands period. After independence, the Sánchez Navarros doubled their colonial inheritance, mainly through foreclosure on loans to other owners of large estates. In 1840 the family acquired the Marquisate of Aguayo, making it the greatest landowner in Mexico, with holdings of over 15 million acres, or about the size of the state of West Virginia.

CONFLICT BETWEEN THE UNITED STATES AND MEXICO

By the early 1830s the experience in Texas had convinced Mexican policymakers that allowing U.S. settlers to grow to a majority in its northern frontier posed a grave danger to the new nation. By this time, immigrants from the United States outnumbered all others in Texas and Alta California. In an attempt to control immigration and bring the northern frontier firmly into its sphere of influence, the Mexican government abolished slavery and imposed high taxes. And in a move that irritated the local settlers, the government began to use convicts to settle the region.

At the same time, the sentiment of Manifest Destiny was sweeping the United States. There was a widespread belief among U.S. citizens—from frontier people to New England poets, northern abolitionists, and southern slaveholders—that it would be beneficial to both countries to absorb Mexico into the United States. Expansion was a pervasive idea in the U.S. culture of the time, widely promoted in newspapers and political speeches. The United States repeatedly offered to buy Texas; Mexico steadily refused to sell territory clearly belonging to that nation under the 1819 Adams-Onís Treaty. Finally, Mexico sent an army to Texas in an attempt to bring the region back into the national fold. When Texas and Mexico went to war, the United States refused to intervene; despite its official neutrality, however, it looked with favor on the volunteers and weapons that poured into Texas to aid the independence movement. Even without overt U.S. support, Texas won its independence in April 1836. Britain, France, and the United States recognized its independence the following year.

For the next nine years, Texas defended its sovereignty against constant saber rattling in Mexico. For its part the United States placed the Texas issue on the back burner until the early 1840s, when increasing European interest in the new republic fueled U.S. concerns about European expansion into the region. California, with its access to the Pacific Ocean for whaling and trade, began to attract the attention of U.S. policymakers. U.S. interest in the West Coast sharpened when France and Great Britain expressed interest in the property. The United States offered to buy California for the price of outstanding U.S. claims against Mexico, but the Mexican government, still outraged over the loss of Texas, declined.

Diplomatic relations between Mexico and the United States deteriorated during the early 1840s. Mexico refused to discuss its debt with U.S. creditors or to reopen negotiations on the boundary established in the 1819 treaty. U.S. policymakers were alarmed by the perceived threat of the potential sale of California by Mexico to Great Britain. Tensions increased when the United States annexed Texas in 1845, an act that Mexico perceived as a declaration of war. Strong factions within Mexico that welcomed a war with the United States influenced other leaders to reject offers of peace; there was a great deal of confidence in the Mexican military's ability to resist the United States. Annexation of Texas became the final act severing the tenuous connection between the two countries. After a skirmish on land that clearly belonged to Mexico, armies from both sides hurriedly moved to the Texas-Mexico border, each preparing for the hostilities that broke out in April 1846.

Between 1846 and 1848 the U.S.-Mexican war was fought to a stalemate. Eventually, Winfield Scott, commander of the U.S. forces in Mexico, occupied Mexico City and forced President López de Santa Anna to terms of agreement. Both sides could make further gains only by bargaining. The occupation of its capital was a great humiliation to Mexico, but the war also cost many U.S. soldiers' lives. Although an All Mexico movement in the United States advocated taking the entire country, some observers worried about the expansion of slavery and the incorporation of a large, mixed-ethnicity population into the United States. The conflict was formally ended with the Treaty of Guadalupe Hidalgo (1848) and the forced sale of one-third of Mexico to the United States. In 1853 the Gadsden Purchase completed the parcelization of Mexican territory, adding approximately thirty thousand square miles to what are now the states of Arizona and New Mexico. All told, about one-half of Mexico, including Texas, was lost to the United States by midcentury. The Treaty of Guadalupe Hidalgo established a new international boundary that had immediate consequences for people residing in the now lost territories. As many as three hundred thousand people, many of them Mexican nationals, lived in the ceded territories and Texas.

EARLY BORDER PHENOMENA

Changes followed immediately upon the establishment of the new border. Many towns located on or near the boundary were transformed by the new reality. Laredo was divided into two, with Nuevo Laredo established on the south bank of the Rio Grande. Tijuana, although it remained a modest village of little consequence until the mid-twentieth century, emerged in 1848, as small ranchers and merchants capitalized on the new back door to California. After the boundary was drawn, many Mexicans migrated south into Mexico, where they founded settlements along the border. This movement was abetted by the insecurity of land tenure, continued rapid U.S. settlement on the U.S. side of the border, and the existence of family land held by returnees on the Mexican side.

One of the most significant stimuli to the growth of border towns was Mexico's campaign to repatriate its citizens to the south side of the border. The Mexican government was eager to populate its border states in an effort to avoid further U.S. incursions into its territory. Beginning in 1848, Mexico began repatriating southwestern families of Mexican descent by providing them with free land. Commissioners traveled to California, New Mexico, and Texas to recruit interested families. Established towns such as Guerrero, Mier, Camargo, Reynosa, and Matamoros grew in population, and new towns such as Nuevo Laredo and Nogales were established. Families repatriating from New Mexico founded several towns in Chihuahua, including Refugio, Guadalupe, La Mesilla, and Santo Tomás. At the turn of the century, perhaps one-quarter of the Mexican-origin population in the northern cities consisted of *repatriados* (repatriates).

New border settlements also sprang up on the U.S. side of the border, across the boundary from repatriate communities, to take advantage of trading and smuggling opportunities. In Texas, Brownsville, Rio Grande City, Eagle Pass, McAllen, El Paso, Del Rio, and other small communities emerged and thrived. In Arizona, Douglas and Nogales grew as commercial centers. U.S. military outposts constructed along the new border also served to encourage the establishment of towns on the Mexican side, as was the case with Fort Duncan and Piedras Negras. The Mexican town of San Diego was transferred to the United States by the Treaty of Guadalupe Hidalgo. Its excellent natural seaport, along with the California boom following the 1848 Gold Rush, assured the growth and importance of this border city.

The most difficult border-region conflicts of the period involved land. Most of the Mexican citizens occupying land grants in the ceded territories held titles that were valid under Mexican law but considered vague and inadequate by U.S. legal traditions. Such circumstances as frequent changes in administration and the slow motion of the Mexican bureaucracy made it difficult for estate holders to obtain clear titles. Within months of the beginning of the gold rush in California, the call was raised to "liberate" property held by Mexicans. Texas proved particularly problematic, as one condition of its 1845 admittance to the United States had been complete control over its own lands. As a result the U.S. Congress approved the Gwin Land Act in 1851. The Board of Land Commissioners was established to analyze the validity of Spanish and Mexican land grants. Grantees had two years to present evidence supporting their titles to occupied territories; if they were unable to document their grants, the land became part of the public domain.

In California the law touched off an orgy of speculation and squatter intrusions, as settlers moved to claim "unused" rancho lands. Mexican estate holders eventually lost the bulk of their property to lawyers, banks, and speculators. In New Mexico, where most of the lands were grants held in common by residents of former pueblos, Congress authorized the surveyor general's office to determine the extent of pueblo holdings. By 1863 only twenty-five grants had been confirmed; by 1880 only 150 of 1,000 claims had been acted upon by the federal government. Two-thirds of all claims were rejected; eventually, only 6 percent of claims were settled in favor of Mexican-era estate owners. In the meantime, as a result of the bribery of corrupt officials and the activities of speculators, thousands of acres of village and township lands passed to the federal government and were then purchased by individuals or corporations. In 1856 a ruling by the U.S. Supreme

Court held that, because the Treaty of Guadalupe Hidalgo applied only to territories held prior to its signing, the treaty did not apply to Texas. In the following years, most Mexican-origin *tejanos* (Texans) lost some part of their property through "a combination of methods including litigation, chicanery, robbery, fraud, and threat."[4]

In most conflicts between Mexican and U.S. landholders over titles, U.S. courts ruled against petitioners of Mexican descent. The Mexican government protested, demanding compensation for damages. Responses to such complaints were ad hoc and limited in scope. The biggest winners in the landgrab were U.S.-owned corporations and the federal government. Private estate owners who built up great fortunes would later invest their capital in border mining, commerce, and industry. The government would use its vast public landholdings to spur development in the West.

Midcentury witnessed the first major economic boom on the border. In January 1848, not two weeks before the signing of the Treaty of Guadalupe Hidalgo, gold was discovered in California. Large numbers of people began moving north and west to take part in the prosperity of the region. Between 1840 and 1860, 300,000 people migrated west on overland trails. The non-indigenous population of California increased from about 14,000 in 1848 to about 225,000 in 1852. This increase fueled rapid growth and development of western agriculture, trade, and industry. In the process many border towns flourished as well, as they became swept up in the boom-time economy. The rush reshaped large areas of the border, as migrants passed through them. Many never made it all the way to California, settling in the border region permanently. This early boom would be followed by one after another, with similar patterns and rates of growth.

During the mid-nineteenth century, the border region was officially recognized by the Mexican government as a special area with distinct and unique needs. Free zones, where goods could be moved back and forth across the border without payment of any duty, were established in Tamaulipas and Chihuahua in 1858. Shortly thereafter the border areas of Nuevo León became free zones as well. These measures led to an economic expansion on the Mexican side as trade and consumption of U.S. manufactures increased. Untaxed trade was eventually expanded to the entire border region in 1885. Although the existence of the free zone in these states brought significant benefits to *fronterizos* (border dwellers), it provoked opposition, particularly from merchants, in both Mexico and the United States. Many Mexicans from the interior argued, with justification, that the free zone stimulated smuggling into the rest of Mexico, that it brought unfair competition for national manufactured goods, and that it prevented the government from collecting import taxes. U.S. border merchants complained of unfair competition and large-scale smuggling into the United States as well.

NOTES

1. Miguel Tinker Salas, *In the Shadow of the Eagles: Sonora and the Transformation of the Border during the Porfiriato* (Berkeley: University of California Press, 1997), 17.

2. This chapter draws heavily on four draft chapters for the historical volume of the University of California, Los Angeles, Borderlands Atlas Project: Miguel León-Portilia, Susan Schroeder, and Michael C. Meyer, "Early Spanish-Indian Contact in the Borderlands"; Paul Ganster, Bernardo García Martínez, and James Lockhart, "Northern New Spain"; David Hornbeck and Cynthia Radding, "The Northern Frontier during the Early Mexican Republic, 1821–1848"; and Richard Griswold del Castillo and Raúl Rodríguez González, "Conflict and Development: The United States–Mexico Borderlands, 1848–1900." Also see Harry W. Crosby, *Antigua California: Mission and Colony on the Peninsular Frontier* (Albuquerque: University of New Mexico Press, 1994).

3. Ida Altman, "A Family and Region in the Northern Fringe Lands," in *Provinces of Early Mexico: Variants of Spanish American Evolution*, ed. Ida Altman and James Lockhart (Los Angeles: University of California, Los Angeles, Latin American Center Publications, 1976), 260.

4. Richard White, *"It's Your Misfortune and None of My Own": A New History of the American West* (Norman: University of Oklahoma Press, 1991), 83.

2

BOOMS AND
BUSTS ON THE BORDER

Economic Development, 1880s to 1920s

During the course of the twentieth century a group of small, scattered outposts along the international boundary between the United States and Mexico, isolated from national and international economies and from one another, merged into one of the most economically and demographically dynamic regions in the world. How did the economy of the U.S.-Mexican border region, so peripheral in 1900, evolve to its present-day dynamism and importance? What are the distinguishing characteristics of this momentous change? This chapter examines the early period of the century to shed light on the border economy's twentieth-century transformation.[1]

THE FIRST BORDER BOOM, 1880–1910

The twentieth century dawned on the border region with great promise. During the last quarter of the nineteenth century its economy had taken off for the first time. With the ascension of Porfirio Díaz to the Mexican presidency in 1876 and his recognition by the United States in 1877, sustained political stability existed along the international line for the first time since Mexico's independence in 1821. Díaz imposed law and order with an eye toward promoting economic development: "Order and Progress" became the motto of his thirty-four-year rule.

Responding to the novel political stability in Mexico, U.S. capital spurred the development of railroads, mining operations, export agriculture, and commercial endeavors throughout the border region. The Porfirian regime of Order and Progress led to an average annual growth rate of 8 percent per year between 1884 and 1900—the longest sustained period of economic growth in Mexico's history as an independent state. In the last quarter of the nineteenth century, closer ties between Mexico and the United States were accompanied by ever-increasing exchange and interdependence in the border region.

The extractive economy of the border region, exemplified early on by colonial silver mining and the nineteenth-century gold rush, was transformed by three principal factors in the late nineteenth century. First, inexpensive transportation by rail revolutionized the relationship between border production and markets. Second, distant markets for border commodities had developed. Silver, copper, salt, lead, and other mineral products; lumber; commercial agricultural products such as wheat and cotton; and livestock were all in great demand as both the U.S. and Mexican economies grew. Border residents increasingly shipped most of what they produced to faraway buyers. Third, labor and capital for extractive activities, both of which originated outside the region and created a distinctly dependent border economy, increased in quantity and flexibility.

The farthest-reaching transformation of the border region in the late nineteenth century resulted from the construction of a railroad network that connected the Mexican North and the U.S. Southwest with the major commercial and population centers in each country. Completion of the first transcontinental line by the Central and Union Pacific railroads in 1869 spurred the formation of many other rival lines throughout the West. The Atchison, Topeka, and Santa Fe railroad as well as the Southern Pacific railroad established major routes in the Southwest that linked most of the important population centers in the border region with one another and with eastern markets.

The first transcontinental railroad to pass directly through the border region was completed in 1881, linking the area to the western and eastern seaboards of the United States. Between 1876 and 1910 the amount of track laid in Mexico increased exponentially. Often the railroad tied Mexican communities more closely to the United States than to the Mexican interior; railroad lines in Sonora, for example, did not reach south to Guadalajara until 1909. By 1900 the Mexican North boasted more miles of track than any other region of Mexico—more than four thousand miles, which constituted one-half the national total.

The iron horse significantly boosted the economic importance of the regions through which it passed. El Paso, Texas, for example, suddenly became a key commercial hub for both the United States and Mexico. Prior to the arrival of the railroad, El Paso was a town of about eight hundred people. When news spread that the railroad was coming in 1880, a floating population of recent arrivals doubled the size of El Paso. "Bankers, merchants, capitalists, real estate dealers, cattlemen, miners, railroad men, gamblers, saloon keepers,

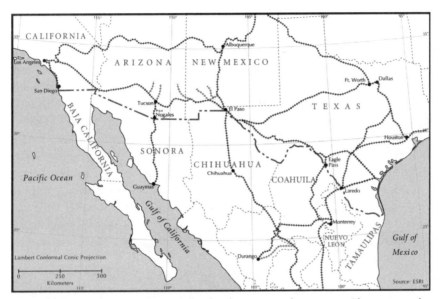

Map 9. *Principal railway lines in the border region, about 1900. There were also many short feeder lines from mining and agricultural areas connecting to the main lines. (Based on "Map of the Railway & Steamship Lines Operated by the Southern Pacific Company, 1884" [Chicago: Poole Brothers] and "Map of the Mexican Central Railway and Connections, 1898" [Chicago: Poole Brothers]).*

and sporting people of both sexes flocked to town. They came in buggies, hacks, wagons, horseback, and even afoot. There was not half enough hotel accommodations to go around, so people just slept and ate any old place."[2] In the four decades following the arrival of the railroads, the population of El Paso grew to eighty thousand, transforming the town into a city with vibrant transportation, mining, trade, and livestock sectors.[3] The railroad profoundly affected land values in El Paso—lots jumped from $100 an acre to $200 per front foot—as both U.S. citizens and Mexicans moved to the area.[4] Between 1885 and 1910 the value of imports and exports passing through the city increased by a factor of seven.

In the interior of the border zone, too, the arrival of the railroad had a great impact on towns. Salinas, Coahuila, for example, grew from a small community of 778 in 1877 to nearly 15,000 by 1910. During the same period, Nuevo Laredo, Tamaulipas, experienced a similar, though not quite so dramatic, expansion from 1,200 to 9,000 inhabitants. Nogales, Sonora, increased its population from under 10 to over 3,600 by 1910 solely because of its rail connection to the South. The arrival of the railroad shifted economic power in local societies all along the border. In Sonora, merchants found it necessary to develop new relationships with suppliers on the U.S. West Coast rather than rely on their traditional European purveyors.[5]

The railroads also increased the value of the border region's natural resources by connecting them to distant processing plants, distribution centers, and markets. With the rail link, mines in Arizona, Sonora, and Chihuahua could ship their ores to smelters in El Paso with no difficulty. Timber stands in the mountains of northern New Mexico and Arizona became lumber for new homes in Southern California and west Texas. The railroads opened up lands for the expansion of agriculture as well. By the turn of the century, the Winter Garden area of south Texas, the Salt River valley in central Arizona, and the Imperial Valley in Southern California and the adjoining Mexicali Valley in Baja California were emerging as important agricultural regions, capitalizing on both new irrigation technology and links to markets. With the decline of the open range, the railroad also became essential to the prosperity of the rancher, providing access to larger markets for sheep and cattle.

Of these border resources, mineral products remained the most important and held the greatest power to shape life throughout the region. Mexico's new mining code of 1884 replaced colonial laws reserving subsoil rights for the state, and U.S. investors led the way in developing Mexican mining ventures. Daniel Guggenheim obtained a concession to build three smelters in 1890 and received further grants in 1891 and 1892. Guggenheim eventually invested $12 million in mining projects in northern Mexico. Overall, the number of concessions increased from 40 in 1884, to 2,384 in 1892, to 6,939 in 1896. During the final years of the Díaz administration, U.S. citizens owned seventeen of thirty-one major mining companies operating in Mexico, controlling 81 percent of the industry's total capital (British investors held 14.5 percent). Guggenheim's American Smelting and Refining Company (ASARCO) was the largest privately owned enterprise in Mexico. Mexican nationals held a few companies, among the largest of which was the Torreón Metallurgical Company, owned by Evaristo Madero, father of future revolutionary and president Francisco I. Madero.

By 1908 the border states of Sonora and Chihuahua had become the most important mining areas in Mexico, rapidly increasing their output of gold, silver, lead, and copper. From 1877 to 1908 the value of gold production in Mexico rose from 1.5 million pesos to over 40 million pesos, and the value of silver production rose from 25 million pesos to over 85 million pesos. Much of that output was concentrated in Sonora and Chihuahua.

Several other areas of the extractive border economy boomed. World demand for petroleum increased with the invention of the gasoline engine

Santa Bárbara Church in Santa Rosalía in Baja California Sur, designed by Gustav Eiffel, prefabricated of iron in France, and assembled on site in 1897. A copper mining concession from the government of Porfirio Díaz to the French company El Boleo resulted in the arrival of French investments and industrial architecture to this area of the border. 2006.

in the 1890s. Two petroleum investors—Edward L. Doheny of the Mexican Petroleum Company and Whitman Pearson of the Mexican Eagle Company (El Águila)—came to control major portions of the border oil industry. Commercial agriculture and livestock raising in northern Mexico also expanded, again with a significant infusion of capital from the other side of the border. California newspaper magnates William Randolph Hearst and Harrison Gray Otis both held extensive rangeland in Chihuahua.

Manufacturing expanded rapidly in the Mexican border states during the late nineteenth century. As an industrial center the city of Monterrey, Nuevo León, became second in importance only to Mexico City during this period. As mining towns boomed, Monterrey satisfied the demand for such goods as nails, windowpanes, bricks, cement, explosives, metal products, clothing, cigarettes, beer, and processed foods. Small family-owned and -operated companies catering to local and regional markets expanded to become large, capital-intensive, vertically integrated firms producing for the national market. The giant steel foundry Fundidora Monterrey, established in 1900, was the first integrated steel plant in Latin America. In contrast to the situation in mining and in petroleum production, the capital in northern manufacturing tended to be Mexican.

The border region boasted valuable natural resources, a network of rail lines, and inexpensive labor, but control of its economy was in the hands of bankers, investors, and corporations in New York, Chicago, Mexico City, and London. A small share of profits flowed back to the border. As San Francisco amassed wealth and power in the wake of the California gold rush, it joined financial powers in the U.S. East and Midwest and in Mexico City in directing the border economy. The border region in this early period was an economic colony, sending its natural resources to more developed areas.

By 1910 about 25 percent of the foreign investment in Mexico was concentrated in Coahuila, Sonora, Chihuahua, and Nuevo León. Only the Federal District had a higher proportion (63 percent) of the foreign capital in the country. By the turn of the century, U.S. investments in Mexico had risen to over $500 million, far outstripping the amount of European involvement. More than a thousand U.S. companies were engaged in Mexican operations, with more than 20 percent of their activities concentrated in the border states of Coahuila, Chihuahua, and Sonora. These investments marked the beginning of significant U.S. economic influence in Mexico. The northern Mexican railroads—the catalyst of the nineteenth-century border boom—were themselves built largely by U.S. companies and were financed by U.S. banks. The rolling stock, railroad ties, and engineers tended to be of U.S. origin. By 1902, U.S. companies controlled 80 percent of Mexican railroad stock. After

1908, responding to increasingly strident nationalism, Díaz began to buy much of the stock in an effort to Mexicanize the railroad.

The state of Sonora provides a striking example of the extent to which U.S. investment dominated the Mexican border economy. At the turn of the century, U.S. investors owned several million acres of land in Sonora and in neighboring Sinaloa. Additionally, U.S. citizens controlled the largest mining enterprises in the state, and they were heavily involved in commercial and ranching activities. Powerful U.S.-owned companies, such as the Cananea Consolidated Copper Company and the Sonora Land and Cattle Company, played an enormous role in Sonora's economy, exercising considerable political influence as well. In Chihuahua the situation was much the same; foreigners obtained millions of acres of choice agricultural, timber, and ranching land, and they invested heavily in mining enterprises. These were not exclusively enclaves of U.S. interest and activity, however. In Minas Prietas–La Colorada, for example, U.S. investment served as a catalyst for regional development in which local Mexican elites built subsidiary industries that generated significant profits.[6] In Baja California, the Porfirian government granted a huge concession of more than 10 million acres to a U.S. company for the colonization and development of Ensenada and the coast to the south. At the same time, large parts of the rich Mexicali Valley passed into the control of U.S. investors.[7]

THE BORDER ECONOMY
DURING THE MEXICAN REVOLUTION

From 1910—the end of the Díaz regime—to the onset of the Great Depression at the end of the 1920s, the economy of the border region continued to develop in what had become its traditional sectors: mining, raising livestock on the vast and arid plains, small-time agriculture, and some manufacturing and petroleum production. But the development paths of the two sides of the international boundary diverged markedly in this period. While the Revolution of 1910 held the economies of the Mexican border states in stasis—they neither grew nor contracted significantly as a whole—the economies of the U.S. border states boomed.

In the Mexican border states, the period from 1910 to 1917 was dominated by the convulsive political upheaval of the Revolution of 1910, which had long-lasting economic impacts for Mexico and for the border region. Peaceful political change was not firmly established until the 1920s, and the destabilizing challenges of regional strongmen remained until the organization of the first official party of the Revolution, the Partido Nacional Revolucionario, in 1929.

The violent phase of the Revolution did not, however, destroy the Mexican economy of the border states. Despite the turbulence along the U.S.-Mexican border, trade and commerce continued. Though trade patterns and goods changed, the magnitude of commercial exchange increased significantly: the value of imports from the United States trebled between 1911 and 1920. The value of exports to the United States was $57.5 million in 1911 and $179.3 million by 1920. Furthermore, official figures conceal the large amount of smuggling that took place. Manufacturing continued in many parts of Mexico throughout the decade, interrupted in some areas but not destroyed. The worst was over by 1915. Far more problematic was the negative effect on investor confidence; the conflict certainly did not encourage long-term investment in or optimism about the border region's economic future.

The Mexican petroleum sector boomed during the Revolution, with output increasing from 3.6 million barrels in 1910 to 157 million in 1920. British and U.S. investment in oil continued despite the violence. Most companies maintained production throughout the period; when oil fields came under the control of revolutionary groups, businesses paid taxes or bribes to stay in operation. By the end of the decade, more U.S. investment than ever before was concentrated in the Mexican oil industry, having grown from 38 percent of total investment in 1911 to 61 percent in 1920. The Mexican petroleum industry, located principally in the border state of Tamaulipas and neighboring Veracruz, was producing over 25 percent of the world's oil by 1921.

The emergence of the oil industry in the early decades of the twentieth century also ranked as an important economic turning point in the U.S. Southwest. Oil had been discovered in the region prior to 1900, but little demand had existed until the invention of the internal combustion engine for use in automobiles and trucks, improvements in heating and lighting techniques, and the use of petroleum by-products in manufacturing. Texas quickly assumed leadership in the new industry, boasting major wells in the northern and eastern parts of the state by 1918. California also became an important oil producer after 1900, with extensive drilling taking place in the central and southern areas of the state.

Mining in Mexico did not fare as well as oil or manufacturing. Mines and equipment throughout the Mexican North were frequently located in areas of extreme turmoil, and some were destroyed as targets of deliberate assaults by revolutionaries. Transportation in this corridor was often interrupted; mining products were sometimes seized from trains. After reaching peaks in mineral output in 1911 and 1912, production levels decreased between 1914 and 1916. Declines were exacerbated by the outbreak of World War I and the disappearance of the German market, the loss of German cyanide (used to extract gold and silver), and a U.S. embargo on dynamite shipments to Mexico. It is estimated that mining production fell by as much as 50 percent during the revolutionary decade.

In the U.S. Southwest, in contrast, mining experienced significant growth. In an important shift, mining increasingly moved away from gold and silver to copper production. Copper was in steady demand for industrial applications; with the shift from precious metals to copper, the U.S. West was evolving in step with the changing technological basis of national industrial development. In Arizona, copper production rose from 23 million pounds in 1883 to 719 million pounds in 1917. Mines and smelters at Bisbee, Morenci, and Douglas busily extracted and processed copper for use in the expanding electrical industry throughout the United States. Border cities such as El Paso became binational mining centers, processing and shipping ores from both sides of the border and selling supplies and services to mining companies and their workers. By the end of the 1920s the U.S. West was responsible for 90 percent of U.S. mineral production, excluding coal.

Mexican agriculture probably experienced the greatest disruption during the Revolution of all economic sectors. Crops were seized and distributed to revolutionary armies. There was a drastic decline in the production of corn and other staple goods. Famine accompanied warfare in some parts of the countryside. In the cities there was panic over staple food prices throughout 1915. Related was the lack of maintenance and the destruction of large portions of the transport infrastructure during the fighting. By the end of 1920 the railroads—the great symbol of Porfirian economic progress—were in a state of disrepair. Half of Mexico's locomotives were out of service.

In the U.S. border states, however, agriculture and transportation boomed during the second decade of the new century. New irrigation works triggered a dramatic rise in crop production. The Reclamation Act of 1902 prompted the U.S. government to construct large irrigation operations in the Southwest, causing desert areas to blossom. In the southern New Mexico–west Texas area, the Elephant Butte Dam project, completed in 1916, which included hundreds of miles of canals, brought eighty thousand new acres of land under cultivation in the El Paso region alone. Steady delivery of Rio Grande water spurred an upsurge in cotton cultivation in El Paso, and the El Paso Valley emerged as one of the leading agricultural areas in the border region in the 1910s. All over the Southwest and West, farmers formerly limited in their capacity to produce crops now expanded their agricultural operations.

Large-scale water projects—the Roosevelt Dam and the Arizona Canal in Arizona, the Imperial Dam for California's Imperial and Coachella valleys, and the Elephant Butte Dam—established both the Bureau of Reclamation and the federal government as main pillars of economic growth in the border states. Western farming reached an all-time peak during World War I.

At the same time, advances in food processing and the development of refrigerated railroad cars in the United States, which made it possible for growers to ship their vegetables and fruits to the vast eastern markets, created the potential for huge profits. In California, orange growers quadrupled their production between 1900 and 1920, and lemon growers quintupled theirs. The revolution in southwestern agriculture caused land values to skyrocket. The average value of an acre of California farmland increased from $25 to $105 during this twenty-year period.

The boom, brought on by water projects and demand sparked by World War I, was followed by a short-term bust in the early 1920s, as the agriculturally based economies of the U.S. West fell into a deep depression. The postwar severe downturn contributed to a massive movement of people from rural to urban areas. Farmers who remained in agriculture shifted steadily toward more capital-intensive, mechanized farming practices in order to remain competitive in an era when farm commodities fetched low prices. Water projects and increasing mechanization led to the rapid growth of agriculture in California's Central Valley, which developed into one of the country's most important centers of cotton, fruit, and vegetable production in the 1920s.

The economies of U.S. border towns flourished during the second decade of the new century. A sizable portion of Mexicans who migrated to the border region during the Revolution brought money and prosperity to the border towns they settled in while they waited for the fighting to end. Unlike earlier immigrants, who were mainly unskilled labor, these refugees from the Revolution included skilled workers, professionals, entrepreneurs with capital, merchants, and others. El Paso thrived as Chihuahua refugees brought their purchasing power to the border. Bank deposits surged, department store business boomed, and hotels filled to capacity. The city's assessed property value increased from $38 million to $61 million between 1914 and 1918. The El Paso Chamber of Commerce established a committee to help refugees cross the border and secure accommodations. El Paso also benefited from trade created by the Revolution. Arms attracted new customers from as far south as Zacatecas and Aguascalientes; local businessmen launched an aggressive campaign to attract Mexican buyers to the region.[8]

As many U.S. border cities thrived, some Mexican border towns declined. In Ciudad Juárez there was a continual flow north across the river to El

Paso, as Juarenses (residents of Ciudad Juárez) left to find work. The disparity between the two sister cities grew more pronounced with the revolutionary fighting; ultimately, the "only available jobs around Juárez were in agriculture and making bricks for construction, both of which paid very little."[9] One observer wrote, "Juárez had featured many tourist attractions before the revolution, but the years of fighting had crippled it sorely. At every turn you come up in ruins—houses riddled with bullet holes or breached with shot and shell; a public library razed to the ground, a mere heap of stones; a post office badly damaged; and, opposite the Juárez monument, a brick building, roofless, with gaping windows and walls."[10]

Development in Mexican border towns tended to focus on entertainment and tourism. A reformist movement in the United States that gained strength early in the century drove significant sectors of the U.S. border entertainment industry south of the boundary during the revolutionary decade. Three cabaret operators forced out of Bakersfield opened bars in Tijuana and quickly became financial powers. Eventually, they financed racetracks, gambling halls, and a brewery in Tijuana and Mexicali. Ciudad Juárez also capitalized on this source of income. In the face of declining economic options and municipal bankruptcy, such opportunities were welcome.

In short, the Revolution retarded development in many economic sectors on the Mexican side of the border between 1910 and the early 1920s. Mexican leaders were preoccupied first with civil war and then with the politics of centralization and the reconstitution of the social fabric of a war-torn country. Mexican border states fell behind in several key areas in which the U.S. border states boomed. The disparity would continue through the twentieth century and into the twenty-first century.

PROHIBITION ON THE BORDER

In the border region as a whole, the 1920s saw the first stirrings of growth based on tourism across the international boundary. Prohibition in the United States, which came with the Volstead Act of 1919 (implemented after 1920), and restrictions on gambling and night life provided the impetus for the development of Mexican border-town economies based on the sale of liquor, gambling, and other services that could not be obtained legally or inexpensively in the United States.[11] Prohibition was the culmination of a moralistic movement that began in the United States in the nineteenth century. During the teens, large nightclubs, gambling casinos, dance halls, and the brewing, traffic, and sale of alcoholic beverages had been at their peak. The movement also represented a reaction against changes in U.S. society—such as women working, driving automobiles, smoking, and drinking—which were deemed undesirable by many influential guardians of public morality.

Prohibition affected the entire nation, but Southwesterners, particularly the residents of the cities close to the international boundary, had the option of crossing to Mexican border towns for pleasures not available in their own backyards. Seeing an opportunity to make money, many U.S. citizens and other foreigners obtained concessions from Mexican officials to open tourist-oriented businesses along the border. Prohibition encouraged owners of U.S. bars, casinos, and related enterprises to move their operations to Ciudad Juárez, Tijuana, and other Mexican border cities where few restrictions existed. For thirteen years, from 1920 to 1933, Mexican border cities boomed in an explosion of U.S. tourism.

The spillover effect was felt in U.S. border cities as well. In order to derive maximum benefits for El Paso, the local chamber of commerce advertised in national magazines and newspapers to promote visits to Ciudad Juárez. As a result, El Paso was frequently chosen as the site for national and international conventions. There was so much tourist traffic in Ciudad Juárez–El Paso that, during a ten-year period, two new international bridges were built. In addition, the El Paso Electric Company owned and operated an iron bridge across the Rio Grande, which produced a small fortune in tolls.

Just as Ciudad Juárez drew tourists from Texas and New Mexico, Tijuana enticed residents of Southern California who sought such diversions as cockfights, bullfights, horse and dog races, nightclubs, casinos, bars, and prostitution. A prime attraction was the casino at Agua Caliente, established in 1928. A large complex, it included gambling rooms, bars, restaurants, theaters for floor shows, a dog racetrack, a horse racetrack, a golf course, and an airport. Its owners, Baron Long, Wirt G. Bowman, and James N. Crofton, had operated nightspots in Southern California prior to Prohibition. The clientele were mostly U.S. citizens, especially prosperous Californians, among them many well-known movie stars of the period. Tijuanenses (residents of Tijuana) who worked at Agua Caliente as waiters, dealers, or bartenders during those years recall serving such stars as Clark Gable, Douglas Fairbanks, Jean Harlow, the Marx brothers, Jimmy Durante, Buster Keaton, Johnny Weissmuller, Bing Crosby, Dick Powell, and the celebrated gangster Al Capone. Many of the establishments in Tijuana were luxurious; their architecture reflected the romantic taste of the times, blending Mexican, Californian, and Moorish styles.

There was no shortage of tourist establishments elsewhere on the Mexican border. Examples in Sonora included the International, Southern, and O.T.B. Bar-Restaurant at San Luis Río Colorado; the Cactus Club and

"A Mexican Belle, Tijuana, Mexico." Colorized picture postcard from the late 1920s advertising the Agua Caliente Casino in Tijuana, which opened in 1928, the Mexican belle, and ABC Beer, all attractions to U.S. visitors during Prohibition. (Andre Williams Collection)

Americano at Sonoyta; the Royal Cafe and High Life at Nogales; the Foreign Club at Naco; and the International Club, Silver Dollar Bar, Curio's Cafe, and the Volstead Bar at Agua Prieta. In Chihuahua there were the Central Bar and Fred's Place at Palomas; the Tivoli Gardens and Central Café at Ciudad Juárez; and the Riverside at Ojinaga. Coahuila included the Washington Bar and Newton's Cave at Ciudad Acuña and the Club International at Piedras Negras. And at Reynosa, Tamaulipas, were the New York Bar and the Crystal Palace. The publicity directed at the U.S. public greatly contributed to the reputation of the Mexican border cities as Sodoms and Gomorrahs. An image largely created by profiteers, this was, in fact, the great attraction of the border towns. The problem with this effective reputation for sin was that a "black legend" of the border persisted for decades after Prohibition.[12]

Although Prohibition tarnished the reputation of the Mexican border, it also benefited the region. Revenues from gambling houses in Ciudad Juárez helped finance numerous city projects. The surge in tourism transformed Ciudad Juárez into the most prosperous Mexican city along the border, boasting a wide range of urban services, including electricity, sewage, and water services, pavements, and trolleys. Advances were made in transportation throughout the North. At Ojinaga, Chihuahua–Presidio, Texas, a new international bridge was inaugurated, uniting the Kansas City–Mexico City railroad line. Economic resurgence from tourism allowed the state of Chihuahua to develop some much needed public works.

Despite the economic and social progress promoted by Prohibition in the 1920s, Mexican border states suffered from uneven, superficial, and incomplete development. There were few systematic or lasting improvements in infrastructure, with the important exception of irrigation (in the late 1920s the central government devoted 6 percent of the federal budget to irrigation, most of it in the border area). Nor did the Prohibition boom underwrite investments in long-term economic enterprises in the industrial sector. Because of communication and transportation bottlenecks, border cities found themselves cut off from the rest of Mexico, nurturing instead commercial, economic, and social ties with cities on the U.S. side of the boundary.

In contrast, several broad and positive economic changes took place in the U.S. border states during the 1920s, including a spectacular growth in agriculture in the U.S. Southwest. Whereas nationally the number of workers in agriculture declined during this period, the border states recorded impressive gains in agricultural employment. At the same time, there was significant growth in nonagricultural activities and employment. Nonagricultural employment increased in the United States by 130 percent between 1900 and 1940, and the U.S. border states far surpassed that rate; Arizona recorded a 272 percent increase; California, 489 percent; New Mexico, 253 percent; and Texas, 392 percent. El Paso was one of many border cities that developed its industrial base during the prosperous 1920s. Over two hundred factories in the city produced a wide variety of products by the end of the decade. Among the industrial establishments the most prominent were the ASARCO plant, which continued to grow in importance as a regional mining processing center, and the new Phelps Dodge refining plant, whose operations converted El Paso into a leading world producer of refined copper.

There were also considerable advances in the transportation sector on the U.S. side of the border during the Prohibition era. El Paso, Albuquerque, and Tucson were among the cities most affected by the increased integration of the Southwest with other parts of the United States by rail. These three cities evolved into important transportation and trading centers. Because of the mild weather and the unique Spanish–Mexican–Native American heritage, they also became tourist attractions. El Paso was in a particularly advantageous position to grow and develop. Enjoying railroad connections with central Mexico and with all parts of the United States, the city became a prominent transshipment and distribution center for raw materials and manufactured goods from Mexico and the U.S. Southwest during the 1920s. Many farming, ranching, mining, and manufacturing concerns in the surrounding territory depended on El Paso for a variety of supplies and services. Capitalizing on its border location, El Paso promoted trade with Mexico.

In Tucson, the Southern Pacific and the Southwestern railroads contributed substantially to the city's prominence in the Arizona-Sonora economy. Farming, mining, and ranching interests in the region looked to Tucson as a source of investment capital, processing plants, shipping facilities, supplies, and services. Again, tourism figured prominently in the economy of the city, as local leaders publicized the plentiful sunshine of the Arizona desert. In the 1920s the Sunshine Climate Club promoted Tucson as the "Climate City of the Nation" and boasted that its tourist facilities were "the best in the West." With a membership of several hundred people and a hefty operating budget, the club conducted very successful advertising campaigns in leading national magazines. The "good life" available in the Tucson oasis appealed to U.S. citizens from other parts of the country; soon thousands moved there permanently, and many others chose Arizona as a vacation spot. Tucson also succeeded in luring large numbers of people who sought a desert climate for health reasons. Affluent patients were especially welcome, and every effort was made to make their lives pleasant and comfortable.

Tourism in the U.S. border states was different from Prohibition-led tourism in the Mexican border cities. People came to the U.S. border states to stay, frequently retiring on steady pension incomes. On the U.S. side of the border, boomtowns combined tourism with deeper-level economic developments.

EARLY FREE TRADE

As early as the economic boom of the Díaz administration, border commerce was enhanced by legislation establishing free trade zones along the Mexican side of the border. Recognizing the distance of border inhabitants from central Mexico, these zones allowed for the importation of goods from the United States at reduced or waived tariff rates. In 1885 the administration of President Díaz extended what had been a free trade area along the Texas-Mexico boundary line to the entire border.

Always controversial, however, free trade experienced a series of government restrictions that reduced the benefits for border communities by the turn of the century. The Díaz regime justified its action, citing the increased integration of the border region with the rest of Mexico brought on by the arrival of the railroads throughout the North. The government eliminated the free zone altogether in 1905.

The end of the free zone changed life in many towns on the Mexican side of the border. In Ciudad Juárez, for example, once prosperous merchants found the rules of the game changed. The city's turn to tourism through the construction of prominent tourist facilities followed the changes in the law. A bullring was built in the city in 1903, a racetrack in 1905. In subsequent years *fronterizos* lobbied for the return of free trade to the region. A 1911 article in a Ciudad Juárez newspaper pointed out that the poor state of farming in the Juárez Valley was due to high prices for oil—used to run irrigation pumps—imported from the United States. But Mexico City did not respond to such pleas until the 1930s, when dire economic conditions in the remote border states made duty-free importation of foreign products an absolute necessity.

It is important to note that the changes in the border region in the first two decades of the twentieth century, including the impressive advances on the U.S. side, were plagued by a major shortcoming: the region as a whole received limited returns from the raw materials it supplied to other areas. Ownership of petroleum fields, mines, smelters, ranches, and railroads remained heavily concentrated in the hands of outsiders. Industrial and financial decisions were the purview of investors, bankers, and federal governments whose interests sometimes opposed those of border dwellers. In effect the border region continued to function as an economic colony of the U.S. Northeast and Midwest, from whence the capital for sustaining the extractive and agricultural industries that dominated the region's economy originated. This situation was to change dramatically with the far-reaching impacts of the Great Depression and World War II.

NOTES

1. The first section of this chapter draws heavily on two draft chapters from the historical volume of the University of California, Los Angeles, Borderlands Atlas Project: Richard Griswold del Castillo and Raúl Rodriguez González, "Conflict and Development: The United States–Mexico Borderlands, 1848–1900," and Oscar J. Martínez and David Piñera, "The Mexico–United States Borderlands, 1900–1940."

2. James B. Gillett, quoted in W. H. Timmons, *El Paso: A Borderlands History* (El Paso: Texas Western Press, University of Texas, El Paso, 2005), 167.

3. Timmons, *El Paso*, 185.

4. Timmons, *El Paso*, 167.

5. Miguel Tinker Salas, *In the Shadow of the Eagles: Sonora and the Transformation of the Border during the Porfiriato* (Berkeley: University of California Press, 1997), 5, 101.

6. Salas, *In the Shadow of the Eagles*, 177.

7. David Piñera, *American and English Influence on the Early Development of Ensenada, Baja California, Mexico* (San Diego: Institute for Regional Studies of the Californias, San Diego State University, 1995).

8. Oscar J. Martínez, *Border Boom Town: Ciudad Juárez since 1848* (Austin: University of Texas Press, 1978), 46.

9. Martínez, *Border Boom Town*, 50.

10. Quoted in Martínez, *Border Boom Town*.

11. Martínez, *Border Boom Town*.

12. Although Mexican authorities generally condoned vice-based tourism at the border, there were times when they acted to curb its negative impact. In 1925, for example, Emilio Portes Gil, governor of Tamaulipas (and later president from 1928 to 1930), prohibited the sale of liquor on Native American *ejidos* (common lands) and in small towns to protect area youths. The construction of bars near churches, hospitals, schools, and workplaces was prohibited.

3

LIFE ON THE BORDER

Social Change, 1880s to 1930s

A t the end of the nineteenth century the U.S.-Mexican border region was still sparsely inhabited; its population grew only slowly and fitfully. By the end of the twentieth century, the ten states of the border region were among the largest and fastest growing in both Mexico and the United States. Moreover, the social importance of the border states increased markedly in the national life of both countries as the proportion of persons living in border states climbed by 2010 to one out of every five in Mexico and one out of every four in the United States. This chapter, which focuses on the period between the coming of the Mexican Revolution and the end of the Great Depression, addresses questions about social change: What are the main features of the social evolution of the U.S.-Mexican border region? What characteristics make border society unique, and how has the social development of the border influenced national reality in both countries?

1880s TO 1910

In the late nineteenth century, rapidly expanding railroad networks connected the border region's natural resources to abundant labor supplies for the first time. The economic growth of the area was greatly facilitated by the availability of a large, inexpensive labor force consisting mostly of Mexican Americans and Mexicans, as well as Chinese who had flocked to the western United States to work in mining and on the railroads. In the mid-1880s the expansion of south Texas cotton acreage and sheep ranches relied on the annual importation by rail of thousands of Mexican migrant workers. At the turn of the century the development of open-pit copper mines in Clifton, Douglas, and Bisbee, Arizona, likewise rested on a mostly Mexican and Mexican American labor force. In the 1880s in California the growth of agriculture in the San Joaquin Valley drew upon a multinational migrant labor force of Asians, European Americans, and Mexicans. The railroads that spanned the region were built primarily by Chinese and Mexican migrant workers.[1]

Large-scale Mexican immigration to the United States began in the 1880s, after the Mexican Central Railroad was connected with the Southern Pacific in El Paso. Enabled by the web of new rail connections, a mass migration in the late nineteenth century transformed the border's small village communities. In the U.S. West, the movement of millions of Europeans, European Americans, African Americans, Mexicans, and Chinese—for the most part by train—rearranged the social landscape. The railroad brought an end to the border region's isolation from distant population centers. Towns like San Antonio and Los Angeles rapidly grew into major cities during the last decades of the nineteenth century; Los Angeles mushroomed from fewer than 6,000 people in 1870 to more than 100,000 by 1900, and San Antonio grew from 12,000 to 53,000 during the same period. As with earlier immigration to the border zone, the river of movement from east to west constituted the majority of the flow; smaller streams of migrants moved from central Mexico to the North and from the Mexican North across the border into the United States.

With the expansion of the railroad network, Mexico experienced a population boom on its peripheries, but especially in the states along the border with the United States. Mining, irrigated agriculture, construction, and other urban service activities drew thousands of migrants to move northward by rail. The rate of population increase in the border states tripled, rising from 1 percent per year between 1857 and 1880 to 3 percent per year during the 1880s. The states of Coahuila and Tamaulipas doubled their populations between 1877 and 1910, while Baja California and Nuevo León quadrupled theirs. Pacesetters in urban growth in the North were the cities of Chihuahua, Hermosillo, La Paz, Saltillo, Ciudad Victoria, and Monterrey, with Monterrey's bustling industrial activities making it Mexico's fastest-growing city in the last quarter of the nineteenth century.[2] Only slightly less dramatic in their railroad-induced expansion were such cities as Sabinas, Piedras Negras, Muzquiz, and Linares. The improvement of port facilities helped spark the growth of La Paz, Mazatlán, and Guaymas on the Pacific coast and Tampico on the Gulf of Mexico. New and expanded mining industries in the North also provided a stimulus for population growth in such places as Santa Rosalía, Cananea, and Navojoa.[3]

As a result of the new migration of the last quarter of the nineteenth century, the Mexicans and Mexican Americans of the southwestern United States—whether recent arrivals or descendants of settlers of former Spanish and Mexican communities—found themselves reduced to minority status and sometimes deprived of power and property by the many thousands of new-comers carried westward by the railroads. *Californios*—as native Californians of predominately Spanish descent came to be called—declined from 82 percent of the population of California in 1850 to 19 percent in 1880. In Texas, *tejanos* remained a majority during the last half of the nineteenth century, but they became an increasingly impoverished majority. By the end of the century, most had become unskilled rural laborers. Although frequently confined to unskilled jobs and segregated barrios, these residual social groups maintained vital and distinctive communities in which their religion, language, and other customs stayed strong. They established newspapers, mutual aid societies, and sports teams that served their own social and cultural needs.

Native Americans, too, became increasingly marginalized during the late nineteenth century. The new international boundary split traditional in-digenous groups, including the Kumeyaay of the California–Baja California border, the Cocopah of the lower Colorado River, and the Tohono O'odham (Papago) of the Arizona-Sonora border region. As the U.S. and Mexican governments restricted the ability of these partitioned groups to cross the border freely, their traditional lifestyles and cultures deteriorated. Under Por-firio Díaz, the power of the Mexican North's indigenous populations to resist further incursions was definitively broken. The Yaqui people, who until the 1870s had lived in the agricultural valleys of the Yaqui River, were crushed by a series of ruthless federal campaigns that dispersed them throughout the state. In addition, thousands of Yaqui were deported to the Yucatán peninsula to work on henequen haciendas.

The most feared Native American group both north and south of the border was the Apache nation, for which nomadic raiding had become a way of life. Divided into many clans in southern Arizona, New Mexico, and south-western Texas, the Apache had lived for hundreds of years in symbiosis with the Spanish-speaking settlers. From the 1860s through the 1880s, sporadic warfare erupted between border settlers and the Apache, the latter inspired by a series of charismatic leaders, including Geronimo, Cochise, and Mangas Coloradas. The U.S. Army failed in its attempt to keep the Apache on reserva-tions. The standard cycle of broken treaties and massacres followed. In 1886, Geronimo surrendered to a joint Mexican and U.S. force in the Sierra Madre of Sonora. Apache raids continued periodically in Mexico into the 1920s, but after 1890 they came to an end in the U.S. Southwest.

A new border elite replaced older groups at the top of the social pyramid. The economic expansion of the North was accompanied by the emergence of many large and wealthy families. In Chihuahua, the Terrazas-Creel clan became one of the most important landowning families in Mexico. The family built its empire of wealth on land and cattle, as well as exports to the United States, and eventually owned 10 million acres of land in Chihuahua, 500,000 head of cattle, the largest meatpacking and flour mills in the region, the state's only brewery, some textile and clothing mills, and an iron foundry. The Terrazas-Creel family dominated state politics for two generations.

CAUSES OF THE MEXICAN REVOLUTION

The Order and Progress brought to Mexico by President Porfirio Díaz between 1876 and 1910 (see chapter 2) embodied the twin, mutually reinforcing causes of the Revolution of 1910 in the Mexican border states. The shape and course of violence in the North—and to some extent also in the U.S. border area—between 1910 and the 1920s ironically reflected signal accomplishments by Díaz. The intersection of long-term and short-term stresses caused the Revolution to occur when and where it did.

Porfirian "order" meant political centralization, which came at the expense of local privileges and customs. The force of centralization was particularly strong in the North, where the federal government had previously had only a tenuous grip on local activities. Throughout the North, an unusual degree of autonomy had been granted to settlers and frontier towns in return for holding the line against nomadic indigenous groups. With the withering of central authority after Mexico's independence, this autonomy had tended to increase.

Attacks on village political institutions under Díaz principally consisted of limiting this traditional autonomy. The central government began to appoint district and municipal officials instead of allowing them to be elected locally. Whereas villagers had historically chosen their own council members and mayors—the officials who allocated access to village lands, water, and pastures and who resolved conflicts in the community—Porfirian leaders took control of even minor municipal appointments. Porfirian politicians also introduced new taxation systems that replaced local with central authorities and old practices with new ones. In particular the northern states of Sonora, Chihuahua, Nuevo León, and Durango—all key foci of the Revolution—were brought under the control of Mexico City.

The dynamic of political centralization in Chihuahua is illustrative. There, the Terrazas clan, working hand in hand with Mexico City politicians, destroyed even the pretense of representative local government over a period of a few years. From 1881 to 1911 a total of only eighty-six men sat in the state legislature, fifty-five of them on two or more occasions. In 1887 the state governor began to appoint *jefes políticos* (political leaders); two years later independent mayorships were abolished.[4] A 1904 law provided that the *jefe municipal* (municipal leader) be appointed by the governor. Because of this rapid political centralization under Díaz, social stresses in the North differed from the conflicts between communities and property owners over land tenure that characterized parts of central Mexico; in the North hostilities tended to express themselves as conflicts between common people and local notables over political power and prerogative. When conflict over power centered on resources, the fencing off of woods and prairies became the focus of the struggle.

Porfirian "progress" meant, above all, the rapid commercialization of agrarian and extractive activities. The key to this process was the expanding rail network that connected once isolated regions, such as the border states, to distant markets, vastly increasing the value of land in the region. Rapidly expanding circles of profitable agricultural and mining operations had swift and profound impacts on villages and towns throughout the North.

The case of Porfirian progress in Chihuahua reveals the sort of agrarian discontent that developed in the North in the period preceding the outbreak of the Revolution.[5] Colonization under the Spanish Crown had given settlers in the region 250,000 acres of land, exemption from taxes, freedom from ethnic discrimination, and the right and obligation to carry arms. After independence these rights continued in autonomous communities. What emerged was quite unusual in Mexico: a territory of small landowners. In the late 1850s and early 1860s, hacendados, led by Luis Terrazas, began to buy up large estates. These landowners were not generally considered expropriators: they took little land from peasants, and they protected them against depredation by the Apaches and the expanding central government, refusing to send state resources to Mexico City.

In 1884, however, the first railroad connection from Chihuahua to the United States was established, and Terrazas, the patrician protector, was ousted. The rail link meant new markets for the state's mineral goods, cattle, and agricultural produce. As land prices increased, suddenly Chihuahua's village property became a very attractive commodity. The intense attack on the traditional rights of communities, followed by attacks on village holdings, eventually reduced the land of the original colony settlements from 250,000 to 50,000 acres. These agrarian stresses, characteristic of both Durango and Chihuahua, would cause the two states to witness the largest popular mobilizations of the Revolution.

Under the Chihuahua governorship of Enrique Creel, Terrazas's son-in-law, a new law was enacted in 1905, declaring that all community-held land—not only collective grazing land but even houses—could be sold on the open market. The law required municipal governments to sell off all municipal properties, including housing plots, fields, and pasture. At the same time, a massive enclosure movement on larger haciendas emerged, reducing the lands available to inhabitants of the region for informal traditional uses. Terrazas had customarily allowed people from neighboring villages on his property. Now these persons were forced to pay or see their cattle confiscated. Small ranchers lost access to irrigation water, increasing their vulnerability to dry spells. When the Revolution broke out, these communities were spearheading the movement in Chihuahua. Many men who assumed command were traditional leaders of the free villagers who had lost autonomy and access to land.

In many areas of the North, the Porfirian government granted or sold large concessions of land as a way to spur economic development. These included sale of lands for Mormon colonization in Chihuahua, an English colonization project in Sonora, and a huge concession to a U.S. company, the International Company of Mexico, for development of the northern part of Baja California. By 1887, about 60 percent of the entire Baja California peninsula had been given in concession to private foreign and Mexican interests.[6]

The long-term effects of Porfirian Order and Progress were accompanied by a growing discontent among working people throughout the North. Here again the railroad played an important role; after its extension through the border states, a well-consolidated mining, construction, and railroad labor pool flowed between northern Mexico and the U.S. Southwest. It is estimated that in 1908 between 60,000 and 100,000 Mexicans entered the United States to work in these sectors. In 1909 Mexican nationals made up 7 percent of the U.S. workforce in mining and 13 percent in smelting. In Arizona the corresponding figures were 26 percent and 61 percent. By 1912, Mexicans were the main source of labor on railroads west of Kansas City.[7]

The ethnically diverse workforce of the Mexican North and U.S. Southwest was often segmented according to geographical provenance, with the Mexican and Chinese populations generally assigned the least skilled, most arduous, and most dangerous work—usually at lower pay than other groups. Resentment festered around these points, exacerbated by Mexican rules that demanded respect toward foreigners and brought stiff penalties for their violation; *faltando respeto a un extranjero* (disrespecting a foreigner) became a common pretext for arresting Mexican workers in the Sonoran mines. Industrial accidents were common, and labor conditions were generally austere. In 1909, to give one example, the Cananea Consolidated Copper Company reported 18 deaths and 769 accidents (47 of them deemed serious). There were no safety laws until 1912, and these were not enforced until the late 1920s. Everyday dangers to employees' health were frequently ignored. Sometimes workers also were caught in dependent relationships with employers; company store purchases were credited to employees' accounts or were automatically deducted from paychecks. In general the commercial nexus in the isolated border states was characterized by strained social relations. Although general stores were not predominantly owned by U.S. or Chinese citizens, there was animosity both toward members of these groups who did own stores and against fixed prices. The small-time Chinese merchants, who, in contrast to their Mexican or U.S. counterparts, sold primarily on credit, were particularly resented.[8]

There was also a dramatic change in the late nineteenth century from traditional to more modern work routines in the Mexican North. The changing Mexican economy placed a premium on laborers who could adapt to consistent hours, routinized activities, and a new work ethic. At the same time, people were increasingly separated from access to subsistence farming as they became dependent on wage incomes. Many Mexican workers traveled regularly to the United States, where they were exposed to various labor-organization and protest strategies, as well as to anarchist and socialist ideas.

Worker dissatisfaction in the North grew with the economic contraction of the first decade of the twentieth century. The Sonoran mining center of Cananea, for example, intricately linked to the U.S. economy, was negatively affected by the financial panic of 1902. Cananea workers, paid in pesos, found their wages worth half their previous value—U.S. staples were now at twice their previous cost. In June 1906 employees of Cananea struck, their grievances based on wage demands, particularly the elimination of the system in which Mexicans received less pay than did U.S. citizens. The manager of the company store fired on the protesting crowd, and in the ensuing melee workers killed managers and burned down the store. With the approval of the Díaz administration, the company brought in by rail several hundred Arizona Rangers from across the border to suppress the strike.

The impact of Porfirian Order and Progress in the North was exacerbated by the sustained demographic increase in the border states during the same period. The population of Chihuahua doubled, an increase caused mostly by the number of immigrants brought by rail to mining towns. Reactions to these various stresses were diverse, including a series of uprisings in the 1890s, the most famous being that at Tomóchic.

Added to the popular discontents and disaffections that resulted from Order and Progress and that helped incite the Revolution of 1910 was significant dissatisfaction with the Porfirian order among the elite in the North. The economic growth of the Porfiriato brought the Mexican North to national economic prominence but accorded it little commensurate political power. Few of the North's powerful families were as successful as the Terrazas-Creel clan of Chihuahua at gaining both economic and political power. The Porfirian political world was an exclusive one. By the first decade of the twentieth century, sectors of this elite were becoming increasingly disillusioned with Porfirian politics. Some began to push for reform. The classic example of the trend is Francisco I. Madero, the son of a wealthy Coahuilan land and mine owner, educated in France and California, who found that he could not break into local politics. In his *The Presidential Succession of 1910*, Madero gave voice to a widespread desire for greater democracy. He believed that a reform of the Porfirian system was needed to provide political opportunities for people such as him.

In addition to the long-term causes outlined above, important short-term causes of the Mexican Revolution existed in the border region. In 1907 a worldwide financial crisis sparked by a U.S. recession brought to a halt many of the economic gains of the Porfirian period. Few people in Mexico escaped the effects of this economic decline, which caused a crisis in mining and in the cotton fields of the Laguna region of the states of Coahuila and Durango. A shortage of capital led to many bank failures, and real wages fell dramatically. Social fallout in the Mexican North was particularly severe. The massive emigration of marginal and displaced persons that had occurred from central areas to the North in the period from 1877 to 1910 created a large pool of unemployed people in the region. Banditry became widespread and fueled the Revolution once the conflict had begun. Pancho Villa (discussed in the next section) is the best example of the many men and women affected by these local blows.

Especially hard hit after 1907 were people and enterprises in the North that were intertwined with the U.S. market. The copper mines at Cananea, Sonora, the state's largest employer, began laying off workers in September and by the end of the year had completely closed down operations.[9] As mines in the United States closed, Mexican miners returned home to face unemployment. Chihuahua, so dependent on foreign capital in its key mining sector, suffered a dramatic increase in unemployment. These changes served to accelerate the growth of militancy among northern workers as the general dislocation of the time proved to be more significant than ideology. The systems of credit and debt that had pervaded the lives of both rich and poor disintegrated. "After the 1907 crisis, the promise of development became increasingly illusory—as the mines closed, as merchants' sales plummeted, and as agriculture declined, old social cleavages acquired new importance."[10]

The world financial crisis of 1907—with its wide-ranging impacts in northern Mexico—was followed by a Mexican subsistence crisis in 1908 and 1909. A serious drought in 1907 led to the loss of half of the wheat harvest in the Bajío region of north-central Mexico, the nation's breadbasket. Alarming reports of food shortages began to appear in the newspapers. Prices for staples skyrocketed, severely cutting into workers' earnings. Corn and wheat imports, which had been steadily increasing between 1902 and 1906, took off in 1908 and 1909. Because food generally constituted 60 to 70 percent of workers' household expenditures, food shortages and concomitant price hikes caused a dramatic decline in the standard of living.

The match that ignited the volatile mix in the North was a succession crisis at the national level. In an interview with foreign journalist James Creelman, Díaz—stating that Mexico was now ready for democracy—indicated that he would step down as president of Mexico in 1910. After months of political maneuvering, however, Díaz decided to run again. A group of middle-class political activists suggested Teodoro Dehesa, governor of Veracruz, as a vice presidential running mate for Díaz. Dehesa had an excellent reputation in middle and popular sectors, including those in the border states. His popularity reflected regional stresses. However, Díaz's proposed vice presidential running mate was Ramón Corral, a city boy associated with the interests of the capital and with the centralization and exclusion of the Díaz regime. Dehesa, in contrast, was believed to better represent provincial reformist interests. Shutting off every hope of the rising northern middle and upper classes, Díaz chose to stick with Corral. Thwarted backers of the Dehesa candidacy threw their support behind Madero as the only possibility for change.[11]

Personifying the growing disenchantment and resentment of a number of the elite factions, Madero called for a revolution against Díaz's exclusive political system after the elections of 1910. But to his considerable surprise, Madero was also able to rally to his side a wide range of popular groups either dissatisfied with long-term economic trends or negatively affected by short-term downturns of the Porfirian period. The mobilization of these groups drastically altered the nature of Madero's efforts to reform the political system, transforming the decade after 1910 into a period of civil war.

THE SOCIAL CHARACTER OF
THE REVOLUTION IN THE MEXICAN NORTH

The best-known expression of Revolution in the Mexican North was the popular mobilization in support of Pancho Villa. Along with Emiliano Zapata, whose actions were restricted to south-central Mexico, Villa would come to symbolize the downtrodden Mexicans fighting between 1910 and 1917. Born Doroteo Arango, Villa came from humble origins, and much of his early history is obscure. Before the Revolution he appears to have made his living in a number of ways not uncommon in the North: through part-time and temporary employment of various sorts, cattle rustling, and perhaps some desultory banditry.

The motivations behind Villa's response to Madero's call to arms when the Revolution began were perhaps as much personal as they were ideological. But by early 1914, Villa commanded the dominant revolutionary force in the North, the División del Norte. Most successfully active in the states of Chihuahua and Durango, it made a number of early strong showings against federal forces. Middle-class revolutionaries were suspicious of Villa's proclaimed allegiance to Madero's cause. Venustiano Carranza, who emerged after 1915 as the leader of middle-sector groups desiring political reform, attempted to restrict Villa's actions by withholding coal and military supplies from his forces. Villa, unlike his contemporary, Zapata, never presented a plan defining his objectives. This inability to publicize his goals, which left some historians questioning whether they existed, prevented Villa from gaining a national base of support. A mystery to many commentators and scholars, Villa came down through the twentieth century with an image as both a violent, villainous opportunist and a popular, populist hero of the common people of the North.

Villa's mobilization capitalized on well-established historical traits of border society. His army included a wide representation of border types, some of whom—such as the descendants of military colonists who had fought Apaches—had acquired particularly useful local skills and knowledge. The ranks of Villa's army were swelled by rural workers, sharecroppers, seasonal hacienda laborers, ranch hands—exactly the sorts of people affected by the long-term and short-term causes of the conflict. Many of Villa's followers may have regularly participated in marginally legal activities. As such they reflected the lawlessness and violence that, in the absence of centralized authority, were endemic in the border region. In Sonora during the period just before the Revolution, the number of people murdered in barroom fights frequently equaled the number who died in mining accidents.[12] Ideology of any kind seems to have been conspicuous in its absence among Villa and his followers. When in Sonora, for example, Villa's men did not distinguish between Mexicans and foreigners; they imposed their depredation on the entire populace.[13]

Villa's rhetoric and practice between 1913 and 1915 illustrate both his accomplishments and his contradictions. In December 1913, after his troops had dominated the state of Chihuahua and he had become governor of the state, Villa issued a decree to confiscate the land and other properties of the wealthiest and most powerful Mexican landowners in Chihuahua, including the Terrazas. Revenues from land expropriation were to go to the public treasury to pay pensions to the widows and orphans of soldiers. Eventually, the lands would be distributed, with one portion divided among veterans of the Revolution, another piece restored to earlier owners from whom the hacendados had stolen them, a third part to remain at the disposal of the state for pensions, and the last section to be used to provide credit to peasants. The main beneficiaries would be the descendants of the military colonists of Chihuahua. Once autonomous municipalities would regain hacienda lands and receive new grants. All long-range plans were to be implemented after a total victory by Villa.

In actual practice under Villa, the lion's share of confiscated haciendas was administered directly by and for the military high command, with the best lands operated by Villa and his lieutenants. Some of Villa's men, such as Tomás Urbina, rented parcels to wealthy landowners; others rented land to sharecroppers on traditional terms. Even though Villa passed a law to prohibit the worst elements of sharecropping, his policy did not, on the whole, drastically alter the conditions of northern labor. For the most part the proceeds of the haciendas that remained under Villa's control were devoted to building his military machine.

Villa did devote some portion of hacienda income to social purposes but generally in a haphazard manner. When he took Chihuahua City, he gave each poor person in the city clothing, shoes, and other apparel taken from a large store confiscated from Spaniards, and from other stores he distributed candy to children. Once he became governor of Chihuahua, Villa decreed low meat prices (he owned a large meatpacking plant himself). He granted provisions to unemployed miners and other workers; he provided meat, milk, and bread to centers run by nuns for poor children. Wheat and maize from confiscated estates were sold at reduced prices. He made plans for further agrarian reforms, but he never carried them out (until mid-1914 Villa accepted the authority of Carranza, who did not yet desire a thoroughgoing agrarian reform).

Villa is famous in border history for a series of incidents that shattered the fragile peace between Mexico and the United States and brought the two countries to the brink of war. He became enraged at the United States for recognizing Carranza as official head of the revolutionary forces and for imposing an embargo on arms shipments for Carranza's rivals. The last straw came when the United States authorized Carranza to transport troops through the U.S. border states, enabling them to repel Villa at Agua Prieta, Sonora. By fall 1915, Villa's strength and status had declined drastically. On January 10,

1916, Villa's soldiers took sixteen U.S. engineers off a train in Santa Ysabel, Chihuahua, and killed them. On March 9, 1916, approximately five hundred Villistas attacked the isolated hamlet of Columbus, New Mexico, killing and injuring U.S. civilians and soldiers alike. Villa himself directed the attack from the safety of the Mexican border town of Palomas, Chihuahua, directly across the international boundary from Columbus. In response, General John J. Pershing led six thousand U.S. troops into Mexico in pursuit of Villa, angering Mexicans who found themselves face to face with armed foreigners. Two skirmishes at Parral and Carrizal, Chihuahua, produced casualties on both sides. The crisis escalated; a U.S. invasion of Mexico seemed imminent, but the two nations engaged in diplomatic negotiations. After prolonged and acrimonious talks, the conflict was resolved. In February 1917, having failed to capture or even catch sight of Villa, the U.S. troops withdrew.

Popular mobilization under Villa was accompanied by an elite mobilization in the Mexican border states. As a result of their activities during the Revolution, upper-class northerners came to dominate Mexico's political landscape for the first time. The main elite leaders of the Revolution and of the postrevolutionary rebuilding of the 1920s—Madero, Carranza, Alvaro Obregón, Plutarco Elías Calles, Emilio Portes Gil, and Abelardo L. Rodríguez—were from border states. The Northern Dynasty, as they came to be called, represented the new economic forces that emerged in the Mexican boundary region during the Porfiriato. Essential to the formation of these forces, the border experience would prove vital to the priorities and policies of the central government until the 1930s.

THE REVOLUTIONARY PERIOD ON THE U.S. SIDE OF THE BORDER

The outbreak of violence in Mexico posed a number of important problems for the United States. As conflicts spawned by the Revolution escalated and spilled over the boundary, relations between the two nations deteriorated. Throughout the decade both revolutionary and counterrevolutionary elements made use of the U.S. border states to promote schemes for seizing power in Mexico. These activities prompted the government in Washington to impose arms embargoes and invoke neutrality laws. Meanwhile, U.S. citizens along the U.S.-Mexico border continued to suffer property loss and personal injury.

Revolutionary instability also affected local business and social life along the international boundary. Texas, where large numbers of people shared the border, was particularly hard hit. As the Revolution broke out in Mexico,

Statue of Pancho Villa at Puerto Palomas, Chihuahua, commemorating the exploits of General Villa and the raid across the border on the U.S. Army garrison in Columbus, New Mexico, in 1916. 2003.

peace along the Texas border began to unravel. The twin cities of Ciudad Juárez–El Paso and Matamoros-Brownsville became staging areas for incursions into Mexico. The arms trade flourished—the value of legal exports of firearms jumped from $270,832 in 1911 to $1.3 million in 1915.[14] Additional weapons were smuggled across the border. Battles between *federales* and *insurrectos* in 1911 heightened tensions along the Baja California–California, the Sonora-Arizona, and the Texas-Chihuahua borders. At the Texas-Tamaulipas frontier, such traditional illegal activities as smuggling, gunrunning, and cattle rustling were overshadowed by organized banditry and raiding.

Revolutionary battles in Mexican border towns were a favorite spectator sport for U.S. residents. These tourists flocked to view the action from the relative safety of the U.S. side of the border while battles raged in the Mexican towns of Ciudad Juárez, Naco, and Tijuana. These events, where an occasional stray bullet felled a tourist, were often captured on picture postcards that were sent all over the United States.[15]

In at least one case, conditions in the U.S. border states, similar in many ways to conditions in Mexico, produced a popular mobilization. South Texas in particular was ripe for violence, if not revolution.[16] Since 1848 the Mexican-origin population in south Texas had experienced profound changes. Annexation had introduced a new elite of U.S. merchants, officials, and ranchers. At first the Mexican ranch society, which had developed over the course of nearly two centuries, was able to accommodate these developments; intermarriages pervaded all levels of society. By the early 1900s, however, this situation had begun to shift.

In the early twentieth century, rapid economic change came to south Texas. The arrival of the railroad and the exhaustion of homestead lands in the Midwest made the more arid regions of south Texas increasingly attractive to farmers. Irrigation works and dry farming techniques abetted development. The combined forces of the railroad, which expanded markets, and irrigation, which extended growing seasons and areas, transformed the region. Irrigated land increased from 54,673 acres in 1909 to 228,020 acres in 1919. In Texas as a whole, this constituted a 32 percent jump, but the increase was 317 percent in the lower Rio Grande Valley and 663 percent in Hidalgo County.

A large migration of midwestern and northern farmers to south Texas followed. This demographic shift, combined with the economic changes, led to the gradual eclipsing of the Mexican ranching population. The population of the lower Rio Grande Valley nearly doubled between 1900 and 1920, with the greatest increase occurring after 1910. Hidalgo County experienced a demographic explosion—450 percent—during the same period. The proportion of U.S. citizens rose from 12 percent to 35 percent. Urban and rural property values soared.

These changes were met by a brief flash of armed insurrection in Texas between 1915 and 1917. The conflict was centered on the controversy surrounding the discovery of the Plan de San Diego. The plan, which called for an armed uprising against the U.S. government on February 20, 1915, apparently had its origins in the south Texas town of San Diego, a community with a majority (75 percent) Mexican-origin population. Supporters of the plan intended to reclaim the territory lost in 1848—Texas, New Mexico, Arizona, Colorado, and California. This region would first become an independent republic and would then be incorporated into Mexico. Every U.S. male over the age of sixteen would be put to death. Backers of the plan were restricted

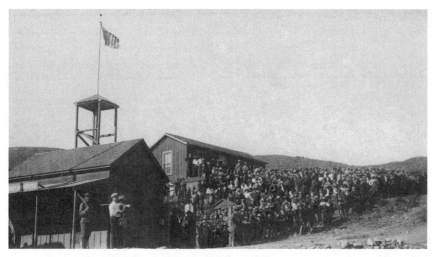

War tourism. "The Crowd Watching the Battle at Tijuana, June 22, 1911." During the Mexican revolutionary period, battles in Mexico's northern border cities attracted crowds of U.S. spectators. In this picture postcard, the crowd is gathered on the U.S. side of the boundary, adjacent to the U.S. Customs House in San Ysidro. (Andre Williams Collection)

to Native Americans, Latinos, African Americans, and Japanese. Once the territory was liberated, six states bordering it would be turned over to the African Americans. The plan promised indigenous groups that, in return for their support, their ancestral territories would be restored to them.

U.S. authorities discovered the Plan de San Diego in early 1915, when Basilio Ramos, one of its authors, was arrested in McAllen, Texas, while trying to organize the uprising. Ramos jumped bail and fled across the border to Matamoros, but others pursued the plan's objectives by initiating raids against south Texas residents in the summer of 1915. Hundreds were killed, thousands were dislocated, and property worth millions of dollars was destroyed in a small area. It is difficult to determine, however, which attacks were perpetrated by adherents of the plan and which were the work of independent bands with separate motives. Groups ranging from twenty-five to one hundred men led incursions, including train derailments, bridge burnings, and the sabotage of irrigation pumping plants.

By the end of 1917 an uneasy calm had been achieved. Vigilantism in south Texas played a major role in the reduction of violence, and with the end of fighting in Mexico, the south Texas movement lost its staging areas. The people of the region paid a heavy price. The raids, which had reinforced existing hatreds, led to severe repression of and general discrimination against

Mexican Americans. Lynchings, hangings, shootings, and other forms of execution perpetrated by unscrupulous lawmen, soldiers, and vigilantes caused the loss of many innocent lives. The Texas Rangers exceeded their authority in many cases, submitting suspected lawbreakers, particularly those of Mexican descent, to unrestrained brutality.

The Plan de San Diego had international repercussions. Carranza apparently used the border troubles in Texas to his advantage in his attempts to gain U.S. recognition for his floundering government. When he finally received de facto recognition in October 1915, the organized raids associated with the plan stopped. Whether Carranza actually instigated or encouraged the 1915 violence is not certain, but following U.S. recognition of the Carranza regime, the border enjoyed a period of relative calm. The Plan de San Diego and the events in south Texas highlight the ease with which the border is transcended by social phenomena. Not only did ideas, arms, troops, and goods flow back and forth, but similar conditions appear to have engendered similar social stresses and responses on both sides of the border as well.

TRANSBOUNDARY POPULATION MOVEMENTS DURING THE REVOLUTION, PROHIBITION, AND THE DEPRESSION

The Revolution of 1910 was one of the greatest early stimuli to population movement and growth along the border. In its violent phase, from 1910 to 1920, it constituted a major push for Mexican migrants caught in the shifting path of disruption and destruction. The U.S. economic boom resulting from preparation for World War I created a complementary migrant pull in both field and factory, drawing people from both the United States and Mexico to the U.S. border states. And the railroads that had linked Mexico to the United States in the 1880s provided inexpensive transportation northward. It is estimated that between 1900 and 1930 almost 10 percent of Mexico's population migrated north to the United States.

The number of persons crossing the border into the United States rose significantly after the outbreak of the Revolution. In 1912 alone, 23,238 Mexicans entered the United States. Legal immigration to the United States from 1910 to 1920 amounted to 890,371, a figure that includes both legal immigrants and temporary workers (206,000 legal immigrants; 628,000 temporary workers). Many others came as refugees and as undocumented workers. The widespread poverty and hunger caused by the Revolution triggered the displacement of countless people. Conditions were poor in the rural areas, where food shortages frequently followed revolutionary violence. In cities, common people waited hours for the opportunity to purchase provisions, and urban food riots erupted in areas of the North.

A wide variety of people were pushed north during the Revolution. Most were unskilled workers; about half were either migrants without jobs, women, or children. But there were also professionals, teachers, architects, and lawyers. Middle- and upper-class persons who entered the United States in search of political asylum settled in such cities as San Antonio, El Paso, Tucson, and Los Angeles. It was not unusual for a whole town of people living directly on the border—poor and rich alike—to cross to the other side before, during, or after a military battle in the area. In October 1913, for example, eight thousand people went from Piedras Negras to Eagle Pass.

The impact of the Revolution on migrant flows was reflected in the modest growth recorded by four of the Mexican border states and the population loss recorded by the other two between 1910 and 1921. On the U.S. side, population increased much more rapidly during the Revolution in Mexico as a result of the considerable economic opportunities throughout the southwestern and western regions of the United States. The U.S. economic boom during World War I offered the unemployed jobs and good wages in the border region.

Until 1917 the only people who were not legally permitted to cross the border were beggars, the physically and mentally disabled, paupers, criminals, anarchists, those deemed incapable of earning a living, and prostitutes. In 1917 the United States passed an immigration act establishing several tests for migrants (among them a literacy test), as well as a head tax of $8. As commercial farming expanded and growers' demands for labor increased, however, restrictions for Mexican workers were reduced. One cotton company executive, writing to President Woodrow Wilson, said, "Personally, I believe that the Mexican laborers are the solution to our common labor problem in this country. Many of their people are here, this was once part of their country, and they can and they will do the work. . . . I personally find them, especially those with families, to be appreciative of fair treatment and to be deserving of it."[17] Employers throughout the Southwest lobbied hard for exceptions to the 1917 act with respect to Mexicans. The literacy test and head tax were lifted as a result of this pressure, beginning a pattern of crisis and response in border labor recruitment and in subsequent migrant flows that is still common today.

Labor contractors—despite a ban on their activities in the Immigration Act of 1917—were very influential in supplying Mexican workers to the U.S. Southwest. Stationed near the border, they approached migrants as soon as they crossed. During the revolutionary period migrant labor continued

Border checkpoint for entering San Ysidro from Tijuana, 1920s. Colorized picture postcard. (Andre Williams Collection)

to dominate agriculture and railroads. In 1909 almost one-fifth of unskilled trackmen in the U.S. West were Mexican; by 1928 Mexicans constituted 60 percent of these workers. Mexican migrants also traveled far from the border states, working, for example, in the steel and meatpacking industries of the Midwest. The 1920s saw even more Mexican immigration to the United States than the previous decade. A brief postwar economic downturn in the early 1920s eliminated many employment opportunities, causing Mexican workers to return, or be sent, home. But the boom of the mid- to late 1920s soon brought migrants back.

The Great Depression slowed these population movements, as hard times fell on the economy of the U.S. West. Hundreds of thousands of Mexicans lost their jobs in the United States, and tens of thousands were sent back across the border to Mexico. Depressed economic conditions in the 1930s, along with an increase in anti-Mexican sentiment, motivated U.S. officials to impose severe restrictions on the entry of immigrants and to pressure Mexicans already in the United States to repatriate to Mexico. A drastic drop in the number of Mexican immigrants entering the United States resulted. Five hundred thousand Mexicans were forcibly repatriated between 1929 and 1935. Foreigners received the blame for employment problems, as local government officials sought to remove Mexican families from relief rolls.[18]

A large percentage of repatriated Mexicans remained near the border, posing a challenge to state and local officials in Mexico from Tamaulipas to Baja California. Often transportation to the interior of Mexico was not readily available or was unaffordable, stranding returnees in such cities as Ciudad Juárez. Many repatriates who ran out of money were forced to depend on charity to meet basic needs. *Juntas de beneficencia* (charity boards) were organized in many border localities to deal with the problems of the *repatriados*.

The Mexican federal government attempted to aid *repatriados* by allowing them to import certain possessions without paying a duty, by providing free transportation to some destinations, and by opening up agricultural colonies for those inclined to take up farming. Although well intentioned, the assistance rendered by the government in Mexico City often fell far short of actual needs. The government's promises surpassed its ability to minister to the large number of migrants. For this reason many *repatriados* remained close to the border, awaiting the opportunity to reenter the United States when economic conditions improved.

Many neighborhoods in border urban centers trace their origin to the arrival of repatriated Mexicans during the Depression. One example is Colonia Libertad in Tijuana, which was settled beginning in 1930. Many of the refugees who founded Colonia Libertad settled unlawfully on vacant land that belonged to a racetrack complex in the process of relocation. The invaders resisted all efforts to remove them. The name Colonia Libertad attracted former Villistas and adherents of anarchist ideology. Its settlement pattern followed the U.S. model of large lots, wide and straight streets, and alleys for services. *Repatriados* who preferred a rural lifestyle settled in the Mexicali Valley, taking advantage of the area's growing focus on agriculture, stimulated by federal water projects and land programs.

The large Mexican immigration into the United States between 1910 and 1930 coincided with a resurgence of anti-Mexican sentiment in the United States that only worsened during the Depression. Attacks on U.S. citizens in Mexico and recurring border incidents during the years of the Mexican Revolution had influenced some U.S. citizens to call for major military intervention in Mexico. Many frustrated U.S. citizens took out their resentment on Mexicans and Mexican Americans along the border. Even when the violence in Mexico subsided and the potential for large-scale confrontation between U.S. citizens and Mexican nationals dissipated, negative attitudes toward Mexicans found expression in the debate over immigration that swept the United States during the 1920s. Opposition to unrestricted immigration into the United States grew in the 1920s and 1930s, and because of their expanding visibility in the labor markets of the Southwest, Mexicans became a principal target.

Table 3.1.   Border-State Population, 1900–1940

State	1900	1910	1920[a]	1930	1940
Baja California	7,583	9,760	23,537	48,327	78,907
Chihuahua	327,784	405,707	401,522	491,792	623,944
Coahuila	296,938	362,092	393,480	436,425	550,717
Nuevo León	327,937	365,150	336,412	417,491	541,147
Sonora	221,682	265,383	275,127	316,271	364,176
Tamaulipas	218,948	249,641	286,904	344,039	458,832
Mexican border	**1,400,872**	**1,657,733**	**1,717,082**	**2,054,345**	**2,617,723**
Mexican total	**13,607,272**	**15,160,369**	**14,334,780**	**16,552,722**	**19,653,552**
Arizona	122,931	204,354	334,162	435,573	499,261
California	1,485,053	2,377,549	3,426,861	5,677,251	6,907,387
New Mexico	195,310	327,301	360,350	423,317	531,818
Texas	3,048,710	3,876,542	4,663,228	5,824,715	6,414,824
U.S. border	**4,852,004**	**6,785,746**	**8,784,601**	**12,360,856**	**14,353,290**
U.S. total	**76,212,168**	**92,228,496**	**106,021,537**	**123,202,624**	**132,164,569**

Source: Lorey, *United States–Mexico Border Statistics since 1900*, table 100.

[a]Data for Mexico are for 1921.

Despite the concerted efforts by labor unions and restrictionists who were motivated by concerns over ethnicity, the U.S. Congress excluded Mexicans and other Latin Americans from the strict quotas imposed by the landmark immigration acts of 1921 and 1924. The border states won the period's debates over immigration. The great need for inexpensive labor in the U.S. border region and the desire to improve relations between the United States and Latin America compelled the United States to allow Mexicans to continue entering the country with relative ease.

This was pleasing to many U.S. border-state employers, but the permissive policy caused distress in other sectors. Opponents of Mexican immigration cited economic, cultural, social, and ethnic differences to make their case. Organized labor, for example, complained that Mexican immigrants depressed wages and interfered with efforts to unionize workers. Other observers focused on an alleged inability and unwillingness among the Mexican people to assimilate into the mainstream culture. These themes, replayed ever since, still shaped debate on a constellation of policy issues at the end of the twentieth century.

In the first forty years of the twentieth century, the population of the border states almost tripled, from a total of about 6 million in 1900 to nearly

Table 3.2.   Population of Selected U.S.-Mexican Border Twin Cities, 1900–1940

	1900	1910	1920	1930	1940
San Diego, California	17,700	39,978	73,683	147,897	203,341
Tijuana, Baja California	242	733	1,028	8,384	16,486
Calexico, California	N/A	797	6,223	6,229	5,415
Mexicali, Baja California	N/A	462	6,782	14,842	18,775
Nogales, Arizona	1,761	3,514	5,199	6,006	5,135
Nogales, Sonora	2,738	3,177	13,445	14,061	13,866
El Paso, Texas	15,906	39,279	77,560	102,421	96,810
Ciudad Juárez, Chihuahua	8,218	10,621	19,457	39,669	48,881
Eagle Pass, Texas	N/A	3,536	5,765	5,069	6,459
Piedras Negras, Coahuila	7,888	8,518	6,941	15,878	15,663
Laredo, Texas	13,492	14,855	22,710	32,618	39,274
Nuevo Laredo, Tamaulipas	6,548	8,143	14,998	21,636	28,872
Brownsville, Texas	6,305	10,517	11,791	22,021	22,083
Matamoros, Tamaulipas	8,347	7,390	9,215	9,733	15,699

Sources: Lorey, *United States–Mexico Border Statistics since 1900*, tables 110 and 104; U.S. Census Bureau,
1990 Census of Population and Housing, Summary Tape File 1 (100% Data), Matrices P1, P11, P12, P28;
Census 2000 Summary File 1, Matrices P13 and PCT12; Table 4: Annual Estimates of the Population for
Incorporated Places in California (SUB-EST2004-04-06), Arizona (SUB-EST2004-04-04), New Mexico
(SUB-EST2004-04-35), and Texas (SUB-EST2004-04-08), April 1, 2000, to July 1, 2004; INEGI, XI Censo
general de población y vivienda 1990/indicadores/sociodemográficos; XII censo general de población y
vivienda/2000/población.

17 million by 1940, an annual rate of 2.5 percent (see table 3.1).[19] In 1900,
Baja California, Chihuahua, Coahuila, Nuevo León, Sonora, and Tamaulipas
had a combined population of about 1.4 million; by 1940 that number had
increased to approximately 2.6 million. The combined population of the U.S.
border states grew from almost 4.9 million in 1900 to almost 14.4 million by
1940. For most of the period, Texas was the giant among the border states,
but by 1940, with a population of nearly 7 million, California had assumed the
lead. Most of the border growth took place on the U.S. side; the 1.6 percent
annual increase on the Mexican side was significantly lower than the overall
rate.

After 1900 the border region became increasingly urbanized, but the
growth of individual cities varied considerably. The Mexican Revolution and
the Great Depression significantly affected cities south of the Rio Grande,
slowing growth or causing population declines. That trend also characterized the U.S. border cities; both El Paso, Texas, and Calexico, California,
lost population in the 1930s. Albuquerque, like El Paso and Tucson, lured
many health seekers by advertising its dry and mild climate and emerged as
the dominant city of New Mexico. Specialists in diseases such as tuberculosis
and asthma moved to the border states to meet the growing demand for their
services; modern medical establishments replaced the health spas and wintering

hotels of an earlier era. Although the largest metropolises of the region developed at some distance from the international boundary, their growth owed much to their proximity to the border. Los Angeles reigned as the largest U.S. city of the border states throughout the first four decades of the century, followed by Houston, San Antonio, and San Diego. On the Mexican side, Monterrey remained the largest border city, but with a population of only 186,092 in 1940, it was far smaller than the leading U.S. cities.

The cities immediately adjacent to the border had grown considerably by 1940, foreshadowing the densely populated binational twin cities that emerged during and after World War II. By 1940, for example, the twin-city pair of Brownsville-Matamoros had nearly 38,000 inhabitants, Laredo–Nuevo Laredo had about 48,000 people, El Paso–Ciudad Juárez had a population of 146,000, and San Diego–Tijuana had 220,000. The settlement pattern of densely urbanized twin cities located on north-south trade routes and separated from other binational pairs by vast empty spaces was consolidated during this period. Table 3.2 details the urban evolution of the immediate border zone.

NOTES

1. This section draws heavily on Griswold del Castillo and Rodríguez González, "Conflict and Development," a draft chapter from the historical volume of the University of California, Los Angeles, Borderlands Atlas Project.

2. David Lorey, "Monterrey, Mexico, during the Porfiriato and Revolution: Population and Migration Trends in Regional Evolution," *Statistical Abstract of Latin America* 2, no. 8 (1990): 1183–704.

3. Del Castillo and González, "Conflict and Development."

4. Ramón Ruíz, *The Great Rebellion: Mexico, 1905–1924* (New York: Norton, 1980), 36–37.

5. This discussion of Chihuahua and the discussion of Francisco (Pancho) Villa in the next section of this chapter are adapted from Friedrich Katz's work, particularly his speech "Was There an Agrarian Problem in the Mexican North on the Eve of the Mexican Revolution?" (given at the Center for U.S.-Mexican Studies, University of California, San Diego, 1995); his "Agrarian Changes in Northern Mexico in the Period of *Villista* Rule," in *Contemporary Mexico*, ed. James Wilkie (Los Angeles: University of California, Los Angeles, Latin American Center Publications, 1976), 259–73; and his *The Life and Times of Pancho Villa* (Stanford, CA: Stanford University Press, 1998). See also Alan Knight, *The Mexican Revolution*, 2 vols. (Lincoln: University of Nebraska Press, 1986).

6. David Piñera, *American and English Influence on the Early Development of Ensenada, Baja California, Mexico* (San Diego: Institute for Regional Studies of the Californias, San Diego State University, 1995), 49.

7. William E. French, *A Peaceful and Working People: Manners, Morals, and Class Formation in Northern Mexico* (Albuquerque: University of New Mexico Press, 1996), 43.

8. Miguel Tinker Salas, *In the Shadow of the Eagles: Sonora and the Transformation of the Border during the Porfiriato* (Berkeley: University of California Press, 1997), 187–88, 196.

9. Salas, *In the Shadow of the Eagles*, 239.

10. Salas, *In the Shadow of the Eagles*, 8.

11. Karl B. Koth, "Crisis Politician and Political Counterweight: Teodoro A. Dehesa in Mexican Federal Politics, 1900–1910," *Mexican Studies/Estudios mexicanos* 11, no. 2 (summer 1995): 243–71.

12. Salas, *In the Shadow of the Eagles*, 193.

13. Salas, *In the Shadow of the Eagles*, 199.

14. Don M. Coerver and Linda B. Hall, *Revolution on the Border: The United States and Mexico, 1910–1920* (Albuquerque: University of New Mexico Press, 1988), 157.

15. Paul Vanderwood, "Writing History with Picture Postcards: Revolution in Tijuana," *Journal of San Diego History* 34, no. 1 (winter 1988).

16. The discussion of the south Texas rebellion is adapted from James A. Sandos, *Rebellion in the Borderlands: Anarchism and the Plan of San Diego, 1904–1923* (Norman: University of Oklahoma Press, 1992); and David Montejano, *Anglos and Mexicans in the Making of Texas, 1836–1986* (Austin: University of Texas Press, 1987).

17. Coerver and Hall, *Revolution on the Border*, 134.

18. On repatriation, see Francisco E. Balderrama and Raymond Rodríguez, *Decade of Betrayal: Mexican Repatriation in the 1930s* (Albuquerque: University of New Mexico Press, 1995); Abraham Hoffman, *Unwanted Mexican Americans in the Great Depression* (Tucson: University of Arizona Press, 1974); Camille Guerin-Gonzales, *Mexican Workers and American Dreams: Immigration, Repatriation and California Farm Labor, 1900–1939* (New Brunswick, NJ: Rutgers University Press, 1994).

19. Implicit compound rate.

4

BOOMS AND
BUSTS ON THE BORDER

The Great Depression and World War II

The Great Depression and World War II brought momentous, lasting change to the U.S.-Mexican border region, transforming it, in the span of twenty years, from an economic backwater into a global powerhouse. The New Deal, designed by Franklin Delano Roosevelt to promote economic recovery and social reform, forever altered the economy of the United States, especially the West. Meanwhile, reforms of the 1930s touched off an impressive economic consolidation in Mexico, one that had far-reaching implications for the development of the Mexican border states. World War II brought dramatic economic changes to both Mexico and the United States, with significant ramifications in the border states. In both countries an active federal government increasingly provided the area with a stable foundation for rapid development and a way to free itself from regional dependencies—from the domination of the East in the United States and from the domination of Mexico City in Mexico.

THE GREAT DEPRESSION

The Depression was a mixed blessing for the border region. Although it caused extensive short-term dislocation for people in both Mexican and U.S. border states, federal responses in both countries provided long-term investments in infrastructure and a precedent of federal support for regional economic growth. Depression-era infrastructure would prove to be one of the foundations for the area's wartime and postwar economic expansion. As in the case of the short-lived boom brought on by Prohibition, however, most Depression-era benefits were experienced north of the international boundary.

During the early 1930s the U.S. border states, paralleling occurrences in other parts of the United States, experienced deep economic disruption as a result of the Great Depression. Banks defaulted, factories closed, businesses failed, and masses of workers lost their jobs. Throughout the Southwest, people from rural and urban areas struggled to make a living in an environment that provided limited opportunities. In El Paso, the Great Depression was first felt in the latter part of 1931, when a prominent bank collapsed. In the years that followed, many factories and stores went out of business, throwing thousands out of work. Between 1929 and 1939 the number of workers employed by major manufacturing establishments in El Paso decreased by 63 percent. The economic pressures became so great that many people left El Paso; the city's population fell from 102,000 in 1930 to 97,000 in 1940. Many Mexicans returned to their homeland when they could no longer make a living in the United States. Although Tucson suffered less than El Paso, the city still had to cope with major disruptions in trade, mining, ranching, and agriculture; tourism sharply declined as well.

Tijuana was also hard hit by the Depression. In the first months of the crisis, 150 of the town's commercial establishments ceased operation. The majority of foreign owners left; some even torched their businesses to collect insurance (two dozen fires were reported in 1935). The number of crossings along the border declined considerably between the late 1920s and the mid-1930s, falling from 27 million in 1928 to 21 million in 1934. In Ciudad Juárez, tourist expenditure dropped from $3.5 million to $2.3 million during the Depression years.

In the United States the most important and longest-lasting impact of the 1930s was the use of federal funds to underwrite infrastructure projects, which supported western economic development in both direct and indirect ways. The Great Depression brought hardship to the U.S. West, but it also brought Roosevelt's New Deal. The federal government subsidized both producers and consumers. Large-scale water projects, such as Boulder Dam (Hoover Dam) and the All American Canal, provided irrigation, inexpensive electric power, and much needed employment.

Both border states and border communities benefited from New Deal relief programs during the difficult years. The Civilian Works Administration provided employment for thousands of El Pasoans by implementing projects ranging from constructing roads to channeling the Rio Grande. The federal government also helped preserve the troubled Middle Rio Grande Conservancy District, an agency that held great importance for Albuquerque. With the availability of federal resources the district was able to undertake numerous activities that improved the environment for commercial agriculture in the

The Works Progress Administration (WPA) funded many Depression-era projects in the border region, including San Diego's County Administrative Center (1936–1938) and the sculpture Guardian of the Waters *(1937–1939) by local artist Donal Hord. 2006.*

Rio Grande Valley. With the arrival of New Deal programs, the situation in Tucson also looked up, and by the late 1930s, the so-called Sunshine Capital of the United States was once again booming as a winter haven for people from the frigid North. New Deal agencies such as the Reconstruction Finance

Corporation, the Federal Relief Emergency Administration, the Works Progress Administration, and the Civilian Conservation Corps invested heavily in a wide variety of endeavors in the western states, stimulating new or restarting disrupted activity in such important regional industries as agriculture, ranching, construction, and mining. Most significantly, large-scale water projects financed by the federal government during the Depression led to the conversion of semiarid areas in the West into some of the most productive farmland in the country.

In comparison with other parts of the United States, the West benefited from a disproportionate share of the New Deal expenditures, with the border states receiving substantial grants and loans. Arizona and New Mexico—which placed in the top five states nationwide in terms of per capita federal funding—particularly felt the helping hand of the government in Washington. These events were the first steps toward a massive shift of federal resources to the western United States.

The world economic crisis of the 1930s prompted Mexican policymakers to institute fundamental changes in the nation's economy. The federal government encouraged internal commerce by establishing associations of merchants and promoting greater integration of the country through improved transportation networks. Banks were reorganized and credit was extended to sectors in need of it, especially agriculture. Import-substitution measures protected existing industries and stimulated new manufacturing activities.

During the Lázaro Cárdenas administration (1934–1940) in particular, Mexico experienced profound economic transformations, which had striking consequences for the northern border states. In the North, land reform, one of the principal objectives of the Cárdenas government, led to the expropriation of millions of acres and the creation of many communally owned and farmed *ejidos*. By 1935 more than 181,000 *ejidatarios* worked in communal agriculture throughout northern Mexico. The years 1936 and 1937 were especially significant on the border, as large-scale land redistribution reached Coahuila, Sonora, and Baja California. In 1937, Cárdenas distributed almost 60,000 acres of land to peasant families in the Mayo Valley and a total of 84,000 acres to settlers and Native American villages on both banks of the Yaqui River (later grants to the Yaqui, between 1937 and 1939, would bring the total to 1.1 million acres).

The government carried out one of its most ambitious agricultural projects in the La Laguna district in the states of Coahuila and Durango. In 1937, land for thirty thousand families was distributed, allowing for *ejido* cultivation of cotton, wheat, alfalfa, and corn. The government gave a major boost to agriculture by building dams to supply irrigation water to the *ejidos*. The construction of schools, hospitals, and community centers allowed for the provision of a variety of social services.

Land reform transformed the Mexicali Valley and the San Luis Río Colorado areas, where for years the powerful Colorado River Land Company had claimed ownership of more than 1.2 million acres. Unaffected by previous agrarian reform efforts by Pancho Villa or by Presidents Venustiano Carranza, Alvaro Obregón, and Plutarco Elías Calles, the company had enjoyed effective economic and political control of the region from 1902 through the Revolution. By the mid-1930s growing Mexican nationalism prompted the firm to sell *ejido* lots to Mexican farmers. At the end of 1937, over 100,000 acres had changed hands, benefiting 4,500 Mexican families who settled permanently in the Mexicali Valley. A decade later the government bought the remainder of the company's holdings, concluding the most important border campaign to provide peasants with land in the form of communal agricultural colonies.

Reclamation projects begun in the late 1920s and stepped up by the Cárdenas government during the Depression created new, and expanded old, agricultural lands in northern Mexico. Between 1926 and 1940, irrigation projects created about 370,000 acres of irrigated land throughout the nation, with a high concentration in the North.

In an attempt to stimulate family-friendly tourism in the Mexican border states, the central government tried to rein in border vice. Especially after Prohibition was repealed in 1933 and particularly during the administration of Cárdenas, local and federal officials banned disreputable diversions. The *El Paso Herald Post* reported a transformation by the mid-1930s:

> Gone are the hundred-odd saloons, the downtown honky-tonks and brothels, and the open gambling. In the Tívoli Casino the visitor can no longer hear the click of dice, the riffle of cards, and the sing-song croupiers at the roulette tables. The place is closed by presidential decree. The Moulin Rouge, once the home of nude dances, is closed. Part of the building is being remodeled for a grocery store. Calle Diablo [a red-light district] is no longer a Mecca for El Paso night-life addicts. A few cabarets remain open on Calle Diablo, but most of the girls have moved to restricted zones. Juárez no longer has vice resorts on her downtown streets.[1]

A federal policy that held great importance for the North during the Depression was the reestablishment of free trade zones along the border. Cities like Tijuana and Ensenada, which strongly depended on U.S. tourism, were left economically depressed by the end of Prohibition in the United States. By the mid-1930s many casinos, bars, and related establishments had closed their doors. Because of their geographic isolation from the rest of Mexico, it was crucial that border residents be allowed to import U.S. goods without having to pay tariffs. Border-state policymakers persuaded the central government that without a free trade zone, there would be a significant decline in both population and local commerce.

As early as 1933 the federal government responded to the concerns of *fronterizos* by declaring Ensenada and Tijuana *perímetros libres* (free perimeters), where U.S. products could be imported without payment of the normal tariffs. Four years later the entire Baja California territory was designated a free zone, allowing the increasingly important town of Mexicali to benefit from free trade as well. In 1939, Agua Prieta and Nogales, Sonora, were included in the free zone, as was Baja California Sur. In effect the entire northwest border region had become a free trade zone by 1939, stimulating commerce in every affected community.

WORLD WAR II

World War II ushered in an era of unparalleled growth in the border region. U.S. border states were catapulted forward by an outpouring of federal expenditure for defense, with the lion's share going to the states along the Pacific coast and in the Southwest. The Depression rapidly faded, as the nation's private sector expanded to meet both pent-up consumer demands and the needs of the defense machine. Federal spending in Mexico, though lower and slower than that in the United States, nonetheless helped transform that country's North into an area of large industries and growing cities in the 1940s and 1950s.

During the three decades following 1939, the U.S. gross national product (GNP) grew at an average annual rate of 4.2 percent. The war effort was primarily responsible for this surge, and the federal government significantly increased its participation in the economy in order to bring the country to peak military strength. Federal expenditures stood below 10 percent of GNP prior to 1941 but jumped to over 40 percent during the war. A significant measure of federal wartime spending was directed toward new commercial enterprises on the cutting edge of technology. Government investments in aircraft, electronics, and nuclear weapons bolstered not only the nation's war effort but also the extraordinary growth of the Allied nuclear power, rocketry, communications, computer, and chemical industries. Technology-based firms such as Boeing, Lockheed, Douglas, and Westinghouse owe their industrial leadership to federal outlays during World War II. The war, therefore, more so than even the Great Depression, made the federal budget an engine of growth and change.

AMERICANOS TODOS
★
LUCHAMOS POR LA
VICTORIA

★ AMERICANS ALL ★
LET'S FIGHT FOR VICTORY

Bilingual World War II poster. The "Uncle Sam" arm and hat, along with the stylized mariachi arm and sombrero, sent the message that Americans and Mexicans needed to fight together. (San Diego History Center)

Although this process affected the entire country, it especially influenced the border states.

Prior to 1940 the U.S. border economy depended heavily on agriculture and mining and relatively little on manufacturing. The western United States as a whole contributed approximately 11 percent of the U.S. manufacturing value added. The four border states contributed even less, and New Mexico ranked last in the nation. This primary-sector emphasis of the prewar border economy had always made development in the region particularly dependent

on the government in Washington, and the expenditures following the outbreak of the war served to reinforce this relationship.

The border economy's primary-sector emphasis was transformed with
the impact of federal wartime spending. The government invested some $40
billion in the western United States during the war, including $29 billion for
weapons and $7 billion for supply depots, training camps, and a variety of
other military facilities. A single border state, California, received 10 percent
of all federal monies expended during the war. From 1940 to 1946, 360 billion federal dollars were spent within the continental United States, $35 bil-
lion in California alone. In 1930 the government in Washington had spent
just $191 million in California; by 1945 federal expenditure in California had
mushroomed to $8.5 billion.

Federal monies launched Southern California as the center of the nation's
war aircraft industry, and the San Francisco Bay Area emerged as a focus of
wartime shipbuilding efforts. By the conflict's end, ships and airplanes had
become California's second most important products, behind only food production in terms of value added and people employed. And since ships and
aircraft required steel, Roosevelt strengthened the regional economy by supporting the establishment of Kaiser steel factories in the Los Angeles suburb
of Fontana.

During World War II, the federal government funded new research
clusters such as the Lawrence Radiation Laboratory at Berkeley and the Los
Alamos Scientific Laboratory in New Mexico. Major research universities
such as Stanford, the California Institute of Technology, and the University
of California campuses at Berkeley and Los Angeles received lavish federal
grants during the war. These institutions also attracted a number of firms that
settled nearby and invested their energies in aerospace, advanced electronics,
rocketry, and similar ventures.

Wartime expenditures accelerated the region's shift from an economy
based primarily on extractive industries to a diversified economy strongest
in manufacturing and service industries. Just as was the case with the more
traditional agricultural and mining activities, the new manufacturing sector
depended heavily on the federal budget; its lead businesses tended to be high-
tech firms associated with defense expenditure. As a result, border industries
and the border economy grew in concert with the government's defense ap-
propriations and experienced industrial cycles distinct from those in the older
and more traditional manufacturing centers of the Northeast and Midwest. It
was perhaps natural that the states along the boundary would particularly benefit from government-stimulated industrialization, since the region's economy
had been closely tied to the federal budget since the Depression (and earlier,

Women workers at the Consolidated Aircraft Corporation plant in San Diego during World War II. In 1941, Consolidated was San Diego's largest employer, with twenty-five thousand workers, a figure that grew to forty-five thousand the following year. Both the PBY Catalina patrol airplane and the B24 Liberator heavy bomber were manufactured at this plant. (San Diego History Center)

with federal support of railroad construction). World War II shifted the government's financial emphasis from primary-sector activities to newer industries. Abundant electricity, made available by such Depression public-works projects as Hoover Dam, made the border states an attractive site for new war industries that required low-cost energy. Such projects as the aqueduct from the Colorado River to the Southern California coastal plain and the All American Canal to the Imperial Valley ensured the availability of water for both agriculture and growing cities.

Wartime migration to the border states fueled the economic upsurge, as people from the East and Midwest responded to the attraction of higher wages. New industries related to the war effort—particularly shipbuilding and airplane production—created a wartime employment boom and provided a foundation for continued growth after the end of the conflict. The war effort expanded the navy presence in the West, with the construction of huge bases in San Diego, San Francisco, and Los Angeles–Long Beach. The army and the marines built up large concentrations of men and matériel at Fort Bliss, Fort Ord, Travis Air Force Base, the Presidio in San Francisco, and Camp Pendleton. Some areas of the Southwest had long served as armed forces training centers and could be quickly mobilized for the war effort. Texas, for example, rapidly became a hub of the wartime air-training effort.

World War II industrialization of the border economy received added impetus from the financial accumulation of the early 1940s. In 1939, California's per capita income was still below its 1930 level, and total personal income was only $5 billion. By 1945 personal income had tripled to some $15 billion. That same year the state's leading financial institution, the Bank of America, held deposits and assets worth $5 billion, establishing it as the world's largest bank and setting the stage for its enormous expansion in the immediate postwar years.

At the same time that the war effort sparked new economic activities, it boosted the demand for the West's traditional extractive products. The call for mineral products such as petroleum, copper, and uranium surged during the war years. Western farms became larger as the number of farms and farming families declined. In 1940, California had 133,000 farms, averaging 230 acres each. By 1985 the total had dropped to 79,000, and the average size had nearly doubled to 418 acres.[2] The war inverted farmers' longtime concern over crop surpluses into worry over shortages.

World War II also stimulated important economic changes in Mexico and in the Mexican border states. The nation embarked on a fifty-year period of radical economic transformation, industrializing on the basis of consumer goods destined for an expanding domestic market. Automobiles, tires, radios, televisions, and home appliances were among the country's new products; foreign technology, investments, and capital were influential in developing production of the items. Mexican investors played a complementary role by establishing ancillary industries with less complex technological requirements or by coinvesting in joint-ownership firms. The Mexican government supported industrialization by protecting the domestic market with tariffs, facilitating the import of needed capital goods, and creating the necessary infrastructure of highways, bridges, and other networks for getting products to their markets.[3]

U.S. involvement in World War II provided two crucial stimuli to Mexican industrial development: implicit protection from imports (because goods previously exported from the United States to Mexico were reserved for the war effort) and increased wartime demand (and consequent high prices) for Mexican exports. Rapidly expanding markets for Mexico's traditional exports in the decade after 1940—particularly minerals, cotton, and oil seeds—fueled a surge in foreign-exchange earnings that could not be exhausted in available imports. The Mexican Miracle of the 1950s and 1960s was established upon these pillars. The gross domestic product (GDP) more than tripled between 1940 and 1960. Mexico sustained average growth rates of 6.7 percent between 1940 and 1950, 5.8 percent between 1950 and 1960, and 6.4 percent from 1960 to 1968. The country employed 58 percent more people in the late 1960s than it had in 1940.

During and after the war the Mexican border states were incorporated into Mexico's industrial boom. Monterrey, Nuevo León, had been one of the country's leading manufacturing centers since the late nineteenth century. When the U.S. war effort blocked the city's access to many manufactured goods, local industrialists responded by investing in new production facilities; they continued to invest in the immediate aftermath of the war. Between 1945 and 1950 industrial investments increased fourfold, and the city emerged as the nation's second manufacturing center, just behind Mexico City. Local leaders founded the private Instituto Tecnológico y de Estudios Superiores de Monterrey (also known as Monterrey Tech) in order to provide technicians and engineers for the new factories; the public Universidad Autónoma de Nuevo León became one of the country's largest public universities. By 1980 more than half of all Mexican industrial workers in the border area were employed in Nuevo León; more than 90 percent of them were employed in Monterrey.[4]

After 1940, agriculture, which had benefited from irrigation policies and land reform in the 1920s and 1930s, experienced increased emphasis on capital-intensive mechanized methods, large-scale irrigation works, and greater use of pesticides and herbicides to raise productivity. One important aspect of government policy that contributed to the Mexican Miracle was substantial outlays for agricultural infrastructure in the border states. The impact of federal expenditures was particularly noticeable in commercial agriculture. During the war and early postwar years, the government stepped up investments in northern irrigation and agriculture. From 1947 to 1960, of Mexico's total expenditures for irrigation, 20 percent were in Tamaulipas, 16 percent were in Baja California Norte, and 25 percent were in Sonora. Dams were constructed to store and divert water, allowing expansion of commercial agriculture, and the North boasted between 70 and 80 percent of the newly irrigated lands. By 1970 the northern Pacific region of Mexico accounted for 53 percent of the nation's irrigated farmland. These large commercial farms attracted labor from central Mexico, stimulating the long-term flow of population to the northern states and to the border region.

As a result of these wartime changes, the border states developed Mexico's most modern, commercial, export-oriented agricultural sector. Scientific farming boomed; the use of fertilizers and pesticides increased yields, contributing to the North's economic prosperity. Between 1940 and 1960 the North received over 50 percent of the country's new paved roads. Crucial to agricultural production and distribution, they created communication corridors that still exist. Private commercial holdings benefited from federal policy to a far greater extent than did smallholdings and *ejidos*, although northern Mexico also received more than 60 percent of the total bank loans to *ejidos*.[5] In the easternmost area of the border region, Matamoros became Mexico's most important cotton-producing region, specializing in the processing of the fiber as well.

As California became the leading agricultural producer in the United States (boasting one-quarter of U.S. irrigated farmland), the agricultural complex of the Mexican North turned increasingly to the U.S. market, first to sell cotton and then fruits and vegetables. The population of Mexican border towns such as Mexicali, Reynosa, Matamoros, and Ciudad Juárez swelled to serve the local agricultural economy as well as the tides of seasonal farmworkers bound for Mexican fields and for the expanding agricultural belt of the U.S. Southwest.

Arid soils on both sides of the border presented a common problem that both countries met by supporting significant irrigation and other infrastructure development. Table 4.1 shows the growth of irrigated lands in the ten border states from 1930 to 1980. The most rapid expansion of irrigation occurred in the Depression and World War II decades, when the irrigated area almost doubled in the border region as a whole. By the 1980s the land under

Table 4.1.   Irrigated Land on the Border, 1930–1980 (thousands of acres)

State	1930	1940	1950	1960	1970	1980
Baja California	227	366	482	568	442	511
Chihuahua	286	336	378	558	457	299
Coahuila	612	597	674	741	494	593
Nuevo León	162	244	232	287	203	84
Sonora	285	376	692	1,371	1,561	1,398
Tamaulipas	91	131	442	785	877	963
Mexican Border	**1,663**	**2,050**	**2,900**	**4,310**	**4,034**	**3,848**

State	1930	1940	1950	1960	1970	1980
Arizona	576	576	964	1,152	1,178	1,099
California	4,745	4,277	6,438	7,396	7,249	8,460
New Mexico	527	436	655	732	823	5,573
Texas	799	895	3,123	5,656	6,888	4,241
U.S. Border	**6,647**	**6,184**	**11,180**	**14,936**	**16,138**	**15,940**

Source: Lorey, *United States–Mexico Border Statistics since 1900*, table 1100.

Artesanías for sale along Avenida Revolución in Tijuana, 1964. Gasoline was 26.9 cents per gallon, and the stores in the background offered liquors, perfume, fireworks, guitars, velvet paintings, Swiss watches, and curios. (Harry W. Crosby)

irrigation was more than twice that in 1930. Because most of the irrigation was made possible by federally funded water projects, the data indicating the amount of irrigated land provide a good gauge of the importance of federal expenditure in the region as a whole.

Roads linking the border region to Mexico's interior facilitated U.S. travel to Mexico via automobile. Between 1940 and 1960 the number of U.S. tourists crossing the border increased by more than 400 percent, from 8 million to 39 million. Border transactions associated with tourism accounted for 15 percent of Mexican exports of goods and services in 1940 and 27 percent by 1960. Many of the goods sold in Mexican border towns were curio crafts and popular crafts work, known as *artesanías*.[6] These products were often brought to the border from central and southern Mexico, but others were manufactured locally in cottage industries. The curio industry took off during the 1930s and 1940s thanks to growing numbers of U.S. tourists. It is still a staple of the economy of many Mexican border towns. The wartime expansion of U.S. military bases along the international boundary helped boost tourism. Fort Bliss, near El Paso, grew from 3,000 soldiers in 1938 to 25,000 in 1941. A return to Prohibition in Texas during the war also stimulated crossings to Mexican border towns.

Some of the economic development of the border region in both traditional and industrial sectors during this period stemmed directly from wartime collaboration between the United States and Mexico. A bilateral commission was established to study problems requiring coordinated bilateral actions. Aided by the United States, Mexico was to maintain and intensify its production of necessary prime materials for the fabrication of munitions and other products for the war effort. Mexico produced substantial amounts of minerals for the U.S. war machine, including copper, lead, and mercury. Antimony for munitions and arsenic for insecticides were also produced. In return for this aid, the United States promised to make scarce machinery available to Mexico and to send technicians to help increase agricultural production. A U.S. and Mexican team also worked to help solve Mexico's transport problems. Long neglected, Mexico's railroads, upgraded with the input of U.S. expertise and rolling stock, were crucial to the transportation of goods from Mexico to the United States during the war years and afterward.[7]

Wartime cooperation was reflected in increased bilateral trade in the border region. Between 1940 and 1945, 1 million tons of goods were transshipped through border cities (the number of tons grew to 2.75 million in 1950 and 3.3 million in 1960). Trade at ports of entry between 1940 and 1960 increased by 153 percent. The increase in Mexicali was 878 percent. These shifts had profound effects in border cities. The labor force doubled in Ciudad Juárez, as inhabitants found employment related to the rise in trade and in other sectors stimulated by the war.

With the outbreak of World War II, a new wave of migrants crossed the border from Mexico, this time under the official auspices of the U.S. government. Prompted by the immediate shortage of labor, farmers in the region pressured the federal government for permission to import temporary workers from Mexico. In 1942 the government in Washington responded with an emergency farm labor plan—the Bracero Program. Initially, the Farm Security Administration (FSA) oversaw the program, but agribusiness, which considered the FSA too pro-union and too radical, pressured the government to transfer control to the more conservative War Food Administration, where growers had more influence. The program was so successful that in April 1943 the United States and Mexico signed an agreement providing for a bracero-type plan for importing railroad workers. Under this arrangement the United States was authorized to bring in 20,000 additional Mexican workers in 1943, 50,000 in 1944, and 75,000 in 1945.

Between 1942 and 1947, as World War II raged, the Bracero Program brought 219,000 agricultural workers into the United States from Mexico. Fully one-half of all the Mexicans labored in California agriculture.[8] After the war the Harry S. Truman administration maintained the Bracero Program in agriculture. With the outbreak of the Korean War, Congress enacted Public Law 78 in 1951, providing formal legislative recognition of a new arrangement with Mexico. Although approved as a wartime emergency measure, the law in fact established a continuing Bracero Program, first renegotiated in 1954 and then renewed regularly until 1964. In the peak year of 1957, California imported 192,438 braceros. These migrant workers were unevenly distributed among large and small farms. In 1959 a mere 5.4 percent of California farms employed 59 percent of total seasonal labor.

This wartime flow of labor north to the U.S. border states and beyond marked the beginning of the massive influx of Mexicans to both the Mexican and U.S. border states. The northward movement of inexpensive Mexican labor, beginning as an implicit subsidy to U.S. agriculture, would gradually mold the economic and social profile of the United States in the late twentieth century.[9]

Within the overall development of the border region during and after the war, California in the United States and Nuevo León, Baja California, and Chihuahua in Mexico saw the most dramatic transformation of their economies. California, which received 10 percent of all government expenditure during the war years, saw its economy boom and its population soar. At the same time, Nuevo León consolidated its position as the center of Mexico's heavy industrial development, with the expansion of facilities for steel, cement, and glass, as well as consumer goods production. Mexican nationals in Monterrey also participated greatly in the industrialization process.

As Monterrey's industrialization gave rise to a large, urban, industrial workforce, it also brought to the fore questions about labor relations. Local employers accepted neither the central government's recognition of organized labor nor its official body, the Confederación de Trabajadores de México. Instead they supported company unions, which often functioned as little more than the personnel departments of Monterrey's firms. In part because of Monterrey's influence throughout the border region, unionization, with only local exceptions, never spread broadly in the Mexican border states.

The era spanning the Great Depression and World War II left an indelible legacy throughout the border region. Considerable government spending and high-tech production in field and factory would characterize the economy of the U.S. West long after the end of the war. Many of the thousands of U.S. military personnel stationed in the U.S. border states during the war years remained after discharge or later returned to fuel the post–World War II Sunbelt population and economic boom. And the Mexican economy's wartime pattern of growth would leave a strong imprint on Mexican development in the 1950s, 1960s, and 1970s. In both Mexico and the United States, the World War II years transformed the regional economies along the international boundary from economies based largely on agriculture and mining to economies based on manufacturing, technological innovation, and services. Growth was made possible by subsidized infrastructure, including—with the Bracero Program—subsidized labor costs. This trend established a long-lasting pattern in which federal expenditure and streams of migrant workers would undergird the development of both the U.S. West and the Mexican North.

NOTES

1. Oscar J. Martínez, *Border Boom Town: Ciudad Juárez since 1848* (Austin: University of Texas Press, 1978), 83.

2. Ellen Liebman, *California Farmland: A History of Large Agricultural Landholdings* (Totowa, NJ: Rowman and Allanheld, 1983), 16–67, 169–73; U.S. Department of Commerce, Bureau of the Census, *Statistical Abstract of the United States, 1950* (Washington, D.C.: Government Printing Office, 1950), 49, 563; U.S. Department of Commerce, Bureau of the Census, *Statistical Abstract of the United States, 1986* (Washington, D.C.: Government Printing Office, 1986), 635, 636.

3. On the Mexican economy and U.S.-Mexican trade relations during World War II and in the postwar period, see Timothy King, *Mexico: Industrial and Trade Policies since 1940* (London: Oxford University Press, 1970); Stephen R. Niblo, *War, Diplomacy, and Development: The United States and Mexico, 1938–1954* (Wilmington, DE: Scholarly Resources, 1995); René Villareal, *El desequilibrio externo en la industrialización de México (1929–1975): Un enfoque estructuralista* (México, D.F.: Fondo de Cultura Económica, 1976); Clark W. Reynolds, *The Mexican Economy: Twentieth-Century Structure and Growth* (New Haven, CT: Yale University Press, 1970); Leopoldo M. Solís, *La realidad económica mexicana: Retrovisión y perspectivas* (México, D.F.: Siglo Veintiuno Editores, 1987).

4. Menno Vellinga, *Desigualdad, poder y cambio social en Monterrey* (México, D.F.: Siglo Veintiuno Editores, 1988), 42.

5. Reynolds, *The Mexican Economy,* 158.

6. Daniel D. Arreola, "Curio Consumerism and Kitsch Culture in the Mexican-American Borderland," *Journal of the West* 40, no. 2 (spring 2001): 24–31, details the development of border curio trade.

7. Niblo, *War, Diplomacy, and Development.*

8. On the Bracero Program, see Ernesto Galarza, *Merchants of Labor: The Mexican Bracero Story* (Charlotte, NC: McNally and Loftin, 1964); Richard Craig, *The Bracero Program: Interest Groups and Foreign Policy* (Austin: University of Texas Press, 1971); Linda C. Majka and Theo J. Majka, *Farm Workers, Agribusiness, and the State* (Philadelphia: Temple University Press, 1982); Rodolfo Acuña, *Occupied America: A History of Chicanos*, 2nd ed. (New York: Harper and Row, 1981).

9. For the classic historical account of these beginnings, see Carey McWilliams, *North from Mexico: The Spanish-Speaking People of the United States* (New York: Greenwood Press, 1968).

5

ECONOMIC TRENDS SINCE 1950

Legacies of War and a Globalizing Economy

The economic significance of the border region for both the United States and Mexico increased dramatically after 1950, then accelerated during the last two decades of the twentieth century and first years of the twenty-first, despite recessions in 1990–1991, 2001, and 2008. After the boom caused by the expanded demand of the war effort, the economy on both sides of the border settled into a prolonged period of sustained growth, the first in its history. New economic pursuits and the stability brought by the increasing diversity of the economic base undergirded this transformed pattern of development. The federal governments in both Mexico and the United States continued to stimulate border economic development by investing in infrastructure. This was particularly the case in the U.S. West, where "the rising federal role as regional financier–resources manager, which had begun so abruptly in 1933–45, was heightened, expanded, and institutionalized."[1] By the end of the century, as the region as a whole became caught up in the world economy's globalization and momentous shift from an Atlantic to a Pacific axis, the border's economy emerged as the focus of scholarly attention, debate among policymakers, and increasing general interest.

THE BORDER ECONOMY COMES OF AGE

Economic trends established during World War II continued into the 1950s, becoming, if anything, more pronounced in peacetime. In the decade and a half following the end of the war, the U.S. federal government invested an additional $150 billion in the U.S. West, most of it in the four border states. Texas and California benefited from federal spending through defense contracts, price supports for farm commodities, and generous outlays for veterans.

Table 5.1. Mexican Border-State Gross Product, by Economic Sector, 1979–2011

	1970		1985		2000		2004		2011	
	Border	Mexico	Border	Mexico	Border	Mexico	Border	Mexico	Border	Mexico
Total gross product (thousands of current pesos)	93,714	444,271	8,787,037	47,402,549	1,205,593,982	4,983,517,681	1,716,976,477	6,964,058,586	3,008,451,353	13,843,758,061
Sector										
					Percentage of Total					
Agriculture	12.7	12.2	9.6	9.1	3.1	4.1	3.2	3.8	3.4	3.5
Mining	3.5	2.5	2.4	4.7	0.8	1.4	1.1	1.5	3.5	10.4
Manufacturing	21.6	23.7	25.7	23.4	24.4	20.3	22.0	18.1	25.2	18.1
Construction	6.0	5.3	4.8	4.4	4.5	5.2	4.2	5.5	8.6	6.7
Trade, restaurants, and hotels	28.0	25.9	32.6	34.8	24.5	21.4	24.8	20.8	16.3	18.7
Utilities	1.2	1.2	1.3	0.8	1.2	1.1	1.6	1.3	1.7	1.2
Transport and communications	N/A	N/A	N/A	N/A	11.5	11.2	10.7	10.4	10.1	10.8
Services	22.0	24.4	23.6	22.8	30.6	36.6	33.1	39.8	29.8	32.8

Sources: Lorey, *United States–Mexico Border Statistics since 1900*, table 52; INEGI, Sistema de cuentas nacionales de México, producto interno bruto por entidad federativa, 1999–2004; INEGI, Sistema de cuentas nacionales de México, producto interno bruto por entidad federativa, 2007–2011, tables 97, 99, 102, 105, 116, 123, 125; calculations by authors. The percentages may not equal 100 percent due to rounding and INEGI's accounting for intermediate financial services that are measured indirectly (SIFMI).

Table 5.2. U.S. Border-State Gross Product, by Economic Sector, 1963–2012

Sector	1963	1970	1975	1980	1985	1990	1995	1997	2000	2004	2012
Total gross product of border states (millions of dollars)	104,785	177,653	300,941	575,466	913,974	1,268,651	1,561,899	1,804,395	2,222,003	2,695,854	3,949,429
Percentage of Total											
Agriculture, forestry, and fishing	3.4	2.7	3.1	2.4	1.9	2.0	1.8	1.5	1.3	1.5	1.3
Farms	3.0	2.2	2.5	1.4	1.4	1.4	1.1	1.2	0.9	1.1	1.0
Mining	5.2	3.8	5.4	8.1	6.2	3.9	2.8	2.5	2.6	3.2	1.4
Construction	5.4	5.1	5.1	5.6	5.0	4.4	3.8	3.9	4.5	4.9	3.8
Manufacturing	19.1	18.0	16.8	16.9	14.7	14.8	14.6	14.1	13.7	10.4	12.5
Durable goods	11.7	11.0	9.9	10.5	9.4	9.0	9.3	9.2	9.3	6.2	6.3
Nondurable goods	7.3	6.9	6.9	6.4	5.3	5.8	5.3	5.0	4.4	4.1	6.2
Transportation and public utilities	9.1	8.9	8.7	8.3	8.5	8.1	8.8	5.2	5.0	4.9	2.9
Wholesale trade	7.3	7.4	7.7	7.3	7.0	6.7	7.0	6.4	6.3	6.0	6.2
Retail trade	10.5	10.7	10.1	9.4	9.8	9.1	9.2	7.3	7.1	7.1	5.7
Finance, insurance, and real estate	14.3	14.6	14.6	15.0	17.9	18.8	18.7	18.7	18.9	17.1	18.0
Services	9.0	13.2	13.3	14.4	16.4	19.7	20.8	26.7	27.9	28.3	30.8
Management of companies	N/A	N/A	N/A	N/A	N/A	N/A	N/A	1.5	1.7	1.5	1.2
Federal government	3.1	3.3	3.1	2.5	2.4	2.3	2.2	2.0	1.7	1.7	1.8
Military	3.1	3.0	2.6	1.8	2.0	1.6	1.3	1.1	1.0	1.1	1.4
State and local government	7.9	9.4	9.4	8.1	8.1	8.6	9.1	8.4	8.3	8.4	9.0

Source: Bureau of Economic Analysis (BEA), Gross State Product by Industry; 1963–1997 data are based on the Standard Industrial Classification (SIC) codes; data for 1997–2012 are based on the North American Industry Classification System (NAICS). Thus, there is a discontinuity between the 1961–1995 data and the 1997–2012 data. See "Regional Economic Accounts," BEA, http://www.bea.gov/regional/index.htm.

Table 5.3.   Mexican Border-State Economically Active Population, by Economic Sector, 1970–2013

Sector	1970 (%)	1980 (%)	1990 (%)	2000[a] (%)	2010[*b] (%)	2013[*c] (%)
Primary activities	29.1	15.4	14.3	8.0	7.0	5.9
Extractive industry	2.4	0.7	1.6	1.0	1.1	1.4
Manufacturing	17.4	15.2	24.1	27.3	19.9	23.7
Construction	5.8	6.7	8.4	6.3	7.9	7.4
Electricity and water	0.4	0.3	0.8	N/A	N/A	N/A
Commerce	11.7	11.1	14.0	17.9	19.6	18.8
Transportation	3.7	4.6	4.8	4.7	5.1	4.8
Services	20.6	17.0	25.1	29.3	42.3	41.4
Government	3.0	N/A	3.6	3.8	4.6	3.7
Unclassified	5.8	29.0	3.2	1.8	2.2	1.5

Source: INEGI, Encuesta nacional de empleo, 2002; Encuesta nacional de ocupación y empleo, 2010, 2014 (http://www.inegi.gob.mx).

[a] Electricity and water figures not specified in 2002 survey.

[b] Values for electricity listed as part of extractive industry for 2010 and 2013.

[c] 2013 values calculated based on first two trimesters of the year.

San Antonio, like San Diego, developed a postwar economy heavily dependent on the military. Los Alamos, New Mexico, continued as a major center of federally funded nuclear research.

Throughout the postwar period, expenditures for defense constituted the largest single item in the federal budget, a national priority that had a profound impact on the border region. Defense-related production, most of which was financed by the federal government, continued to lead the border's industrial development. Federal support of high-tech industries also characterized the period after 1950. Government financing of high-risk research and development helped provide a competitive edge to U.S. industries. The importance of military spending was felt well into the 1980s. In 1984, California led all states in garnering federal military dollars, with 20 percent of the total allocation. Of the funds set aside for military contracts, the state's producers received 23 percent of the U.S. total. The country's active-duty military personnel, 15 percent of whom were stationed in California, also contributed to numerous local economies.

Although the end of the Cold War and tensions in the early 1990s between the United States and its allies and the Soviet Union and its bloc brought a slowdown in defense expenditures, U.S. involvement in the Persian Gulf War (1990–1991) and the Iraq War (2003–2011) kept military expenditures at a high level, including for the defense industry and military bases

Table 5.4.   U.S. Border-State Employed Persons, by Economic Sector, 1970–2012

Sector	1970 (%)	1980 (%)	1990* (%)	2001 (%)	2005 (%)	2010 (%)	2012 (%)
Agriculture, forestry, and fisheries	3.7	3.1	3.0	1.8	1.8	0.8	0.7
Mining	1.3	1.7	1.0	0.7	0.8	1.3	1.4
Construction	6.3	6.9	6.8	5.9	6.4	5.2	5.1
Manufacturing	19.9	18.7	15.8	11.5	9.6	6.2	6.2
Transportation, communication, and public utilities	7.0	7.2	7.0	3.7	3.5	5.5	5.6
Wholesale trade	4.5	4.6	4.7	4.7	4.6	3.7	3.7
Retail trade	17.0	16.6	16.8	11.5	11.6	9.0	5.3
Finance, insurance, and real estate	5.6	6.7	7.3	5.9	6.3	10.6	11.1
Services	28.5	29.4	33.2	38.8	41.1	41.3	42.1
Management**	N/A	N/A	N/A	1.3	1.1	0.9	0.9
Unclassified**	N/A	N/A	N/A	0.2	0.3	N/A	N/A
Public administration	6.2	5.1	4.6	14.0	12.9	12.8	11.8

Source: Lorey, *United States–Mexico Border Statistics since* 1900, table 702; Bureau of Economic Analysis (BEA), regional data. Interactive data tables are available online at "Regional Economic Accounts," BEA, http://www.bea.gov/regional/index.htm.

* Data do not include Arizona.

** There was a change from Standard Industrial Classification (SIC) definitions to the North American Industry Classification System (NAICS) definitions beginning in 1997. For this table, the two systems were combined, except in the management and unclassified categories. For 2010 and 2012 data, there was no unclassified categorical measurement.

in the border states. Moreover, after the September 11, 2001, terrorist attacks on New York and Washington, D.C., expenditures along the U.S.-Mexican border increased rapidly. Congress mandated installation of border fencing that covered some 700 miles by 2014, a nearly tenfold increase from 2000. Moreover, by 2014 the border with Mexico also had 146 miles of new all-weather roads, hundreds of miles of access roads, 70 miles of the border with powerful stadium lights, nearly 12,000 underground sensors, 273 remote video surveillance systems, 220 mobile surveillance systems, and an expanded fleet of watercraft, aircraft, and vehicles, along with 8 unmanned aerial systems (drones). By 2014, more than 18,000 Border Patrol agents were stationed along the southern border.[2] The economic impact of acquisition, installation, and maintenance of security infrastructure and housing well-paid federal employees along the border, many in poor communities, was significant for the region.

The postwar federal budget never returned to prewar levels. Firms such as Lockheed, McDonnell-Douglas, Rockwell International, Motorola, Sperry

Corporation, Hughes Aircraft, General Dynamics, and later Texas Instruments took advantage of government largesse to become leaders in the new U.S. economy. The border area gained some of the country's most technologically sophisticated firms. Many aerospace, computer, and communications industries were established in or relocated to Silicon Valley in Northern California (the area of the San Francisco peninsula that stretches from Menlo Park to San Jose), as well as Los Angeles, Phoenix, San Diego, San Jose, Houston, Austin, and the Dallas–Fort Worth area. Although federal underwriting of western development shifted its focus from providing inexpensive land and water to building freeway networks and financing aerospace and high-tech research and development, government support continued uninterrupted.

In Mexico, the postwar period saw a deepening of the patterns of development initiated during the war years. Mexican federal investment in the border states, which stimulated growth and contributed to changing patterns of employment, remained one of the main pillars of border development in the country after 1950. Postwar budgets for communications and public works, which had averaged 13 percent under Lázaro Cárdenas in the 1930s, hovered between 18 and 23 percent. From the 1960s, the federal government initiated public-private partnerships for the construction of key highways in the border region and elsewhere. This model provides concessions for up to thirty years for the construction and operation of specific toll roads. Some include partial federal funding to offset construction costs, but the model has been successful in bringing needed infrastructure to the border. Examples include the Tijuana-Mexicali highway and sections that connect key border cities with central Mexico.

The period after 1950 saw remarkable changes in the size and shape of state economies all along the U.S.-Mexican border. Data on the evolution of gross state product—the total value of all goods and services produced (see tables 5.1 and 5.2)—reveal impressive absolute growth in both the United States and Mexico. The structure of regional production changed markedly over the course of the postwar period, as figures for the economically active population in different sectors of the ten border states show (see tables 5.3 and 5.4). By 1990 only about 14 percent of Mexicans in border states were working in agriculture; fully one-quarter were employed in the industries and another one-quarter in services. In the United States, the shift away from primary activities was even more impressive: in 1990 only 2.9 percent of the economically active population worked in agriculture, forestry, and fisheries, while one-fifth were employed in industry, and almost one-third worked in services.

Agriculture boomed on both sides of the border in the postwar period, as large capital-intensive farms benefited from massive investment in irrigation works. From 1947 to 1960, of Mexico's total expenditure for irrigation, 20 percent was devoted to Tamaulipas, 16 percent to Baja California, and 25 percent to Sonora. While Tijuana was growing as the center of the West Coast industrial hub in Mexico, Mexicali prospered from major expansion of irrigation and mechanized agriculture linked to the U.S. market. The area around Mexicali became one of Mexico's most productive agricultural regions and attracted numerous national and international manufacturing concerns as well.

The four U.S. border states together came to account for one-fifth of U.S. farm production.[3] After 1949, California remained consistently the nation's number one agricultural state in cash income, and by 1989 it accounted for 13 percent of total U.S. farm production. By 1960, Mexico's northern region was producing 44 percent of the gross value of agriculture, livestock, fishery, and forestry production in Mexico.[4] The four Mexican border states depended more on farm production than did Mexico as a whole. Whereas agriculture accounted for 8 percent of Mexico's gross domestic product in 1980, it represented 17 percent of the gross state product in Sonora, 12 percent in Tamaulipas, 12 percent in Chihuahua, and 9 percent in Baja California.

In both the Mexican and the U.S. border states, the agricultural boom was accompanied by a progressive concentration of farmlands, as family farms gave way to large, vertically integrated agribusinesses. By the 1970s, it is estimated that 70 percent of *ejidos* in Sonora rented their lands to private producers. A 1992 change to the Mexican constitution allowed the sale of *ejido* lands, accelerating the growth of large private farms in the border region. The most dynamic sectors in Mexican border agriculture were increasingly geared toward the cultivation of fruits and vegetables for export to the United States during the winter months. In the period from 1960 to 1983, the Mexican border states also experienced striking growth in the production of animal-feed grains.

Manufacturing was increasingly a mainstay of the U.S.-Mexican border economy after 1950. In the U.S. border states, clean industry led the way after the 1960s. Mexican industry was more concentrated in such basic industrial sectors as food processing and mineral refining. Production was concentrated geographically. By the mid-1980s, Los Angeles was the most important manufacturing center in the United States. Together, the Monterrey industrial conglomerates—controlled by a small clique of interconnected families—were responsible for about one-quarter of Mexico's industrial output. By the mid-1950s the Mexican North generated most of the country's industrial production outside central Mexico; of the nation's twenty-five leading industrial centers, seventeen were northern cities.

Table 5.5. Three Primary Branches of Manufacturing in Mexican and U.S. Border States, 2011

State	Branches of Manufacturing
Baja California	Machinery and equipment
	Food, beverages, and tobacco
	Metals
Chihuahua	Machinery and equipment
	Food, beverages, and tobacco
	Wood and its products
Coahuila	Machinery and equipment
	Metals
	Food, beverages, and tobacco
Nuevo León	Machinery and equipment
	Metals
	Food, beverages, and tobacco
Sonora	Metals
	Machinery and equipment
	Food, beverages, and tobacco
Tamaulipas	Machinery and equipment
	Chemicals, petroleum derivatives, rubber, and plastic
	Food, beverages, and tobacco
Arizona	Computer and electronic products
	Transportation equipment
	Food, beverages, and tobacco
California	Computer and electronic products
	Petroleum and coal products
	Chemical products
New Mexico	Computer and electronic products
	Food, beverages, and tobacco
	Chemical products
Texas	Petroleum and coal products
	Chemical products
	Computer and electronic products

Sources: INEGI, Sistema de cuentas nacionales de México, producto interno bruto por entidad federativa 2007–2011, 2012; Bureau of Economic Analysis, U.S. Department of Commerce, 2011 (http://www.bea.gov); State Manufacturing Data for Arizona, California, New Mexico, and Texas, National Association of Manufacturers (NAM) (http://nam.org/statedata).

Highly specialized links between the two national economies in the border region were particularly striking in such areas as the industrial corridor between San Antonio, Texas, and Monterrey, Nuevo León. In Monterrey, factories and assembly plants combined U.S. capital goods and high-tech know-how with Mexican production skills and inexpensive labor. Monterrey was the origin of 60 percent of all manufactured goods entering the United States from Mexico. North of the border, San Antonio was a top distribution center and supplier of U.S. services to manufacturers in Monterrey. Law firms and accounting firms opened offices in San Antonio to serve the growing Mexican market.

When older U.S. industries such as textiles, automobiles, and steel began to suffer from slow growth and increased foreign competition in the 1960s and 1970s, the newer high-tech firms continued to be buoyant. Often located in the Southwest, they helped the region's economy remain relatively strong through the 1970s and 1980s. By the 1980s the United States exported only a small amount of steel; aerospace products and computer equipment—produced predominantly in border states—became the nation's leading exports. With many of the new firms in the border area, the four states north of the international boundary together outperformed the rest of the U.S. industrial economy after 1970. These industries developed in close relationship with the Pentagon's priorities and were built upon the high-tech industrial base already well established in the border states. Largely because of Silicon Valley—one of the leading sites of the emerging computer, communications, and software industrial complex—the border states continued to lead the nation in high-tech products, processes, services, and exports.[5] The trend toward high-tech production was also notable in Baja California and Chihuahua. Electronic and computer industries often drove the border economy in a symbiotic manner, with innovation taking place in the United States and assembly carried out in Mexico.

The first decade and a half of the twenty-first century saw continued evolution and adaptation in the economy. In the U.S. border states, defense contractors adjusted to meet the needs of the growing security concerns produced by international terrorism after the events of 9/11 and congressional priorities to "defend the southern border." Emerging biotech industries likewise had a strong presence in border cities such as San Diego. The Mexican border economy mirrored some of these trends, with increasing sophistication in manufacturing, supplanting the old model of labor-intensive assembly work. Tijuana, Mexicali, and Ciudad Juárez were important leaders in Mexico's growing aerospace manufacturing, which produced high-quality components for the world's civilian and military aerospace industry.[6]

Both U.S. citizens of Mexican descent and undocumented Mexican immigrants played a major part in the postwar economic boom on the border, particularly in the growth of the manufacturing and service sectors. Data on the occupations of Mexican immigrants show that more than one-third of the men who arrived after 1975 and about 45 percent of the women were employed in manufacturing in 1980 (see table 5.6), a marked change from the years of the Bracero Program. Data on the employment of undocumented

Table 5.6. Percentage of Mexican-Origin Population in the United States Employed in Industry, 1980, 2000, 2011

	1980			
	Males		Females	
	Immigrant Status		Immigrant Status	
Industry	I[a]	II[b]	I[a]	II[b]
Agriculture, mining	17.3	9.0	10.4	4.0
Construction	11.1	13.0	0.6	0.9
Manufacturing	35.3	23.7	44.5	19.2
Transportation, communication, and utilities	2.4	9.3	1.0	3.7
Wholesaling and nonfood retailing	8.7	12.9	8.4	13.5
Food retailing	12.2	7.1	8.0	11.0
Business, repair, and personal services	8.7	7.7	15.3	10.8
Professional services, finance, and government	4.3	17.4	11.8	37.0

Source: Lorey, *United States–Mexico Border Statistics since 1900*, table 1009.

[a] Mexican-born noncitizens who immigrated to the United States in 1975 or later.

[b] U.S.-born persons who identify themselves as being of Mexican origin.

| | 2000 | |
	Males	Females
Farming, forestry, and fishing	11.3	2.7
Machine operators, assemblers, and inspectors	10.4	10.2
Transportation and material moving	6.6	0.8
Executive, administrative, and managerial	5.0	8.9
Professional specialty	3.9	7.3
Technical and related support	1.3	3.1
Sales	6.6	11.3
Administrative support, including clerical	4.9	23.4
Precision production, craft, and repair	23.3	4.0
Handlers, equipment cleaners, helpers, and laborers	11.8	2.8
Service workers, private household	0.0	3.2
Service workers, except private household	15.0	22.3

Source: U.S. Census Bureau, Current Population Survey, March 2000.

Table 5.7. Employment Characteristics of Mexican-Origin Population in the United States, 2011

Industries	Percentage of Labor Force
Construction, agriculture, and mining	18.6
Manufacturing	10.7
Trade and transportation	9.3
Information, finance, and other services	8.2
Occupations	
Management, professional, and related occupations	4.6
Services	14.7
Sales and office support	8.2
Construction, extraction, and farming	23.3
Maintenance, production, transportation, and material moving	13.4

Source: Pew Hispanic Center, *Hispanics of Mexican Origin, 2011* (tabulations of the U.S. Census Bureau 2011 American Community Survey).

workers in the United States (see table 5.8) reveal that recent immigrants were concentrated in some of the lowest-paying and least secure sectors: farming, building cleaning, construction, and food preparation and serving. Unauthorized workers, of which 56 percent were Mexican, dominated some of the most arduous jobs in these sectors. By 2005, undocumented workers made up 36 percent of insulation workers, 29 percent of roofers, 29 percent of miscellaneous agricultural workers, 28 percent of drywall installers, 27 percent of construction helpers, and 27 percent of all butchers and meat-processing workers.[7]

Table 5.8. Proportion of Undocumented Workers in Select Occupation Groups, March 2005

Occupation Group	Percentage Undocumented	Approximate Percentage Mexican Undocumented[a]
Farming, fishing, and forestry	24	13.4
Building cleaning and maintenance	17	9.5
Construction and extractive	14	7.8
Food preparation and serving	12	6.7
Production	9	5.0
Transport and material moving	7	3.9
Total percentage of U.S. workers	4.9	2.7

Source: Jeffrey S. Passel, "The Size and Characteristics of the Unauthorized Migrant Population in the U.S.," Pew Hispanic Center Research Report, March 7, 2006.

[a] Mexicans make up 56 percent of all unauthorized migrants in the United States.

On both sides of the border some of the most traditional economic pursuits fell into decline relative to the rest of the economy in the years after 1960. The most important traditional sector to experience a long-term slump was that of copper, silver, and gold mining. At one time the lifeblood of the border states, the extraction of almost all minerals decreased in relative importance after a short-lived boom in the 1950s, while the ownership of mining operations became increasingly concentrated. Arizona and New Mexico continued as important producers of copper through the last decades of the twentieth century and the first part of the twenty-first century, usually accounting for two-thirds of U.S. total production.[8]

A few Mexican states remained leading national and international sources of key metals and minerals. The state of Chihuahua, for example, continued to produce large quantities of lead, silver, gold, copper, and fluorite, while Coahuila became a critical source of coal for the nearby steel factories in Monclova and Monterrey. Tamaulipas possessed little of Mexico's traditional mineral wealth but served as one of the main centers of the country's oil industry into the 1970s. Sonora and Arizona continued to be important sources of copper, although public outcry over air pollution forced the closure of a number of mines and smelters in the region during the 1980s.

Sitting atop the same oil and natural gas reserves, the states of Texas and Tamaulipas have shared the booms and busts of that industry. In the 1940s and 1950s, discoveries of natural gas near Reynosa provided added wealth for Tamaulipas.[9] In recent decades, Mexican oil and gas production has stagnated, mainly due to a regulatory framework that largely prohibits foreign investment. Texas oil and gas production peaked in the 1970s and then declined rather steeply due to played-out formations until about 2010, when the state still produced about 15 percent of U.S. totals. Hydraulic fracturing, or "fracking," is a new drilling technique that injects fluid into shale beds under pressure to fracture the shale formations and free up additional gas and petroleum resources. This has unleashed a new boom in Texas, and in 2014 the state produced about 30 percent of the national total. Much of the production is in the Eagle Ford shale formation that underlies the Texas-Tamaulipas border. As Mexico under President Enrique Peña Nieto moves forward with legislation to enable significant foreign investment in oil and gas, Tamaulipas will likely experience a similar resurgence of these products.[10]

Tourism, another traditional activity of the border region, which had touched off or contributed to economic booms during Prohibition and World War II, continued as one of the mainstays of the border economy after 1950. Tourism was important on both sides of the boundary: a great majority of Mexican tourists journeyed to the U.S. border states, and the number of tourists traveling from U.S. border states to Mexico grew twenty-four-fold between 1935 and 1970. Most went to Mexico to indulge in such traditional pursuits as entertainment (principally food and drink) and bargain hunting (apparel and personal-care items). Tourism was the greatest source of foreign exchange in Tijuana and in several other border cities.[11] In the case of Tijuana, most of the foreign visitors only spent part of a day and a relatively small amount of money on purchases, but the cumulative effect was significant. Tijuana benefited from San Diego's growing tourism industry, as many out-of-state visitors to San Diego included a visit south of the border as one of their activities.

The flow of foreign visitors to Tijuana and other Mexican border cities was curtailed radically by increasing drug-related violence in Mexican border cities and after 9/11 by waits of several hours to cross back into the United States due to tightened U.S. border inspections. By 2008, for example, the areas that catered to foreign visitors were empty, with shops shuttered; locals in Tijuana reported that tourism had declined by some 90 percent since 2005.[12] After even further declines, by 2014 Tijuana's tourism industry began to show signs of slow recovery.[13]

Border commerce typically experienced periodic downturns, however. Retail sales to Mexican shoppers on the U.S. side of the border were extremely sensitive to fluctuations in the dollar-peso exchange rate, plunging dramatically with each major postwar devaluation of the Mexican peso (1976, 1982, 1985, 1994–1995). After the Mexican crisis of 1982, U.S. border merchants sought federal assistance, and President Ronald Reagan responded by creating a border aid program. Along with the tourism sector, a wide range of services—law, finance, health, entertainment, education, and transportation, to name a few—began to employ large segments of the U.S. and Mexican border-state workforce.

MEXICAN GOVERNMENT POLICY AND THE BORDER: PRONAF AND BIP—THE MAQUILADORAS

Beginning in the 1960s the Mexican federal government played an increasingly active role in managing the economic growth of the country's North. This change came with the massive transformation of the region as its population grew. Also involved was the desire to secure income (by ensuring that money would be spent on the Mexican rather than the U.S. side of the border), to provide for the absorption of excess labor in the region, and to attract family tourism as vice-based tourism waned.

Mexican government policy reflected changes in global production as well, particularly shifts in the United States. As goods produced in Europe and Asia began to flood the U.S. market, the value of imports as a share of U.S. domestic production rose from 14 percent to 40 percent (in the 1970–1979 period). Mexican policymakers' desire to compete with these imports was aided by a new U.S. tariff law in 1965, which exempted from general import duties U.S. goods assembled in whole or in part outside the United States. With a tariff to be paid only on value added in manufacture, in many cases it became cheaper to have goods assembled abroad and import them than to produce or assemble them in the United States. Most U.S. foreign investment in Mexico prior to the 1960s had been in extractive industries, but in the 1970s U.S. factories began to shift assembly and even some production to Mexico.

In 1961, Mexico established a national border program, the Programa Nacional Fronterizo (PRONAF). Under the auspices of the publicly owned national development bank NAFINSA, PRONAF sought to substitute Mexican manufactured goods for imports in the border states, boost the sale of Mexican manufactures to foreign consumers, stimulate tourism in the border states, and upgrade living conditions along the boundary.

The program was most successful in the area of commerce. By the mid-1960s the number of Mexicans shopping on the U.S. side of the border had begun to grow dramatically, outpacing the number of U.S. citizens who shopped south of the border. Studies indicated that 70 percent of Juarenses visited El Paso to shop, their expenditures on food, clothing, and furniture constituting 62 percent of the total spending on these items in El Paso. This trend revealed the inadequate commercial infrastructure of cities like Ciudad Juárez. In response, PRONAF supported the construction of such shopping complexes as Rio Grande Mall in Ciudad Juárez, where shoppers could find both Mexican-made and U.S. and other foreign goods. In a further, controversial effort to strengthen Mexican retailing, streetcar service between Ciudad Juárez and El Paso was discontinued in 1977.

Despite the efforts of PRONAF, Mexican merchants could never compete with merchants across the border in the U.S. cities. Due to large-scale purchases and better distribution systems, U.S. merchants consistently were able to provide a greater selection of goods at lower prices than their competitors south of the border. Mexican border merchants were also disadvantaged by the outrageous interest rates—often 30 percent per year or more—they had to pay Mexican banks to finance inventory purchases for their stores. Mexican government policy received an unexpected boost when the 1976 devaluation of the peso stimulated the sale of Mexican goods and services to U.S. consumers. The devaluation also triggered a boom in U.S. tourism, as

In 1964 tourists flocked to Tijuana to the curio shops, restaurants, and bars on Avenida Revolución. In addition, they brought their automobiles for low-cost and high-quality upholstery. The Jai Alai Palace is in the background, where the Basque game was a favorite of visitors. (Harry W. Crosby)

travelers took advantage of a strengthened dollar. The same year saw an 80 percent increase in vehicular flow between El Paso and Ciudad Juárez; by the end of 1976, commerce in Ciudad Juárez had increased 60 percent over 1975. The devaluation was calamitous for El Paso merchants, however, who had grown to depend on Mexican pesos and shoppers. Some store owners in the downtown area experienced a 50 percent drop in sales.

The Mexican government initiated a Border Industrialization Program (BIP) in 1965 with the twin goals of stimulating the manufacturing sector of the depressed economies in the northern states and providing employment for workers displaced by the end of the Bracero Program in 1964. Mexican policy

and business leaders recognized that a number of Asian economies were being transformed through assembly manufacturing and sought to emulate their
example. As flexible inter- and intrafirm networks developed to provide on-
time deliveries and carefully managed quality control, Mexico became a more
attractive location for assembly operations for the neighboring U.S. market. In
addition, new communications technologies made it possible for firms to carry
out production efficiently at diverse world sites.[14]

The main feature of the BIP was the establishment of *maquilas* or maquiladoras, assembly plants that imported components and raw goods from
the United States, assembled them into finished products, and then exported
them back across the border for sale. The phenomenon was sometimes called
"in-bond" industry because the components and machinery were brought in
under a bonded status that prohibited their sale in Mexico and mandated their
reexport for sale abroad. In some ways the maquiladora program represented
the logical extension of Mexico's earlier free trade zone. Just as the free trade
zone recognized that people in the border cities needed preferential access to
the U.S. market, the maquiladora program recognized the special importance
of the U.S. market for Mexican industrial development.[15] The *maquila* innovation was developed at roughly the same time as, and at least in part as a
response to, the emergence of the export processing zones and special economic zones of Asia.

The attractions of *maquila* operations for U.S. and Asian investors were
several. The enabling legislation provided for the duty-free importation into
Mexico of materials, supplies, and machinery as long as the whole of the product was for export; tariffs on goods returning to the United States were paid
solely on the value added by manufacture in Mexico (mainly labor), generat-
ing a substantial savings. *Maquilas* were also the only firms exempt from the
Mexican laws requiring majority Mexican ownership. Labor organization was
less entrenched in the Mexican border cities than in either the United States
or central Mexico. Few strikes were threatened or carried out in border-state
manufacturing plants. Most important was the location of the maquiladoras
next to the largest consumer market in the world and ready access to the
advanced communications and transportation infrastructure on the U.S. side
of the border. For these reasons the *maquila* plants came to constitute an increasingly important link in the booming intra-industry trade reshaping global
investment and commercial flows. In contrast with other global locations, the
Mexican border area offered managers the advantage of living on the U.S. side,
where families had access to U.S. schools, health care, and other public services.

The maquiladora program gathered steam slowly at first. Between 1965
and the mid-1970s, a gradual increase in investments in *maquilas* in Tijuana,

"Help wanted" sign for a maquila *in Tecate, Baja California. The sign says that the company is currently hiring men, as "women" is taped over. This indicates that the company has flexible hiring practices, depending on the type of work available. 2002.*

Mexicali, Nogales, Ciudad Juárez, and Matamoros gave rise to some twin plants: labor-intensive work took place on the Mexican side, capital- and development-intensive work on the U.S. side. Even with a sluggish start, by 1972 nearly one-third of the value of all U.S. components sent abroad for assembly was going to border plants in Mexico. After 1972, *maquilas* were no longer legally limited to the border region. Although 80 percent were still concentrated in the border states, and almost all of that activity took place in five cities along the border, *maquilas* spread slowly to other areas, notably Guadalajara. An overvalued Mexican peso and higher labor costs led to job losses in the maquiladoras in the mid-1970s. Nevertheless, by 1979, maquiladora production accounted for one-quarter of Mexico's manufacturing exports. With the Mexican national economic crisis of the early 1980s, the maquiladora program became a crucial part of the government's economic strategy to attract foreign capital to Mexican manufacturing.

The number of border *maquila* plants and the number of workers they employed grew rapidly after the early 1980s (see table 5.9). From a total of 12 plants in 1965, *maquila* operations multiplied to 1,500 by 1996; the number of employees increased from 3,000 to about 400,000 in the same period. The majority of the plants were concentrated in Tijuana and Ciudad Juárez and increasingly located in formal industrial parks. Although only 1 percent of Mexico's economically active population worked in border maquiladora plants, these workers constituted more than one in every ten Mexicans in manufacturing jobs. By the turn of the century, assembly plants employed well over 1 million workers throughout Mexico, and half of those jobs were concentrated in the six border cities of Ciudad Juárez, Tijuana, Matamoros, Reynosa, Mexicali, and Nuevo Laredo.

Maquilas produced a wide variety of goods for export to the United States, including electric and electronic goods, clothing, transportation equipment, furniture, toys, and processed foods (see table 5.10). By the early 1980s the majority of television sets, refrigerators, and computer keyboards sold in the United States were assembled in border maquiladoras. Imports to the United States from *maquilas* grew from 9 percent of total U.S. imports in 1979 to 17 percent in 1987. Soon European, Japanese, Taiwanese, and South Korean investors joined U.S. and Mexican entrepreneurs in establishing border industries under the maquiladora program.[16]

It turned out to be beneficial to the Mexican national economy to have *maquilas* in times of crisis—particularly in 1982 and 1995. As Mexico's 1980s economic crisis deepened, the number of *maquilas* grew, and the number of *maquila* workers increased significantly. During the 1995 Mexican economic decline, the maquiladora industry actually expanded by 20 percent. In that year *maquilas* produced $5 billion in exports, accounting for almost 70 percent of Mexico's trade surplus with the United States. Because statistics on Mexican exports include *maquila* production, they are sometimes misleading. One-half of the annual imports and exports claimed by the Mexican government in 1995, for example, came from the dollar-denominated, foreign-owned assembly plants.

The 2001 recession in the United States had strong reverberations in the maquiladora industry. Lack of clarity in the new rules that Mexico was crafting to eliminate special protections for the maquiladora sector in order to comply with the North American Free Trade Agreement (NAFTA) compounded the effects of the economic cycle. This uncertainty resulted in investment delays while subsidies and lower labor costs in Asia encouraged relocation of some existing operations from the Mexican border to China and other countries. From October 2000 to June 2002, more than 240,000 jobs and about 420

Table 5.9.   Number of Maquiladora Employees in Top Six Border Municipalities, 1975–2006

Municipality	1975	1980	1985	1990	1995	2000	2006[a]
Juárez	19,775	39,402	77,592	122,231	155,422	249,380	239,166
Nuevo Laredo	1,928	2,462	3,603	14,747	18,619	22,591	21,434
Matamoros	9,778	15,231	20,686	38,361	43,553	66,075	55,455
Mexicali	6,324	7,146	10,876	20,729	24,965	62,938	54,235
Reynosa	1,255	5,450	12,761	24,801	41,466	65,984	96,830
Tijuana	7,844	12,343	25,913	59,871	93,557	188,054	170,535
Total in Mexico	67,214	119,546	211,968	446,436	639,979	1,291,232	1,202,134

Source: Lorey, *United States–Mexico Border Statistics since 1900*, table 715; INEGI, Estadísticas económicas de la industria maquiladora de exportación, 2000–2006, February 2007.

[a] Preliminary data.

Table 5.10.   Maquiladora Goods Produced in Border Municipalities, by Type, 1980–2006

	1980	1985	1990	2000[a]	2006[a]
Number of Maquiladoras	551	672	1,477	1,581	1,293
Type of Goods	Percentage Share				
Prepared foods	2.2	1.8	2.2	2.3	1.4
Clothes and textiles	17.1	12.1	11.2	30.3	19.7
Shoes and leather goods	3.3	4.8	2.8	1.7	0.8
Furniture	10.2	11.0	17.1	10.9	10.3
Chemical products	0.7	N/A	4.7	4.3	5.2
Transportation equipment	9.1	8.0	8.3	6.9	10.3
Tools and equipment	2.9	3.1	2.3	1.3	2.5
Electric and electronic equipment	11.4	10.9	5.9	4.4	6.2
Electric and electronic materials and accessories	24.9	26.3	24.0	15.5	15.4
Toys and sports materials	3.8	3.9	2.0	1.7	1.3
Other manufactures	9.6	12.8	14.9	14.1	16.4
Services	4.9	5.1	4.6	6.6	10.6

Source: Lorey, *United States–Mexico Border Statistics since 1900*, table 1502; INEGI, Estadísticas económicas de la industria maquiladora de exportación, 2000–2006, February 2007.

[a] Percentage share data for 2000 and 2006 are national.

plants were lost in the Mexican industry, some 76 percent in the border states. In 2002 maquiladoras began to add jobs and by 2006 had recovered about half of the jobs that had been lost.[17] The U.S. recession of 2008 also had consequences for the maquiladora industry, as employment dipped again in 2008, 2009, and 2010, and recovered slowly so that by 2014 jobs were near the levels of 2000.[18]

More companies moved plants south of the border in the 1980s, transforming even towns at some distance from the international boundary. One example was Cananea, the mining town whose 1906 social and political eruption had seemed to many a precursor of the Mexican Revolution of 1910. There, several large maquiladoras opened, attracting workers from the interior of Sonora and from surrounding states.

After 1983 *maquilas* were allowed to sell 20 percent of their production in Mexico; in 1989 this amount was increased to 50 percent. Beginning in 2001, under NAFTA rules, firms were able to sell any portion of their production duty-free in any North American domestic market.

Since the maquiladoras were largely foreign-owned firms, their principal local impact was on employment and wages. *Maquila* wages (about $3 a day in the late 1980s), although low by average manufacturing standards in the United States, were 25 percent higher than in other regions of Mexico and typically were two and a half times the federally established minimum wage. Maquiladora wages did include required benefits such as social security, health insurance, and a housing fund. Because low pay was the key to their success, *maquila* owners struggled to keep unions out of the plants. Some firms initially preferred to employ young, female workers, considering them less likely to organize. Managers argued that women were more efficient than men at most assembly tasks that required manual dexterity and close eye-hand coordination. The preference for women workers may have unintentionally encouraged the male labor force to seek employment opportunities on the other side of the border, stimulating both legal and unauthorized migration to the United States. A program that had been touted as an answer to undocumented migration may thus have added to it. Although women remained in the majority in the maquiladora workforce for some years, the ratio changed over time; by 1988, for example, men constituted 41 percent of the assembly-plant workforce in Baja California. By January 2006, men made up 51.3 percent of the maquiladora workforce.[19] Workers in the maquiladoras are classified into three basic categories: operators, or assembly-line workers; technical and engineering staff; and administrative personnel. Typically, in border plants, the line workers have been about 80 to 85 percent of the employees.[20]

The consequences of *maquila*-led economic development of the northern Mexican states were much debated, both in Mexico and in the United States. As discussion of the implementation of a free trade agreement between the United States and Mexico intensified in the early 1990s, the fear that Mexico would become a "maquiladora country" was voiced. Critics charged that *maquila* production constituted a U.S. enclave on Mexican soil, that the basis of the industry in low-wage labor indicated hyperexploitation of Mexican nationals in the interest of the U.S. consumer, and that the maquiladoras brought little long-term benefit to Mexican industrial infrastructure through the transfer of technology. The impact of maquiladoras on the environment and on the health of workers also caused concern among some observers.[21] One critic pointed out that the social infrastructure remained underdeveloped in Mexican border cities, while the U.S. government received enormous revenues from taxes on goods produced in *maquilas* by U.S. firms (businesses that were taxed at their home location in the United States). The revenues did not make their way back to the border region.[22] Labor experts noted that, until 1998, none of the maquiladora plants was represented by an independent workers' union; even the single, short-lived exception at a Hyundai plant in Tijuana in 1998 served to prove the general rule. In January 1998 the U.S. Labor Department—in response to a complaint filed under NAFTA rules—reported that thousands of *maquilas* administered tests to weed out pregnant applicants for assembly jobs and harassed pregnant workers to force them to resign.[23]

Despite the concerns raised, the *maquila* program did create an enormous number of jobs that produced low unemployment rates in border communities. Mexican border technical schools and universities adjusted their programs, sending graduates to engineering, technical, and management positions in the *maquilas*. Many companies responded to criticism and conditions in the labor market by hiring both men and women. The industry also improved environmental compliance measures, and many firms established internal environmental programs that met international standards.

Early worries that the *maquilas* were "runaway" assembly plants that would move on at the earliest sign of lower-cost or less troublesome labor elsewhere, leaving little benefit for Mexico, proved unfounded: the assembly plants expanded their operations and appeared to be on the border to stay. Accompanying the growth in the number of *maquilas* was a reorientation of the industry; more and more maquiladora plants expanded from assembly operations to full-scale manufacturing, bringing significant wage and technological benefits. The industry also became more diverse. Even agricultural enterprises began to use the *maquila* option to export such products as houseplants and onion powder to U.S. markets.[24]

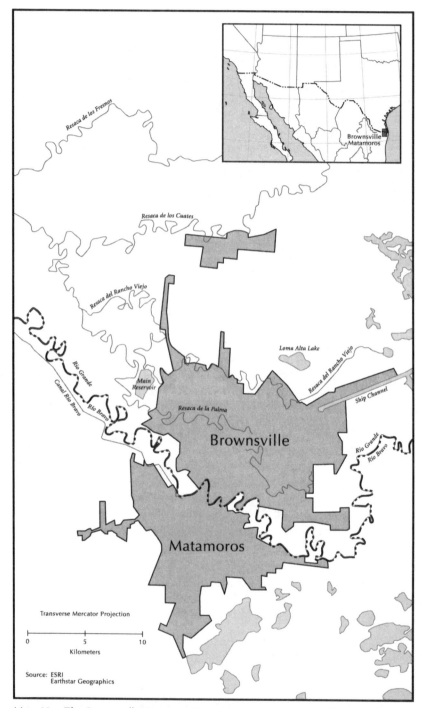

Map 10.   The Brownsville/Cameron County–Matamoros region. Of a population of
840,000 in 2005, some 55,000 people were employed in maquilas in Matamoros, an
important factor in regional population growth.

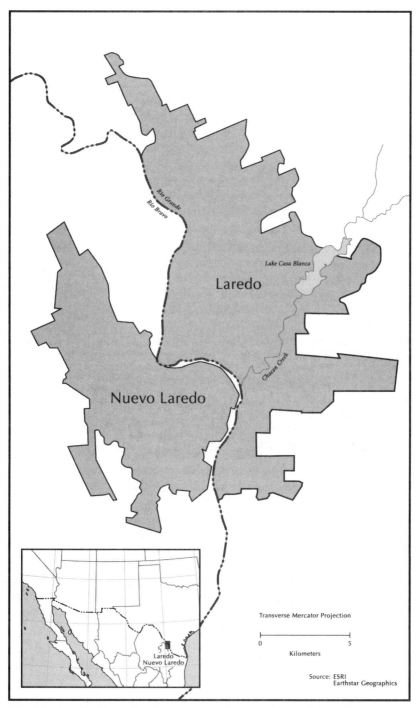

Map 11. Laredo–Nuevo Laredo twin cities. The regional population was 433,000 in 2005; maquilas *in Nuevo Laredo employed 22,000 workers.*

There has been an evolution in the sophistication of many maquiladoras since the industry emerged in 1965. Researchers have identified three classifications of maquiladoras based on their manufacturing operations. First-generation plants perform labor-intensive operations such as clothing assembly. Second-generation maquiladoras are oriented less toward assembly and more toward manufacturing using machine automation to produce products such as television sets and electrical appliances. Third-generation plants are oriented toward research, design, and development of products, using highly skilled labor and engineers. These maquiladoras tend to be quite autonomous from the parent firms.[25]

NAFTA required that Mexico phase out special protections and subsidies for the maquiladora industry and level the playing field with Mexican domestic producers for the internal market and for export. In 2007, Mexico merged the maquiladora program with the Program for Temporary Imports to Promote Exports (PITEX), which had been established in 1990 to help domestic companies export part of their output. The combined program is called Maquiladora Manufacturing Industry and Export Services (IMMEX). Mexico's national statistical agency, the Instituto Nacional de Estadística y Geografía (INEGI), began reporting the combined IMMEX data in categories of manufacturing and nonmanufacturing. This does not accurately reflect the old maquiladora data because IMMEX data include manufacturing firms that do not export and nonmanufacturing firms that do export, such as the former *maquilas* that processed data or sorted coupons.[26] While many trade organizations use the IMMEX manufacturing category as a proxy for *maquilas*, these data overstate the numbers for what traditionally have been *maquilas*. However, the new IMMEX data do provide an excellent view of manufacturing in Mexican border cities and more accurately reflect the growing sophistication of border industry.

The dynamic nature of manufacturing along the border in Mexico is demonstrated by increasing sophistication in technology and greater investment in capital goods and training for workers. This has been accompanied by increased output by skilled workers in some sectors. A notable development has been the growth of the aerospace industry in Mexico, especially in the border states and in the border locations of Tijuana and Ciudad Juárez. By 2014, the border states had 207 of Mexico's 289 aerospace companies, with 80 in Baja California, 45 in Sonora, and 38 in Chihuahua.[27]

Some criticisms remained valid, however. By far the most serious was that *maquila* operations did not, on the whole, create backward and forward economic linkages as hoped. Policymakers had expected the emergence of large numbers of Mexican companies that would supply parts and supporting

Table 5.11. Number of IMMEX Employees in Top Six Border Municipalities, 2007–2010

Municipality	2007	2008	2009	2010	2011	2012	2013	2014
Juárez	216,940	193,420	156,801	183,239	178,118	190,031	201,616	217,871
Nuevo Laredo	17,583	17,806	16,067	19,840	18,455	21,504	19,822	24,602
Matamoros	52,292	47,324	39,909	39,523	42,084	43,301	45,834	50,927
Mexicali	57,490	54,470	44,381	46,727	47,186	48,650	51,418	54,126
Reynosa	100,996	92,998	71,735	81,041	84,913	85,613	91,764	94,601
Tijuana	176,954	164,683	137,247	152,191	151,433	159,846	171,950	186,505
Total six municipalities	622,255	570,701	466,140	522,561	522,189	548,945	582,404	628,632
Total in Mexico	1,940,574	1,853,093	1,618,951	1,818,263	1,880,450	1,993,183	2,108,823	2,221,322

Source: Table 5.9 in this volume; INEGI, Banco de Información Económica, http://www.inegi.org.mx/sistemas/bie.

Note: After 2006, the maquiladora industry was combined with other programs for manufacturing export, PITEX and IMMEX. From 2007 on, IMMEX data include the former facilities under the maquiladora regulations but do not include operations such as call centers. IMMEX data are a good measure of all export-oriented industry but are not equivalent to maquiladora data. See "Indicadores de establecimientos con programa Immex: Cifras durante Noviembre de 2014," INEGI, http://www.inegi.org.mx/inegi/contenidos/notasinformativas/est_immex/ni-immex.pdf.

services to the *maquila* industry. These expectations went largely unfulfilled. The average Mexican share of inputs was about 1.5 percent, even though that figure rose to almost 20 percent in plants proximate to Monterrey. Problems with quality, price, and delivery time plagued potential Mexican suppliers. Particularly in the border states, the *maquilas* were largely enclaves that did not lead automatically to significant technological innovations in Mexican industry.

Along with the creation of the *maquila* program, other political measures created an economic life on the border distinct from that in the interior of the country. In 1971, President Luis Echeverría modified the law enabling businesses on the border to import some consumer goods so that local residents would not have to do their shopping in the United States.[28] Mexican law permitted residents in border municipalities outside the free trade zone to import small quantities of consumer goods (*artículos ganchos*) for resale, as an exception to standard customs regulations. Under this program, consumers could buy, duty-free, some eighty articles that could not be manufactured in Mexico as inexpensively as in the United States. Allowing Mexican merchants to buy goods at wholesale prices in the United States and import them freely was intended to stimulate retail sales on the Mexican side of the border. The program was such a success that the Mexican government eventually generalized it to all of the border states.

THE U.S. BORDER ECONOMY

The slowing of the U.S. economy after 1969 affected the border states in a number of different ways. U.S. growth rates during the 1970s were the most sluggish they had been since the 1930s; meanwhile, inflation surged. From 1973 to 1981 world oil prices rose dramatically, lifting the Texas economy to new heights but causing other border states to experience industrial decline and unemployment between mid-1981 and 1983. International oil prices began to slide in 1982 and then nose-dived in 1986. Throughout the 1980s, Texas banks and savings institutions suffered severely from inflated real estate investment made during the earlier boom. The crisis of the 1980s caused price deflation in real estate, which led much of the financial sector into bankruptcy.[29] By the late 1980s and early 1990s the Texas boom-and-bust cycle began repeating itself nationally and then throughout the border states. Some of the symptoms were the same—overinvestment in inflated real estate markets and overproduction of domestic goods for a public determined to buy foreign products.

High-tech maquila *in Tijuana—IMAC's clean room for the manufacture of blank CDs and DVDs. Note the use of robotics and minimal hand labor, which is typical of many newer maquilas. 2004.*

The coup de grace for the U.S. border states came with the economic and political collapse of the Soviet Union after 1989, which in turn led to massive cuts in federal spending in the United States. Just as the West generally and border states in particular had benefited from war-related federal spending, they now reeled from the ripple effect of reduced defense expenditures and other shifts in the economy.[30] Even California's famously diverse economy proved unable to rise above the tide.

Unemployment in the four border states climbed from 5.7 percent in 1989 to 7.2 percent by the end of 1991. In California the rate of unemployment hit 7.4 percent, second only to Arizona's 7.7 percent, and by April 1992 it had risen to 8 percent, seventh in the nation (tied with Louisiana and Mississippi) and first in the U.S. border states. Not surprisingly, by September 1992, California led the four border states once again, with borrowers behind in payments or bank foreclosures on 8.5 percent of its real estate loans.[31] By the mid-1990s the bust appeared to be waning, and the California economy accelerated quickly after 1997.

It is clear that after World War II a true border economy emerged, reflecting a boundary that united rather than divided. With government initiatives, including the establishment of the maquiladora program, the economy of the Mexican North became increasingly tied to that of the U.S. Southwest. In the late 1990s, Mexico was second only to Canada as a U.S. trading partner. This change in the relationship between the two countries was articulated most clearly at the U.S.-Mexican border, as the region found itself at the center of the economic elements of the bilateral relationship. By the early twenty-first century, the border was no longer a line surveyed through scattered outposts of traditional economic pursuits, as it had been in 1900; instead it was a sensitive membrane of utmost importance for the economies of both the United States and Mexico, a permeable barrier through which goods and services were exchanged at an ever increasing rate.

NOTES

1. Michael T. Malone and Richard W. Etulain, *The American West: A Twentieth-Century History* (Lincoln: University of Nebraska Press, 1989), 262.

2. "Border Security in the 21st Century," U.S. Department of Homeland Security, October 9, 2014, https://www.dhs.gov.

3. U.S. Department of Commerce, Bureau of the Census, *Statistical Abstract of the United States, 1991* (Washington, D.C.: Government Printing Office, 1991), 655.

4. Oscar J. Martínez, *Border Boom Town: Ciudad Juárez since 1848* (Austin: University of Texas Press, 1978), 95.

5. Roger Miller and Marcel Cáte, *Growing the Next Silicon Valley: A Guide for Successful Regional Planning* (Lexington, MA: Lexington Books, 1987), 16, 27; Arizona Office of Economic Planning and Development, *High Technology in Arizona: A Market Analysis of Suppliers in Arizona and the Southwest* (Phoenix: Arizona Office of Economic Planning and Development, 1984), 8–15; Annalee Saxenian, "Silicon Valley and Route 128: Regional Prototypes or Historic Exceptions?" in *High Technology, Space, and Society*, ed. Manuel Castells (Beverly Hills, CA: Sage Publications, 1985), 82–93, 99; Ann R. Markusen and Robin Bloch, "Defensive Cities: Military Spending, High Technology, and Human Settlement," in Castells, *High Technology, Space, and Society*, 106–20.

6. *Pro-Aéreo 2012–2020: Programa estratégico de la industria aeroespacial* (México, D.F.: Secretaría de Economía and FEMIA, 2011). Available at https://profesores.ing.unab.cl/~gbadillo/archivos/cursos/it-strategic-plan/Case%20Study/Plan%20Estrategico%20FEMIA.pdf.

7. Jeffrey S. Passel, "The Size and Characteristics of the Unauthorized Migrant Population in the U.S.," Pew Hispanic Center Research Report, March 7, 2006.

8. See "Copper Statistics and Information," U.S. Geological Survey, http://minerals.er.usgs.gov/minerals/pubs/commodity/copper.

9. Juan Fidel Zorrilla and Manuel Ignacio Salinas Domíngues, "Tamaulipas," in *Visión histórica de la frontera norte de México*, ed. David Piñera Ramírez, 3 vols. (Mexi-

cali: Universidad Autónoma de Baja California, Centro de Investigaciones Históricas, UNAM-UABC, 1987), 3:321.

10. Clare Ribando Seelke, Coordinator, "Mexico's Oil and Gas Sector: Background, Reform Efforts, and Implications for the United States," Congressional Research Service, October 23, 2014, 7-5700, R43313, http://fpc.state.gov/documents/organization/218980.pdf.

11. Paul Ganster and Alan Sweedler, "The United States–Mexico Border Region: Security and Interdependence," in *United States–Mexico Border Statistics since 1900*, ed. David E. Lorey (Los Angeles: UCLA Latin American Center Publications, UCLA Program on Mexico, University of California, Los Angeles, 1990), 437.

12. Richard Marosi, "A Real Tijuana Hangover: Drug Violence Seems to Have Chased Most Tourists from the Former Party Mecca, Leaving Businesses That Cater to Them High and Dry," *Los Angeles Times*, February 17, 2008.

13. Paul Ganster, David Piñera Ramírez, and Antonio Padilla Corona, "A Reflection at 50 Years: 1964–2014," in *Tijuana 1964: A Photographic and Historic View/Una visión fotográfica e histórica*, ed. Paul Ganster, 2nd ed. (Tijuana and San Diego: Centro Cultural Tijuana and San Diego State University Press, 2014).

14. See Sam Dillon, "A Twenty-Year G.M. Parts Migration to Mexico," *New York Times*, June 24, 1998.

15. Jesús Tamayo and José Luis Fernández, *Zonas fronterizas (México–Estados Unidos)* (México, D.F.: Centro de Investigación y Docencia Económicas, 1983), 71.

16. James D. Cockcroft, *Outlaws in the Promised Land: Mexican Immigrant Workers and America's Future* (New York: Grove Press, 1986), 109; Dalia Barrera Bassols, *Condiciones de vida de los trabajadores de Tijuana, 1970–1978* (México, D.F.: Instituto Nacional de Antropología e Historia, 1987), table 11; María Patricia Fernández-Kelly, *For We Are Sold, I and My People: Women and Industry in Mexico's Frontier* (Albany: State University of New York Press, 1983), 192.

17. Jesus Cañas and Roberto Coronado, "Maquiladora Industry: Past, Present, and Future," *Business Frontier* 2 (2002); Instituto Nacional de Estadística y Geografía (INEGI), "Estadística de la industria maquiladora de la exportación," http://www.inegi.org.mx.

18. See INEGI, Bancos de datos, IMME (http://www.inegi.org.mx).

19. INEGI, *Estadística de la industria maquiladora de exportación, 1975–1984* (México, D.F.: INEGI, 1986), 5; United Nations, Comisión Económica para América Latina, *Evolución de la frontera norte, 1940–1986* (Mexico, D.F.: United Nations, 1987), 30; Jorge Carrillo, ed., *Mercados de trabajo en la industria maquiladora de exportación* (Mexico: Secretaría del Trabajo y Previsión Social/Colegio de la Frontera Norte, 1991); Norris C. Clement and Stephen Jenner, "La industria maquiladora de México y la economía de California," in *Las maquiladoras: Ajuste estructural y desarrollo regional*, ed. Bernardo González Aréchiga and Rocío Barajas Escamilla (Tijuana: Colegio de la Frontera Norte, Fundación Friedrich Ebert, 1989), 125; Universidad Autónoma de Baja California, *Estadísticas sobre la fuerza de trabajo femenina en Mexicali: Participación en la industria de transfirmación y repercusiones en la familia* (Mexicali: Universidad Autónoma de Baja

California, Instituto de Investigaciones Sociales, 1984), 16–35; Norris C. Clement et al., *Maquiladora Resource Guide: Exploring the Maquiladora/In-Bond Option in Baja California, Mexico* (San Diego: Institute for Regional Studies of the Californias, San Diego State University, 1989), 17; Vicki L. Ruíz and Susan Tiano, eds., *Women on the U.S.-Mexico Border: Responses to Change* (Boston: Allen & Unwin, 1987).

20. INEGI, *Estadísticas económicas de la industria maquiladora de exportación, 2000–2006* (Mexico, D.F.: INEGI, February 2007); INEGI, Banco de Información Económica (http://www.inegi.org.mx).

21. Ellwyn R. Stoddard, *Maquila: Assembly Plants in Northern Mexico* (El Paso: Texas Western Press, University of Texas, El Paso, 1987); Mitchell Selligson and Edward J. Williams, *Maquiladoras and Migration: Workers in the Mexico–United States Border Industrialization Program* (Austin: University of Texas Press, 1981); Leslie Sklair, *Assembling for Development: The Maquila Industry in Mexico and the United States* (San Diego: Center for U.S.-Mexican Studies, University of California, 1993); Clement et al., *Maquiladora Resource Guide*; Richard Rothstein, "A Hand for Mexico, a Slap for Us," *Los Angeles Times*, November 23, 1990; Patricia Ann Wilson, *Exports and Local Development: Mexico's New Maquiladoras* (Austin: University of Texas Press, 1992).

22. See George Baker, "Social Costs and Revenues of the Maquiladora Industry," in Lorey, *United States–Mexico Border Statistics since 1900*, 465.

23. Sam Dillon, "Sex Bias Is Reported by U.S. at Border Plants in Mexico," *New York Times*, January 13, 1998.

24. Joel Millman, "There's Your Solution," *Forbes*, January 7, 1991, 72, 76.

25. Jorge Carrillo and Alfredo Hualde, "Third Generation Maquiladoras? The Delphi–General Motors Case," *Journal of Borderlands Studies* 13 (spring 1988): 79–98; see also Cañas and Coronado, "Maquiladora Industry: Past, Present and Future."

26. Jesus Cañas and Robert W. Gilmer, "Mexico Regulatory Change Redefines Maquiladora," *Crossroads, Economic Trends in the Desert Southwest* 1 (2007).

27. *Pro-Aéreo 2012–2020*; also see "Aerospace Cluster of Baja California," *Business Conexión* (Tijuana, Baja California: 2014), http://www.bajaaerospace.org.

28. Tamayo and Fernández, *Zonas fronterizas*, 71–72.

29. Chandler Davidson, *Race and Class in Texas Politics* (Princeton, NJ: Princeton University Press, 1990), 262–66; Max R. Sherman, ed., *The Future of Texas* (Austin: Texas Monthly Press, 1988), 5–32, 87–110; M. Ray Perryman, *Survive and Conquer—Texas in the '80s* (Dallas, TX: Taylor Publishing, 1990).

30. See Jesus Sanchez, "Boeing to Slash Aircraft Production 35%," *Los Angeles Times*, January 27, 1993.

31. California Department of Finance, *Economic Report of the Governor, 1988* (Sacramento: California Governor's Office, 1988), 32–35; California Department of Finance, *Economic Report of the Governor, 1990* (Sacramento: California Governor's Office, 1990), 1–2, 21–24, 59–60; California Department of Finance, *Economic Report of the Governor, 1991* (Sacramento: California Governor's Office, 1991), 1–2, 13–31, A15; *New Mexico Business: Current Economic Report* (March 1990): 1–2; *Arizona's Economy* (April 1991): 1–4; *Arizona Progress* (1990): 1–2, 4; U.S. Department of Com-

merce, Bureau of the Census, *Statistical Abstract of the United States, 1989* (Washington, D.C.: Government Printing Office, 1989), 367, 377–78, 396; U.S. Department of Labor, Bureau of Labor Statistics, *Employment and Earnings* (February 1992): 160–64; U.S. Department of Labor, Bureau of Labor Statistics, *Employment and Earnings* (July 1992): 155–59.

6

THE CONSEQUENCES OF RAPID GROWTH IN THE BORDER REGION

Social and Cultural Change since the 1940s

After World War II, industrialization, rapid population growth, and urban-ization reshaped the daily lives of border dwellers. Border natives were joined by millions of new immigrants from other areas of the United States, from central Mexico, and from many other parts of the world. The experiences of border life became more common in both countries, as the states along the boundary claimed an ever larger share of Mexican and U.S. national populations. In the postwar period a complex social mosaic spanning the international boundary emerged from what had been at the beginning of the century two distinct social avant-gardes. In the 1990s no one could describe Los Angeles—or anywhere else along the border—as Octavio Paz had in his 1957 *Labyrinth of Solitude*: "Mexicanism . . . floats in the air . . . 'floats' because it never mixes or unites with the other world, the North American world."[1] The impact of century-long migratory trends and economic integration resulted in a true Mex-America along the international boundary. The region, consisting of the ten U.S. and Mexican border states, was the most populated in North America by the beginning of the twenty-first century. The sheer number of people is certain to place the social evolution of the border onto both domestic and bilateral agendas. With its social complexities and challenges, life in the region is a portent of future life in the Americas.

POPULATION AND MIGRATION

During the fifty-year period from 1950 to 2010, the population of the Mexican border states multiplied 5.2 times, while that of the U.S. border states multiplied 3.6 times (see table 6.1). The pattern had reversed since the period before 1940, when the rate of increase on the Mexican side of the border was

129

Table 6.1. Border-State Population, 1950–2010

State	1950	1960	1970	1980	1990	2000	2010
Baja California	226,965	520,165	870,421	1,177,886	1,660,855	2,487,367	3,115,070
Chihuahua	846,414	1,226,793	1,612,525	2,005,477	2,441,873	3,052,907	3,406,465
Coahuila	720,619	907,734	1,114,956	1,557,265	1,972,340	2,298,070	2,748,391
Nuevo León	740,191	1,078,848	1,694,689	2,513,044	3,098,736	3,834,141	4,653,458
Sonora	510,607	783,378	1,098,720	1,512,731	1,823,606	2,216,969	2,662,480
Tamaulipas	718,167	1,024,182	1,456,858	1,924,484	2,249,581	2,753,222	3,268,554
Mexican Border	3,762,963	5,541,100	7,848,169	10,691,887	13,246,991	16,642,676	19,854,418
Mexican Total	25,791,017	34,923,129	48,225,238	66,846,833	81,249,645	97,483,412	112,336,538
Arizona	749,587	1,302,161	1,775,399	2,718,215	3,665,228	5,130,632	6,392,017
California	10,586,223	15,717,204	19,871,069	23,667,902	29,760,021	33,871,698	37,253,956
New Mexico	681,187	951,023	1,017,055	1,302,894	1,515,069	1,819,046	2,059,179
Texas	7,711,194	9,579,677	11,188,655	14,229,191	16,986,510	20,851,820	25,145,561
U.S. Border	19,728,191	27,550,065	33,852,178	41,918,202	51,926,828	61,673,146	70,850,713
U.S. Total	151,325,798	179,323,175	203,302,031	226,545,805	248,709,873	281,421,906	308,745,538

Source: Lorey, *United States–Mexico Border Statistics since 1990*, table 100; INEGI, XII censo general de población y vivienda, 2000 and 2010; U.S. Census 2000 and 2010.

significantly lower than that on the U.S. side. From 1950 forward, the population of the Mexican border states rose considerably faster than that of the U.S. border states. Between 1950 and 2000, annual growth was 3.0 percent in the Mexican state region and 2.5 percent in the U.S. state region.[2] For the first decade of the twenty-first century, the annual growth rate for both Mexican and U.S. border states had slipped to 1.2 percent. The rapid demographic upsurge in the Mexican border states was due to both internal migration and higher rates of natural increase than those across the boundary, where growth was fueled primarily by migration, both domestic and international.

As a whole the area along the international boundary came to claim an ever greater share of the total national populations of both countries. The four U.S. border states grew from 6.4 percent of the national total in 1900 to 23 percent by 2010. California, which had become the most populous U.S. state by the early 1960s, claimed 52.6 percent of the U.S. border population in 2010; one of every eight U.S. citizens lived in California. In Mexico the border states accounted for 10.3 percent of the national population in 1900 and 17.8 percent in 2010. By 2010 the ten border states in the two countries were home to 90.7 million people. Unlike the U.S. region, with its concentration of people in the two states of California and Texas, the Mexican region had a relatively even distribution in its six northernmost states.

The dimensions of the migrant flows to the boundary area—from east to west within the United States, to the north within Mexico, and across the border—expanded dramatically after the early 1940s. Large numbers of new migrants were pushed out of central Mexico by rapid population growth, declining opportunity in the countryside, and insufficient employment in industry in comparison with the number of people entering the job market. Frequently, migrants were drawn by significantly greater opportunity—more jobs and higher wage levels—in both the Mexican and U.S. border states. Building on both personal experiences of migration and the social networks created by earlier migrant populations, the flow of people grew and changed apace with the increasing economic integration of Mexico and the United States.

In the United States, World War II and the jobs it created drew an enormous number of people west. In the brief period of the war years alone, 2 million migrants headed to California, attracted by high-paying jobs in wartime industries such as steel, shipbuilding, aircraft manufacture, textiles, and services. In the war decade from 1940 to 1950, 8 million people moved to states west of the Mississippi River, 44 percent of them to California.

The wartime economic boom in the United States drew Mexican migrants north. Inhabitants of rural areas in Mexico, many of whom had been negatively affected by the rapid commercialization of agriculture after the

1930s and the lack of technical and financial aid for small farmers, moved first to regional urban centers and then frequently toward the border. Swiftly growing cities on the Mexican side of the international boundary—Tijuana, Hermosillo, and Mexicali, for instance—became staging areas for migrants seeking to relocate to both the Mexican cities and U.S. urban conglomerations north of the border.[3]

Mexican migration to the border states in the postwar period was not uniform throughout the region; rather, it tended to follow economic developments in the United States. In the late nineteenth and early twentieth centuries, when Texas experienced significant development, the largest cities in the Mexican North had been Ciudad Juárez and Monterrey. During and after World War II, as California overtook Texas in economic development, an enormous migration began in a more westerly direction. In Baja California, the previously small towns of Tijuana and Mexicali became major cities, while Ensenada, Tecate, San Luis Río Colorado, Hermosillo, and Nogales also increased in size. The extraordinary growth of Tijuana and Mexicali led to the achievement of statehood for the province of Baja California Norte, which entered the federal republic as Baja California in 1952. Statehood followed for Baja California Sur in 1974.[4]

The bracero agreements between the United States and Mexico, which arranged for the legal transfer of hundreds of thousands of Mexican temporary workers across the border, facilitated migration to the United States throughout the entire postwar period. Many braceros stayed permanently in the United States and then brought their extended families north. The Bracero Program established an advance guard and also stimulated networks that continue to direct a flow of Mexicans to the United States to this day.

Beyond its direct effects, the Bracero Program had important social consequences. The seemingly inexhaustible supply of hard-working Mexican laborers kept wages low in U.S. agriculture and conditioned U.S. employers to the immediate availability of inexpensive field labor. Large agribusinesses were among the major supporters of flexible immigration policy; the pressure they brought to bear helped maintain a steady supply of low-cost Mexican labor throughout the postwar era. The program also encouraged an increased flow of both documented and undocumented migrants to the United States after the 1940s.

The Bracero Program left a definite imprint on border towns. Men brought north to work in the program passed through border towns in a steady stream. Those who stayed on in Mexico's North swelled the population of those cities, frequently moving their families from the interior in order to be close to them during the off-season. The deportations carried out by the

A field in California's Imperial Valley being prepared for the next crop. The agriculture in this region is a mix of mechanized operations for field preparation and labor-intensive operations for cultivation and harvesting of vegetables. 2006.

U.S. Immigration and Naturalization Service, which took apprehended migrants native to central and southern Mexico and dropped them at the border, further contributed to the population of border cities because many of these people remained there permanently.

The Bracero Program also encouraged the attitude that Mexican workers could be returned to Mexico when they were no longer needed, a belief that had important social ramifications. The infamous Operation Wetback of 1953 to 1955 deported 2 million Mexicans (and many U.S. citizens of Mexican heritage) to the region across the boundary. This massive repatriation effort had the effect of transferring to the Mexican border states the social dislocations caused by the economic slowdown in U.S. agriculture following the Korean War.[5] But even the deportation of 2 million Mexicans had little effect on the overall trend of rapid population growth and migration in the border states.

Critics of the Bracero Program alleged numerous abuses, including the failure by employers to pay wages, the forced deportation of laborers after work had been performed, pesticide and herbicide poisoning, lengthy workdays, and unhealthful and unsafe conditions. Formal provisions for wages, hours, transportation, and housing were frequently violated. Migrant farm

Immigrant laborers in the Imperial Valley weeding a vegetable crop. A significant part of the agricultural production of the region is in vegetables, which require large amounts of hand labor. 1999.

laborers tended to live in generalized poverty.[6] In fact, both domestic agricultural workers in the U.S. border states and migrants had long endured low pay, piecework rates that resulted in excessive hours, unenforced contracts, exposure to pesticides, and unfavorable conditions. Critics affiliated with a wide spectrum of labor, civil rights, church, and social activist organizations argued that the migration of Mexican farmhands depressed wages further, undermined the bargaining power of U.S. workers, and denied employment to U.S. citizens.

Both the promises and the pitfalls of migration during the 1940s and 1950s are borne out by the personal experiences of braceros. Manuel Padilla, interviewed by border historian Oscar Martínez, tells of his constant conflicts with employers over the letter and the spirit of the bracero contract system. Beginning in 1946, Padilla, who originally had registered as a bracero in Aguascalientes and then signed up three additional times in Mexicali, worked for a decade picking and loading lemons, oranges, and apples in California and the state of Washington. After a time, Padilla deserted his bracero contract, spent many years in the United States as an undocumented laborer, and eventually became a permanent U.S. resident in 1956.[7]

Crossing the border was difficult and could be treacherous for those without documents. In a classic story by Ted Conover about these hazards, the migrant Jesús and his comrades are tormented by Mexican migration and customs inspectors, who extort money from them, and by the Mexican state police, who beat up some members of the party and demand bribe money. After paying a series of coyotes, who smuggle immigrants into the United States, Jesús passes through Arizona only to be stopped in Utah and returned to Mexico. After several more days attempting to cross and making additional payoffs, Jesús arrives in Idaho, where he had arranged for a number of years of regular employment on a ranch. After a few months of work, Jesús returns to Mexico for the winter.[8]

In the last thirty or so years of the twentieth century, a sizable share of the internal migration of Mexicans to the country's North, and some part of the migration across the international boundary, related to the development of *maquila* assembly plants along the far northern rim of Mexico after 1965. The principal social impact of *maquila* development in the Mexican border states was the provision of steady employment with what were, at least in the Mexican context, high wages and generous nonwage benefits. In the period from 1978 to 1993, *maquila* jobs grew at an annual rate of 14 percent, far outpacing the rate of job creation in Mexico as a whole. Despite a severe recession in Mexico and one in the United States, during the period from 1995 to 2006, maquiladora employment expanded by an average of 6.9 percent per year. In addition, unemployment in the Mexican border states was generally far below central Mexican levels.

Firsthand accounts from the 1980s and 1990s, by which time whole families were frequently caught up in the migrant flow, give testimony to the social and cultural difficulties attendant upon those who lived the transboundary experience, whether in the field or in the factory. For thirty-one-year-old Zacatecan Jesús Avila, his twenty-nine-year-old wife, and their three children, ages seven to eleven, repeat migration to the United States became a way of life. The family lived in the United States one year and returned to Mexico the next. Even with migration, Avila's earnings barely sustained the family. Avila invested some of his wages in a peach-growing venture in Mexico, but a constant income from migrant employment was needed to sustain the operation. Although he hoped to settle permanently in California, thirty-three-year-old Luis López used migrant earnings to make additions on his house in Mexico. Despite evident economic gains from migration, López told an interviewer, "It is very sad to go [to the United States], and in my heart I would not go except for the necessity which obliges one to do such things. . . . My children respect me because they know that they should; but . . . my family has begun to distance itself from me."[9]

Family members separated by the border meet on a Sunday through the fence between Border Field State Park in San Diego and Playas de Tijuana at the Tijuana lighthouse. Excessive waiting times at the ports of entry and lack of proper documentation keep many border families apart. 2006.

URBANIZATION

Although many North Americans think of the U.S. West as made up of wide-open, sparsely populated spaces and pastoral occupations, a highly urban profile characterizes the area. The West is in fact the most urban region of the United States, perhaps because such concentration was inevitable in the development of a "hydraulic society" in the border states. The border states of the West, already more urban than rural by 1930, grew from 55.1 percent urban in 1930 to 56.9 percent in 1940, 71.5 percent in 1950, 81.2 percent in 1960, 86 percent in 1970, 86.3 percent in 1980, and 87.7 percent in 1990. The percentage of persons living in urban areas of the United States as a whole was significantly lower in 2000 at 79.0 percent.

The great postwar migration of Mexican and U.S. citizens to the border states was overwhelmingly to urban areas. Whereas the Bracero Program of the 1940s led Mexican migrants, legal and illegal, primarily to rural areas and agricultural employment, by the 1960s the flow was to large urban concentrations for jobs in manufacturing, construction, hotels, restaurants, and services. In Mexico, peasants fleeing crushing rural poverty could either migrate to Mexico's cities or search for work north of the border. Many of those who headed north got no farther than Mexico's border cities, contributing to accelerated urbanization in that region. It is estimated that in 1974 one-quarter to one-third of the population of Mexico's border cities consisted of recent migrants.[10] In the 1970s and 1980s and on into the 1990s, Mexicans increasingly pursued opportunities in U.S. border cities—a natural shift, given the changing economies of the border states—especially in the service sector and in industry. New cities sprouted up throughout the U.S. West, while previously small towns such as Phoenix boomed and old cities such as Los Angeles grew into megalopolises. Fully 80 percent of all Mexican migrants to California, for example, settled in urban areas in both the northern and southern parts of the state; 55 percent settled in Los Angeles. In the 1990s and into the first years of the following century, large numbers of Mexican immigrants continued to settle in the border states. In addition, important communities of Mexican migrants emerged elsewhere in the United States, including the South, Midwest, Northwest, and Northeast.[11]

The Mexican North, where small towns and villages had been more common, also experienced the development of urban concentrations. Monterrey, Nuevo León, already a large city by the standards of the Mexican North in 1940, with almost 200,000 inhabitants, grew to more than 1 million by 1980. Desert cities such as Chihuahua and Hermosillo grew rapidly, as they expanded beyond traditional rural economic pursuits into industry and services. By 1990, 84.7 percent of the population of the Mexican border states lived in urban areas, in contrast with 42.5 percent in 1940. Mirroring a national reality, the rapidly growing urban populations of the Mexican North came to be dominated by recent migrants from rural areas. By the 1980s the nonnative population of Ciudad Juárez was 53 percent, and that of Tijuana was 66 percent. The urban areas on the Mexican side of the border were densely populated, with the cores of the municipalities (*municipios*) generally claiming at least 65 percent and sometimes as much as 95 percent of the municipal population.

As with the western United States, urbanization in Mexico's North was a natural consequence of the arid environment, since development depended on vast, capital-intensive, centrally managed waterworks. Additionally, Mexico and much of the U.S. Southwest were influenced by the Hispanic tradition of such centralizing outposts as missions, pueblos, and presidios, which also included the practice of superimposing settlements over preexisting indigenous communities or bringing scattered indigenous villages together into a single regional settlement. Because of this urban emphasis, Mexico's northern tier of states remained relatively unpopulated outside the cities. This urban concentration of population is reflected in the 2010 census, with Baja California at 92.3 percent, Sonora at 86.0 percent, Chihuahua at 84.8 percent, Coahuila at 90.0 percent, Nuevo León at 94.7 percent, and Tamaulipas at 87.8 percent urban. By 2010, the Mexican border states had some ten cities with over 500,000 in population, including three that were over 1 million. The metropolitan region of Monterrey, the largest urban area of the North, had 4.1 million in 2010.[12]

By midcentury a pattern of twin cities had emerged all along the international boundary from Tijuana–San Diego on the Pacific to Matamoros-Brownsville on the Gulf of Mexico (see table 6.2). Each twin-city pair shared some characteristics of expansion and differed in others. San Diego grew with World War II and the expansion of area military bases, while Tijuana grew apace as a tourist center for both military personnel and Southern Californians interested in the gambling and the nightlife. Ciudad Juárez and El Paso expanded together as an important commercial hub straddling the lines of communication from northern Mexico to the U.S. Midwest. This development would facilitate the transformation of Ciudad Juárez into the most important center of the maquiladora industry in the 1970s, 1980s, 1990s, and into the twenty-first century.[13] Over time, growth shifted from a larger urban center in the U.S. twin city to a larger urban center on the Mexican side of the border.

The twin-city pairs developed complex interrelationships and interdependencies. Table 6.3 shows the massive flow of people back and forth across the border between U.S. and Mexican border cities. By 1990 northbound traffic crossing the border, most of it commuters, tourists, and shoppers, exceeded 274 million per year—a number greater than the 1990 population of the United States and three times that of Mexico in that year.[14] Mexican laborers, particularly those employed in services, traveled daily from one twin city to the other to work in U.S. hotels, restaurants, and private homes. An estimated 10 percent of the San Diego civilian workforce in 1976 consisted of undocumented Mexican nationals, many of whom came from permanent homes south of the border to work. For the period from 1992 to 2002, an average of 7.3 percent of the workers of Tijuana—about forty thousand—actually were employed in San Diego and nearby areas of California. This pattern of commuter workers was repeated in other twin cities along the border, although in lower percentages of the Mexican city's workforce. These commuter workers included Americans living in Mexico, Mexicans with work permits, and unauthorized Mexican workers who crossed the border ostensibly to shop or visit relatives but actually to work. An estimate from 1998 suggests that Tijuana's then 35,000 commuter workers generated annual income of U.S. $437.5 million, while the city's 100,000 maquiladora workers had a total annual income of about U.S. $180 million. This is a good illustration of the importance of the commuter workers to the economies of Mexican border cities.[15]

Twin cities were populated by a fascinating array of people. In his *Border People*, Oscar Martínez has developed a schema for understanding the social landscape of the border's urban world. He includes in his typology of border social experience the following groups: transient migrants (Mexicans or U.S. citizens residing only briefly in the border region); newcomers (Mexicans or U.S. citizens newly arrived in the region); nationalists (long-term residents of the border who do not participate in the culture of the other side of the boundary, strongly preferring customs that they identify as either Mexican or American); uniculturalists (people who live wholly in the culture of one side); binational consumers (people whose main experience with the other side of the border is commercial); settler migrants; commuters who move back and forth across the border on a regular (frequently daily) basis to work; biculturalists (persons, generally bilingual, who have roots in and live adult lives on both sides of the border); binationalists (frequently businesspeople and professionals who live and do business on both sides of the border, operating at a very high level of transboundary social integration); winter residents (U.S. citizens who spend winter months in the region); and U.S. citizens who reside permanently (frequently after retirement) in the Mexican border states. In addition, Martínez describes some cities along the U.S. border—Laredo, for example—in which the Mexican-origin population has dominated politics and business and the European-origin population has sometimes felt marginal or marginalized.[16]

Table 6.2. Total Population of U.S.-Mexican Border Cities, 1900–2010

	1900	1910	1920	1930	1940	1950	1960	1970	1980	1990	2000	2010
San Diego, California	17,700	39,978	73,683	147,897	203,341	334,387	573,224	697,027	875,538	1,110,549	1,223,400	1,307,402
Tijuana, Baja California	242	733	1,028	8,384	16,486	59,950	165,690	340,583	429,500	698,752	1,210,820	1,559,683
Calexico, California	N/A	797	6,223	6,229	5,415	6,433	7,992	10,625	14,412	18,633	27,109	38,572
Mexicali, Baja California	N/A	462	6,782	14,842	18,775	64,658	281,333	396,324	341,559	438,377	764,602	936,826
Yuma, Arizona	N/A	2,918	4,237	4,892	5,325	9,415	23,974	20,997	42,443	54,923	77,515	93,064
San Luis Río Colorado, Sonora	N/A	N/A	N/A	N/A	N/A	4,079	28,545	49,990	76,673	95,461	145,006	178,380
Nogales, Arizona	1,761	3,514	5,199	6,006	5,135	6,153	7,286	8,946	15,683	19,489	20,878	20,837
Nogales, Sonora	2,738	3,177	13,445	14,061	13,866	24,480	39,812	53,494	65,603	105,873	159,787	220,292
Naco, Arizona	N/A	N/A	N/A	N/A	N/A	N/A	N/A	N/A	N/A	N/A	833	1,046
Naco, Sonora	N/A	N/A	N/A	N/A	N/A	N/A	N/A	N/A	N/A	4,645	5,370	6,401
Douglas, Arizona	N/A	6,437	9,916	9,828	8,623	9,442	11,925	12,462	13,058	12,822	14,312	17,378
Agua Prieta, Sonora	N/A	N/A	3,236	4,674	4,106	10,471	15,339	20,754	28,866	37,644	61,944	79,138
Columbus, New Mexico	N/A	N/A	N/A	N/A	N/A	N/A	N/A	N/A	N/A	641	1,765	N/A
Puerto Palomas, Chihuahua	N/A	N/A	N/A	N/A	N/A	N/A	N/A	N/A	N/A	N/A	5,210	23,975

El Paso, Texas	15,906	39,279	77,560	102,421	96,810	130,485	276,687	322,261	425,259	515,342	563,662	649,121
Ciudad Juárez, Chihuahua	8,218	10,621	19,457	39,669	48,881	122,566	276,995	424,135	385,603	789,522	1,218,817	1,332,131
Presidio, Texas	N/A	N/A	N/A	N/A	N/A	N/A	N/A	N/A	N/A	3,072	4,167	4,426
Ojinaga, Chihuahua	1,709	N/A	N/A	N/A	N/A	4,568	8,252	N/A	18,144	18,177	24,307	26,304
Del Rio, Texas	N/A	N/A	N/A	5,350	N/A	N/A	N/A	N/A	N/A	30,705	33,867	35,591
Acuña, Coahuila	N/A	N/A	N/A	N/A	N/A	11,372	20,048	30,276	38,887	52,983	110,487	136,755
Eagle Pass, Texas	N/A	3,536	5,765	5,059	6,459	7,267	12,094	15,364	21,407	20,651	22,413	26,248
Piedras Negras, Coahuila	7,888	8,518	6,941	15,878	15,663	27,578	48,408	46,698	67,455	96,178	128,130	152,806
Laredo, Texas	13,429	14,855	22,710	32,618	39,274	51,510	60,678	69,024	91,449	122,899	176,576	236,091
Nuevo Laredo, Tamaulipas	6,548	8,143	14,998	21,636	28,872	57,669	96,043	151,253	201,731	218,413	310,915	384,033
McAllen, Texas	N/A	N/A	5,331	9,074	11,877	20,067	32,728	37,636	66,281	84,021	106,414	129,877
Reynosa, Tamaulipas	1,915	1,475	2,107	4,840	9,412	34,076	134,869	150,786	194,693	265,663	420,463	608,891
Brownsville, Texas	6,305	10,517	11,791	22,021	22,083	36,066	48,040	52,522	84,997	98,962	139,722	175,023
Matamoros, Tamaulipas	8,347	7,390	9,215	9,733	15,699	45,737	143,043	186,146	188,745	266,055	418,141	489,193

Sources: For U.S. and Mexican border cities, 1900–1990, see Lorey, *United States–Mexico Border Statistics since 1990*, tables 110 and 104; for U.S. border cities, 2000 and 2010, see U.S. Census Bureau, 2000 Census of Population and Housing and 2010 Census of Population and Housing; for Mexican border cities, 2000 and 2010, see INEGI, Series históricas: http://www.inegi.org.mx/lib/olap/consulta/general_ver4/MDXQueryDatos.asp?#Regreso&c=17161.

Note: Mexican data for 2000 and 2010 pertain to municipalities rather than to cities.

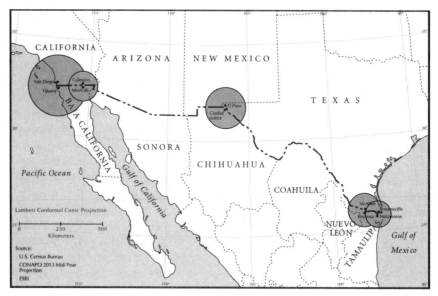

County (Border City) Municipality (Border City)	2013 Population	Binational Region Total
San Diego (San Diego)	3,211,252	4,881,616
Tijuana (Tijuana)	1,670,364	
El Paso (El Paso)	827,718	2,227,796
Juárez (Ciudad Juárez)	1,400,079	
Hidalgo (McAllen)	815,996	1,475,165
Reynosa (Reynosa)	659,169	
Imperial (Calexico)	176,584	1,174,939
Mexicali (Mexicali)	998,355	
Cameron (Brownsville)	417,276	930,933
Matamoros (Matamoros)	513,657	

Sources: U.S.Census Bureau; CONAPO 2013 mid-year projections.

Map 12. Most populous border metropolitan regions, 2013.

Table 6.3.   Entry of Mexicans and U.S. Citizens at U.S. Border, 1928–2013 (in millions)

Years	Total	Mexicans	U.S. Citizens
1928–1930	81	49	32
1931–1940	224	137	87
1941–1950	360	195	165
1950	48	24	24
1955	71	36	35
1960	98	59	39
1965	116	69	47
1970	145	87	58
1975	159	98	61
1980	163	104	59
1985	177	108	69
1990	274	173	101
1995	204	N/A	N/A
2000	290	N/A	N/A
2005	235	N/A	N/A
2010	168	N/A	N/A
2013	166	N/A	N/A

Source: Lorey, *United States–Mexico Border Statistics since 1900*, table 900; U.S. Department of Transportation, Bureau of Transportation Statistics (BTS). From 1995 on, U.S. or Mexican citizenship for crossers is not listed in the data. From 1970 to 1990, Mexicans made up approximately 62 percent of the northbound crossers into the United States.

In the twin-city complexes Mexican consumers on both sides of the border became an important market for North American businesses. Many U.S. firms attributed one-half of their income to Mexican customers traveling from the twin city across the border. It has been estimated that, in 2004, cash-carrying Mexican crossers spent some $8 billion in U.S. border communities. These expenditures generated over $1 billion in taxes and helped to support over 153,000 jobs in the U.S. border region. At the same time, a reverse flow brought U.S. citizens daily into Mexico. In 2003, U.S. residents spent some $2.4 billion in the Mexican border region, with nearly a third of this spent in Tijuana.[17] Visitors from the United States crossed the border to eat, shop, and take advantage of low prices for prescription drugs and for services such as dental hygiene, automobile repair, and medical consultation.

Much disparity existed between border cities sharing these important interconnections. A view from the air at any point over the international boundary revealed a sprawling, hastily built, partly unpaved Mexican city with a significant number of temporary shanties inhabited by the most recent and poorest migrants. Rapid growth, combined with the lack of a robust tax base

and Mexican federal policy that impoverished municipal and state governments, outpaced the ability of border communities to provide urban services,
housing, and social programs to incorporate new migrants. The U.S. side
showed a smaller urban settlement with modern public services and transportation facilities. Within this general pattern of asymmetry were significant
differences in wages.[18]

With rapid population growth in the U.S. cities along the international
boundary came serious social problems that would soon characterize the West
and the border region as a whole: traffic congestion, environmental degradation, a rise in crime, increases in divorce rates, ethnic strife (in an area of great
and growing ethnic diversity), and the rapid spread of diseases, including HIV/
AIDS. All of these problems and more stemmed from the frenetic pace of development along the border and from human interactions in its urban oases—
from both economic booms and massive population movements. Informal
settlements—generally called *colonias*—sprang up all along the U.S. side of the
border, particularly in Texas near the Rio Grande. For the most part illegal,
they lacked even the most basic human services, as evidenced by county health
and other social indicators ranking the settlements at the bottom of the nation.

The meteoric growth of Mexican border cities after 1950 resulted in
pressing social problems. The most severe challenges concerned underdeveloped public-service infrastructure. From early in the postwar period, the rapid
increase in population outpaced the development of social and urban services
in the region. In 1942, forty-five hundred students in Ciudad Juárez were left
without classrooms. This number tripled by the early 1950s. With respect to
housing, *El Continental* reported on the conditions of twelve thousand persons
in Ciudad Juárez in 1948, saying, "[They live] in a very critical situation . .
. suffering horrible needs. In July of 1953, three quarters of the population
of Juárez was without drinking water and sewage services: 400 poor children
died in a three-month period. They lack the most indispensable services, such
as water, sewage, light, police service, telephone, transportation, etc."[19] *El
Fronterizo* reported, "Thousands live under incredible conditions, in shacks . .
. built on public lands . . . having no public services. The residents lack sufficient elements to maintain their health and are in need of adequate food. In
those areas where conditions are the worst, an alarming rate of infant mortality
has been recorded."[20] The public-services crisis on the border is clearly not a
new phenomenon; rather, it emerged in the immediate postwar era as a function of the border's pattern of rapid urban growth.

The lack of basic services for a significant portion of the urban population along the Mexican border created an enormous public-health problem,
and waterborne diseases became a leading cause of death, particularly among

A neighborhood in Tijuana with no paved streets, piped-in water, or sewage services. Eventually, most new neighborhoods such as this acquire municipal services, a process that is slowed considerably by the difficult terrain. 1996.

Business district in Calexico, California, where retail sales are oriented toward customers from across the border in Mexicali, Baja California. Note the "Tienda del Army," or U.S. Army Store. All except one of the vehicles in the photograph have Baja California license plates. 2006.

infants. The significantly higher mortality rate of children in Mexican border communities compared to U.S. border communities is detailed in table 6.4. Intestinal infections, respiratory diseases, and nutritional deficiencies, which were the leading causes of mortality in Mexico, were not even on the U.S. list.[21] In addition, the rate of death from all causes was much higher on the Mexican side than on the U.S. side. As a consequence of these and other factors, there was a five-year difference between the average life expectancy in the Mexican and the U.S. border states between 1980 and 1984 (life expectancy was 69.4 years in Mexico and 74.4 in the United States). By 2000, Mexico's life expectancy at birth had improved to 73.0 years, and the figure for the United States was 77.0; in 2012, the figures were 77.0 years for Mexico and 79.0 years for the United States. All the Mexican border states in 2000 were one to two years above the national average. California was one year above the U.S. average, while Arizona and New Mexico were just above and Texas was just below the average U.S. life expectancy in 2000.[22]

On the Mexican side of the border, poverty appeared to have increased during the 1970s and 1980s. Minimum-wage data suggest that, after the mid-1970s, real wages for unskilled work declined precipitously in the bor-

Tijuana pharmacy window advertising products for U.S. customers, including human growth hormone, the morning-after pill, and other medicines. 2003.

der region. From 1981 to 1986—during the darkest moments of the 1980s economic crisis in Mexico—the real purchasing power of the minimum wage on the Mexican side of the border dropped by half, diminishing to precarious levels in comparison with the income of Mexico's northern neighbors. By the mid-1980s, Mexicans had fewer dollars to spend in San Diego, yet felt greater pressure to find work both there and in neighboring Los Angeles.[23] Because of the proximity of the Mexican North to the United States, the cost of living was significantly higher than in other areas of Mexico.

Most Mexican immigrants in the border region initially lived in rudimentary, self-built houses on plots of land made available by local authorities; electricity was often hooked up within a year, but potable water or sewage lines usually did not reach these neighborhoods for nearly a decade. The homeowners improved and added on to their houses largely through "sweat equity," providing their own labor and buying materials when possible. In

Table 6.4. Mortality Rates of Border Children, Ages One to Four, in U.S. and Mexican Border States and Counties/Municipalities, 2000

United States	7.1	Mexico	24.9
California	5.4	**Baja California**	18.1
San Diego	5.9	Tijuana	18.1
Imperial	4.7	Mexicali	17.9
Arizona	6.7	**Sonora**	22.6
Yuma	5.3	San Luis Río Colorado	20.9
Pima	6.1	Nogales	19.5
Santa Cruz (Nogales)	3.8	**Chihuahua**	23.4
Cochise	6.3	Asención	22.8
New Mexico	6.9	Juárez	20.7
Doña Ana	5.0	Ojinaga	21.7
Luna	21.0	**Coahuila**	22.3
Texas	5.7	Acuña	23.8
El Paso	4.4	Piedras Negras	21.0
Presidio	N/A	**Nuevo León**	11.3
Valverde (Del Rio)	4.5	**Tamaulipas**	23.9
Maverick (Eagle Pass)	6.0	Nuevo Laredo	22.1
Webb (Laredo)	6.1	Reynosa	21.9
Hidalgo (Edinburg, McAllen)	5.0	Matamoros	21.1
Cameron (Brownsville)	3.6		

Source: Basic Indicators, 2003 (Washington, D.C.: Pan American Health Organization, n.d.).

Note: Data are for U.S. counties and Mexican municipalities. The major city or cities of U.S. counties are indicated in parentheses. The Mexican states of Tamaulipas, Nuevo León, Coahuila, and Chihuahua border on Texas.

Tijuana the average number of inhabitants residing in individual housing units increased by one-third between 1960 and the mid-1980s.[24] Natural disasters, such as the winter storms and floods of 1992 and 1993, made the weaknesses of both housing and the health-care infrastructure painfully obvious.[25] Although the situation gradually improved after 1950, even by 1990 only 80 percent of houses in border areas were equipped with piped water, and only 57 percent had sewerage. During the late 1980s in Tijuana, these social conditions and the lack of public services to address them gave rise to a broad political mobilization by the city's popular sectors to gain the attention of regional and national leaders. By 2000, delivery of piped water remained at about 80 percent, which was noteworthy given the mushrooming populations of Mexican border cities. By 2009, Mexico's border cities were at 96 percent coverage for drinking water, above the national average of 89 percent. The biggest gains were in sewage collection infrastructure, with coverages of 84.7 percent in Tijuana, 81.1 percent in Mexicali, 88.3 percent in Nogales, 93.2 percent in

Migrants to Mexico's northern border cities typically found shelter by squatting on government-owned land and using a mix of scrap and new materials to build houses. Often it was years before all urban services were available. Tijuana, 2006.

Ciudad Juárez, 87.4 in Nuevo Laredo, and 78.2 percent in Matamoros. By 2009, Mexico's border cities had sewerage coverage of 88 percent, ahead of the national average of 86 percent. However, in that same year the Mexican border cities only treated 82.2 percent of the sewage collected, far ahead of the national average of 38 percent. By the end of the first decade of the twenty-first century, Mexican authorities had made remarkable progress in providing basic urban infrastructure to the expanding cities of the northern border.[26]

As Mexico's border cities matured socially and economically, and as their social problems grew, they began to play a greater role in regional and national politics. Although Mexican politics had long been characterized by centralization and control from Mexico City, the North had traditionally been among the more recalcitrant regions. The 1810 independence movement began in what had been the North of that period, and the leaders of the Revolution of 1910 included such northerners as Madero, Carranza, Obregón, and Calles. Admittedly, during the postrevolutionary period the northern states generally remained firmly under the control of the ruling party, the Partido Revolucionario Institucional (PRI). But by the 1980s significant opposition challenged the PRI's hegemony.

Political resistance to the central government and increasing demands for tax receipts and other aid—stimulated in part by the country's economic crisis

During the administration of President Vicente Fox (2000–2006), many low-cost housing projects were completed in the northern border cities, offering a viable alternative for low-income residents. Tijuana, 2005.

and in part by the North's social and economic maturation—expressed itself dramatically at the polls beginning in the 1980s. The conservative Partido de Acción Nacional (PAN) claimed several election victories, particularly in Chihuahua, where it won the sharply contested mayor's office in Ciudad Juárez in 1983. In 1989 the first non-PRI candidate ever to win a gubernatorial election in Mexico, PAN's Ernesto Ruffo, former mayor of Ensenada, became the governor of Baja California. In 1992 another PAN candidate, Francisco Barrio, took the statehouse in Chihuahua. These victories in the North were soon joined by PAN victories on the national level, in central states, and in the Mexican Congress. In 1997, PAN governed six of Mexico's thirty-one states and the second- and third-largest urban areas: Guadalajara and Monterrey. In 1998, PRI recaptured the Chihuahua governorship, resulting in the first democratic alternation in Mexico's postrevolutionary history. A social consolidation based on geographical distance from Mexico City and increasing interdependence with the United States thus created a distinct political culture in the Mexican North. By the closing years of the twentieth century, the North's politics and politicians were again shaping the nation's evolution. Although the PRI or PRI-led coalitions were able to recapture governorships in Sonora and Nuevo León in 2003, in Chihuahua in 2004, and in Coahuila in 2005, the PAN remained strong in the North. In the 2006 presidential elections in Mexico, the northern border states were solidly in the PAN column, contributing greatly to the PAN's landmark victory.

The 2012 national elections saw a return of the PRI to national power as Enrique Peña Nieto won by a narrow margin over Manuel López Obrador, the candidate of the left-leaning Partido de la Revolución Democrática (PRD), although PRI failed to capture a simple majority in either chamber of congress. Voters, disenchanted with the conservative PAN's ability to address economic and security issues, opted for a return to the PRI after twelve years of PAN in the presidency. By early 2015, the PRI held four of the governorships of Mexico's border states, and the PAN held the other two. Peña Nieto tackled key problems in Mexico such as the overhaul of the country's energy, banking, and education sectors, all long-term efforts. However, with Peña Nieto's inability to quell the violence and improve social and economic conditions in the short term, it is likely that opposition parties will make gains at state and local elections to be held in 2015 and 2016.[27]

MEXICAN AMERICANS

The Mexican-origin population in the U.S. border states grew steadily throughout the twentieth century, as a tide of Mexicans was drawn by the economic expansion of the U.S. West and the progressive integration of the two national economies. Gradually, they moved north through Mexico, crossed the border, and spread throughout the U.S. Southwest, eventually settling as far as Colorado, Washington State, and Chicago. Between 1900 and 2010 the Mexican-origin population in California grew more than 1,412 times, in Texas it increased more than 111 times, and in the United States as a whole it grew about 100 times (see table 6.5). By the early twenty-first century, the Mexican-origin population had also spread in considerable numbers to the Midwest and the southern states.[28]

By the second half of the century—as a consequence of both natural increase and continued population movements from Mexico to the United States that resulted in naturalization and permanent residence—the Mexican-born and Mexican-origin populations of the U.S. border states were already large and still growing rapidly. According to the census of 1980, 60 percent of all U.S. Hispanics were found in the four border states and Colorado. The urban centers of the late-twentieth-century West were characterized by their Mexican American population concentrations. In the early 2000s, 25.4 percent of residents in San Diego, 46.5 percent in Los Angeles, 76.6 percent in El Paso, 91.3 percent in Brownsville, and 94.1 percent in Laredo identified themselves as Hispanic.[29] Although the Mexican-origin population of the

Table 6.5.　U.S. Population of Mexican Origin, by State, 1900–2010

Year	Arizona	California	New Mexico	Texas
1900	14,172	8,086	6,649	71,062
1910	29,987	33,694	11,918	125,016
1920	61,580	8,871	20,272	251,827
1930	47,855	191,346	15,983	262,672
1940	24,902	134,312	8,875	159,266
1950	24,917	162,309	9,666	196,077
1960	105,342	695,643	34,459	655,523
1970	239,811	1,857,267	119,049	1,619,064
1980	396,410	3,637,466	223,772	2,752,487
1990	616,195	6,070,637	328,836	3,890,820
2000	1,065,278	8,455,926	330,049	5,071,963
2010	1,657,668	11,423,146	590,890	7,951,193

Source: Lorey, *United States–Mexico Border Statistics since 1900*, tables 120 and 122; U.S. Census 2000, 2010; U.S. Census Bureau, *The Hispanic Population: 2010 Census Briefs*, 2011.

border region is the focus here, it is noteworthy that the U.S. border states were characterized in general by the largest foreign-born and foreign-origin populations in the country.

By 2010 the border's Mexican-origin population was 38.6 percent of the total population in Arizona, 30.7 percent in California, 28.7 percent in New Mexico, and 31.6 percent in Texas. One of the most noticeable impacts of these large numbers was on the language of the border region: between 2006 and 2008, 21.7 percent of Arizonans, 28.2 percent of Californians, 30.0 percent of Texans, and 28.3 percent of New Mexicans spoke Spanish at home.[30] By 2013, there were 37 million Hispanic Spanish speakers in the United States, and many non-Hispanic Americans also spoke Spanish, which enabled Spanish-language television networks to frequently beat their English-language rivals in ratings.[31]

In *Border People*, Martínez includes the following groups in his typology of Mexican Americans: disadvantaged immigrants (upwardly mobile persons from poorer Mexican-origin U.S. families), advantaged immigrants (U.S. citizens originating in advantaged sectors of Mexican society), binational consumers, commuters who cross the border on a regular basis to work, biculturalists, binationalists, and U.S.-born Mexican Americans who live and work on the Mexican side of the border.[32]

For the substantial minority of Mexican Americans employed in agriculture and living in the countryside in the U.S. border states, life was difficult; insecurity—both physical and financial—was ever present. The plight of Mexican and Mexican American farmworkers, both legal and undocumented residents of the United States, led to increased political organization and militancy. The 1966 victories of agricultural labor leader César Chávez against grape growers in California led to the growing solidarity of Mexican and Mexican American farmworkers throughout California and other border states. That same year, partially in response to issues in border agriculture, the U.S. Congress extended federal minimum-wage laws to agricultural work. Migrant Mexican American field laborers, who were often segregated residentially, confronted a frequently hostile environment by creating mutual aid societies, churches, and organizations to promote patriotic and social activities. They and their families reinforced a sense of identity and community by establishing Spanish-language newspapers, some of which exist to this day. Distinct cultural forms came to characterize life for Mexican migrants north of the border. New challenges presented themselves from the 1980s and 1990s and into the twenty-first century, and old problems resurfaced, as non-Spanish-speaking migrants from deep in Mexico's interior—particularly from Oaxaca state—moved to the fields of the Californias.

The poverty of Mexican farmworkers was frequently matched by that of some urban-dwelling Mexican Americans. Data show that poverty was widespread among Mexican American families and that, among all ethnic groups, Mexican Americans were generally the poorest.[33] The occupational structure of El Paso, Texas, in the period from 1910 to 1970 sheds light on the long-term evolution of the employment profile of the Mexican American population in the United States. While the number of persons with Spanish surnames employed in unskilled and domestic occupations declined from 57.4 percent in 1910 to 23.5 percent in 1970, the number of those employed in skilled positions decreased as well, from 12.8 to 7.4 percent. Those workers did not move far, however: employment in semiskilled and service occupations rose from 17 to 33.7 percent over the same period. Movement into the uppermost strata was slow but steady, from 11.2 to 29.2 percent in lower white-collar occupations and from 1.6 to 6.3 percent in upper white-collar positions between 1910 and 1970.[34]

Not all urban families of Mexican origin were poor; some had experienced significant social mobility from one generation to another. Although the prevailing popular conception was of poor and downtrodden immigrant families, several studies in the 1990s revealed a large and stable Mexican American middle class in border cities such as Los Angeles. In the mid-1990s, middle-class Latino families purchased more than one-half of the houses in Los Angeles County and owned one-quarter of all businesses in the Los Angeles–Long Beach metro area (up from 10 percent in the 1980s). Fifty percent of U.S.-born Latino families had household incomes above the national average. The wealth of second-generation migrant families was increasingly reflected in political clout. In the 1996 California state elections, Latinos won fourteen of eighty seats as well as the top leadership posts in the lower house of the legislature. By 2003, the number of Latino state legislators had increased to twenty-seven, nearly doubling from 1996.[35] After the 2008 elections, the border states had a total of 143 Latino elected officials in the U.S. Congress and state senates and legislatures.[36]

THE IMPACT OF
MIGRATION ON SENDING COMMUNITIES

Debates over migration in the postwar period tended to focus on its putative effects on the economy and society of the U.S. border states. Observers only infrequently pondered the impacts south of the international boundary. Was migration (and reliance on migrant earnings) a benefit or a detriment to areas of origin? What was the impact of migration to the United States on families and communities in the Mexican border states? These questions are crucial to an understanding of the larger border world. Because migration and migrant remittances are structural features of local economies throughout Mexico and the United States, both national economies are greatly affected by migrant flows. In many sending communities, 41 percent of all household heads had made at least one trip to work in the United States; 81 percent of household heads had a friend or relative living in the United States.[37]

One recent study of Zacatecas and Coahuila shows that well over one-half of all families in both states participated in migration to the United States at some point. Communities with the most diversified local economies tended to have the highest rate of migration. Migrants tended to be male and were younger and more educated than nonmigrants. Within these general parameters there were many regional differences. In Zacatecas, migrants generally came from rural backgrounds and were married with young children. In Coahuila, migrants were more likely to be from urban backgrounds and were less compelled by economic necessity.

Families of migrants in Mexico earned more and owned more than families without this link to the United States. Migrant wages, instead of being wasted in conspicuous consumption, were generally invested in human capital—such as education and medical care—and in sustaining and improving rural livelihoods through the purchase of tractors, land, insecticides, fertilizers, seed, and the like. Income was also dedicated to such family businesses as markets, restaurants, pharmacies, and studios. Commercial knowledge gained through migration frequently proved as important as savings in these cases.

Analysts also found some troubling effects of migration on the sending communities. Clearly, migration benefited families and individuals, for example, but earnings were not generally used to support community projects such as recreation centers or churches. Although migrant earnings reduced the gap between rural and urban incomes, they tended to increase the disparity among families within communities. And as its importance as a strategy of human-capital investment registered, migration sometimes discouraged the pursuit of education in Mexican sending communities. Not everyone viewed such effects as bad, however. The replacement of a narrow social elite with a broad-based migrant economic group, breaking the subservience of the peasant classes in rural Mexico, seemed to some observers as a trend that boded well for Mexico. Migration could serve as an alternative mobility ladder.[38]

Remittances from migrants to their families in Mexico made both indirect and direct positive contributions to the sending communities. Through increased consumption and investment, savings were transmitted to other households in migrant-sending areas, including some that did not participate directly in international migration. By providing access to liquid savings, such earnings influenced the use of other income, loosening credit constraints on investment and local production. Migrants promoted investment by offering informal insurance against loss, promising to assist in times of economic distress or in the event that new investments failed.[39] These economic bonds between migrants and sending communities created entire transboundary social worlds. Encarnación Allende, age thirty-nine and a U.S. citizen, is a good example. In the 1980s, Allende worked as a groundskeeper at a San Antonio golf course, commuting back to Mexico every few weeks to be with his wife and three children in Coahuila, where he invested much of his earnings. Allende's transboundary life, made possible by remittances and investment of income, was a result of his wife's feelings of estrangement and rejection in the United States, which had led to her insistence on living in Mexico.[40]

Migration is thus woven into the fabric of societies on both sides of the border, "linking villages in Mexico and the U.S. economy so pervasively that the two form a single economic space that transcends the . . . border." Through migration, communities in Mexico and communities in the United States became part of a transboundary organism, a web of relationships bound by the northward flow of migrants and by the southward flow of remittances.[41]

The following figures give some idea of the scope of the migration web. In 1994, Latin American remittances were estimated at $5.5 billion, $3.7 billion of which came from Mexican migrants to family members in Mexico. From 1960 to 2000, remittances from the United States to Mexico grew at an average annual rate of 12.8 percent. By 2002, remittances were $9.8 billion, and by 2003 they had increased 35 percent to $13.3 billion. In 2005, remittances reached an astounding $20 billion, which was 128 percent of the total foreign exchange generated by Mexico's petroleum industry. The level reached $26.8 billion in 2007, declined in 2009 to 22.1 after the 2008 recession, and rebounded by 2014 to $24.3 billion.

The impact of these funds in Mexico is significant. One study suggests that 80 percent of the remittances are used for food, clothing, health care, transportation, education, and housing. Another study indicates that throughout Mexico as much as 27 percent of investment in microenterprises in urban areas comes from remittances and that the figure is as high as 40 percent in major migrant sending states such as Zacatecas and Michoacán. In Michoacán during 2001, remittances accounted for 15.7 percent of the state's economic activity (gross state product).[42]

CULTURAL EVOLUTIONS

Reflecting the economic and social consolidation described here and in previous chapters, the culture of the U.S.-Mexican border region grew increasingly rich and varied in the twentieth century, particularly after World War II. Cultural expression was shaped by three factors: geographical mobility (primarily the circular and one-way migrant flows between the United States and Mexico), the characteristic livelihoods of the area, and the growing social and political awareness of the people. In contrast to earlier periods, the border itself—as both a barrier and a unifier—came to figure prominently in regional cultural expression. Cultural manifestations in the border states were characterized by a sense of both pride and ambiguity about the area encompassed in the elusive and shifting boundary. In ethnic terms, border culture reflected a social milieu that was both a melting pot and a salad bowl. There were mixed feelings about Mexico, the United States, Mexicans, Americans, Mexican Americans, *fronterizos*, Americanization, Mexicanization, and, in general, the multicultural, multiethnic society that was an inescapable facet of daily experience in the region.[43]

Culturally, "the border" is much more than just the international boundary and the immediate adjacent national territory. The cultural border be-

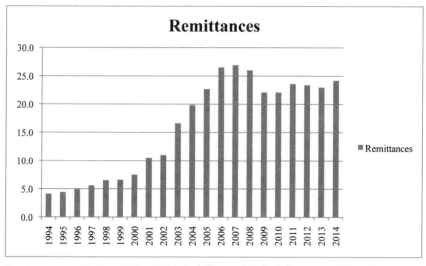

Remittances to Mexico, 1994–2014, in billions of U.S. dollars. (World Bank Migration and Remittances Data)

tween the United States and Mexico extends northward beyond San Ysidro or Brownsville; at the very least, it reaches as far north as San Francisco and as far east as San Antonio and Houston. There are, additionally, significant pockets of border life and culture in nonborder states, most noticeably in Colorado, Washington, and Illinois and in the metropolitan area surrounding Chicago. In the 1990s, the six southern states of Arkansas, Alabama, Georgia, North Carolina, and Tennessee saw an increase of 308 percent in their Hispanic populations, which contrasts with the 43 percent increase in California for the same period. Those born in Mexico made up 73 percent of these Latino immigrants.[44] From the 1940s, the cultural border area expanded with agriculture into California's central and coastal valleys, southwest to the agricultural areas of Baja California and Sonora, and southeast to Chihuahua, Coahuila, Tamaulipas, and Texas. Border culture also responded to the shifts in regional industrialization, most recently to the shift of maquiladora assembly and manufacturing plants to the interior of Mexico. Southward, border culture meandered from the Mexican Far North down highways to the Central Plateau. Even the Yucatán peninsula, traditionally a world apart but now caught up in the second wave of maquiladora expansion, came to exhibit distinctive border-culture traits. It can be argued that the boundary extends into the Gulf of Mexico, which separates the Yucatán from the U.S. South and Florida as an extension of the Rio Grande.

Complicating—and enriching—this picture of an extensive border culture is the fact that it is not monolithic; it takes myriad forms. As Martínez has shown, different groups participate in different aspects of border life and social interaction and consequently display a great variety of cultural traits. "Border society reflect[s] an ongoing process of conflict, exchange, adaptation, and reinvention propelled by class, the character of economic exchange, the area's relation to the national economy, gender, and immigration."[45] The forms of cultural expression are as diverse as the region's population, ranging from habits of dress and social style, to celebrations of community solidarity, to milestones in popular music, film, poetry, and painting. They all share a complex and fruitful interchange among popular tradition and expression, the forms and conventions of high art, and the influence of the national cultures of Mexico and the United States.

As the twentieth century approached, railroad transportation made it increasingly easy for U.S. citizens to travel through Mexico and for Mexicans to travel north. Thousands of U.S. citizens visited or settled in Mexico beginning in the 1880s. On the eve of the fall of the Porfirio Díaz government, approximately sixty thousand Americans lived in Mexico, while the railroads brought multitudes of Mexicans north. A historian of Sonora notes that the railroad itself produced increased social interaction. Interpersonal contact, music, sports, and vacationing all increased along its tracks. The railroad created whole new towns and border communities throughout the region, in many places defining for the first time the boundary, which had previously not existed in a social or cultural sense. Sonoran elites began to vacation in Santa Monica; the middle classes traveled to Tucson. The United States became associated with progress, which influenced the selection of names for stores and services throughout the Mexican border states.[46]

Although it is common to see the increasing intensity of interaction among U.S. citizens and Mexicans as an aspect of U.S.-Mexican relations, growing economic integration had its most profound effects locally, on communities on both sides of the border. Because of the presence of U.S. citizens in the Mexican North, Mexicans became familiar with the ways of the *norteamericanos* (North Americans). At the same time, Mexican words, foods, and agricultural and pastoral practices entered U.S. lexicons, lifestyles, and toolboxes. English became the language of business in the border region from the 1880s; it became necessary to learn English to obtain the best jobs in mining, commerce, and commercial agriculture. Globalization of the economy in the twentieth century only reinforced the already dominant position of English as the language of trade in Mexico. By the early twenty-first century in the border region, knowledge of both Spanish and English increasingly was a requirement for employment in many positions in the public and private sectors on both sides of the border. Businesses of all types had to address the needs of both their English- and Spanish-speaking clients. Government agencies at all levels found that serving regional populations and interacting with counterpart organizations on the other side of the border required additional linguistic and cultural skills.

Material influences were important in shaping border culture as well. With the arrival of the railroad in the nineteenth century, availability of U.S. goods altered patterns of consumption throughout the Mexican North. Fashions and foods replaced and shaped local habits, in particular supplanting European varieties, which became much more expensive than their U.S. counterparts.[47] The bicycle craze sweeping Europe and the United States also arrived in the border states, and cycling clubs abounded by the turn of the twentieth century. Elites may have held on to French styles and language, but they increasingly sent their children to school in the United States. Migrants and merchants introduced the phonograph, which greatly expanded the repertoire of musical styles, and the motion picture projector, which offered a window to lifestyles and happenings around the world.

In Sonora commemorative events reflected this early confluence of cultural currents. Residents of towns and villages all over the state celebrated Independence Day (September 16) and Cinco de Mayo (May 5) with speeches and parades. But they also increasingly observed Thanksgiving (after 1901) and U.S. Christmas practices, both introduced from north of the border. By the turn of the century, baseball was played in towns and villages throughout the region. As practices were widely adopted in the area, Mexicans became no more anglicized or Americanized than U.S. citizens became Mexicanized; rather, an expanded cultural repertoire allowed border residents to fashion new cultural worlds and to function in the worlds of others.[48]

Over time, economic and social asymmetries developed along the international boundary and, with them, more cultural differences and distinction than had existed previously. The towns on the U.S. side of the border experienced a more profound and sustained economic expansion, for reasons noted in earlier chapters. Inequalities and inequities followed and were reflected in popular and elite cultural expression. Differences were particularly noticeable in architecture and public services—from schools and other public buildings to housing and recreation areas. Conflicts between—or within—communities straddling the border became endemic and remain so. Conflicts ranged from small-time violence to the occasional international incident. Only in very recent times has a culture of cooperation and exchange gradually emerged in local transboundary conflict resolution, although it faces an entrenched legacy of mistrust and misapprehension.

After the terrorist attacks in the United States on September 11, 2001, a certain estrangement took place all along the border, increasing the separation and barriers between the halves of the sister cities. Increased security at the border that produced waiting times of up to two to three hours for pedestrians and vehicles, the 2002 and 2008 recessions in the United States, and growing insecurity in Mexican border cities related to drug cartels and criminal gangs all came together to dampen cross-border cooperation and interactions. U.S. local, state, and federal agencies made it very difficult for their employees to cross the border to meet with counterparts in Mexico, even when addressing shared issues and opportunities. Most U.S. border universities prohibited their faculty and students from engaging in traditional research and educational activities in Mexican border cities. Tourists to Mexican border cities from adjacent areas in the United States dwindled to a trickle, although visitors from Europe and Asia continued to visit border Mexico. International tourism to sites elsewhere in Mexico, however, continued to grow after a dip in 2009 due to the 2008 U.S. recession.[49]

One effect of this hardening of the border in Mexico's largest border city of Tijuana was to facilitate a number of interesting cultural and economic developments. As the residents of Baja California began to feel more secure with declining levels of violence, residents of Tijuana ventured out into new public spaces for cultural activities and to socialize in restaurants and bars. A new cuisine, called Baja Med, emerged, fusing traditional Mexican and Mediterranean cuisine with Asian elements, all featuring fresh local produce and seafood. New restaurants owned by Mexican investors and highlighting chefs from the region, from Mexico City, and from New York attracted regional and international attention. Part of the food movement was the emergence of the nearby Guadalupe Valley as Mexico's premier fine-wine-producing region. The many small and large wineries, coupled with boutique hotels and excellent restaurants, produced a lively wine tourism, with most of the visitors from Mexico. In the traditional sites visited daily by foreigners, such as Avenida Revolución in Tijuana, many shops that had formerly sold *artesanías* fell vacant or were made available to new restaurants and bars catering to local people and also as spaces for artists' studios.[50] Isolated somewhat from the United States by the hardened border, Tijuana underwent a cultural transformation.

Popular music forms are among the most deeply rooted traditions along the boundary. The border ballad, with its characteristic focus on regional ethnic and cultural conflict, emerged during the 1846–1848 Mexican-American War. The border *corrido* form dates to the same period. In Sonora, formal musical groups originated with local civilian militias in the last third of the nineteenth century. Popular sectors and wealthier residents of border com-

Traditional musical groups, such as "Los Navegantes," from Palomas, Chihuahua, are still to be found in many areas on both sides of the border. 2003.

munities had their own musical groups, styles, and events, but there was plenty of crossover. European introductions like the waltz, mazurka, and polka were adapted by local bands and eventually formed the basis of Mexico's classic *norteño* (northern) style.[51]

In their traditional forms, the ballad and *corrido* lasted through the Revolution, celebrating revolutionary actors and events, and into the Depression era. After World War II the *corrido* underwent a major change in its subject matter, which reflected the evolving social milieu of the border states: the Mexican avenger transformed into helpless victim. In the 1960s and 1970s the

Chicano movement adopted the *corrido* as a strong mobilizing force, replacing the traditional *corrido* hero—frustrated and powerless—with a hero who actively resists.[52] In the 1990s the *corrido* took up the theme of drug trafficking and its social impacts. After World War II two types of musical groups characteristic of the border continued in popularity: the *conjunto* (ensemble), anchored by the European accordion, and the larger *orquesta* (orchestra).

In the 1980s popular music of the border elbowed its way into the national cultural arena as Los Angeles–based musicians such as Linda Ronstadt and Los Lobos—following in the footsteps of many lesser-known innovators before them—found national audiences for musical explorations of their Mexican, Mexican American, and border-region roots.[53] The music of Carlos Santana, a fusion of rock and Latin American music from the 1970s and continuing in 2015, was likewise influenced by his years growing up in Tijuana. The 1995 death of Texas pop phenomenon Selena was mourned by millions of fans on both sides of the border. The genre of Nortec music emerged in 2001 as a fusion of electronic music and traditional Mexican sounds and has had a wide impact in Mexico and the United States. Nortec illustrates the dynamic nature of border culture.[54]

Mural painting—like music, a staple of the Mexican popular artistic tradition—found dramatic expression in the border states during the postwar period. The early activism of the Chicano movement inspired many community mural projects, the most famous of which were those in San Diego. Painted during the 1960s and 1970s, freeway-overpass murals in Barrio Logan and wall murals in Balboa Park combined the message of the radical Chicano experience with traditional themes of Mexican popular art. In the Barrio Logan paintings, the cult-icon Mexican painter Frida Kahlo and the Virgin of Guadalupe are found within a few yards of each other, while reinterpretations of border history are juxtaposed with scenes of daily life in Mexico. Murals have also emerged as a form of regional expression in many other border communities, such as Calexico, California, and Mexicali, Baja California. Themes such as shared regional history and religion are common.[55]

Film, like music and visual expressions, provides rich insights into cultural perceptions on both sides of the U.S.-Mexican border. Early films about the border included Charlie Chaplin's silent film *The Pilgrim* (1923) and *In Caliente*, a 1935 film with Hollywood and Mexican star Dolores del Rio, set at the Agua Caliente Casino in Tijuana. Film about the border region reached a mass audience in the postwar period with its combination of popular and high-art expressions. Postwar U.S. filmic treatments of the border had an auspicious beginning with the 1949 Metro Goldwyn Mayer production *Border Incident*. The movie was an important landmark for several reasons: the director was the well-respected Arthur Mann; the film was generally devoid of the negative stereotyping typical of the Hollywood cinema of the previous decades; the plot revealed at least some knowledge of and sensibility toward Mexican immigrants in the United States; and Mexican-origin actors were cast in feature roles.[56]

Mexican films about the border had an equally propitious beginning. The first major commercial production was Alejandro Galindo's *Espaldas mojadas*, which premiered in 1954. It was among the most accurate Mexican portrayals of border themes because of its dispassionate look at the socioeconomic problems of Mexico, the hopelessness experienced by countless Mexicans, the need for many to emigrate to the United States, and the conditions in the Mexican American barrios on the U.S. side of the border.

In terms of quantity, Mexico dominated the production of border films in the postwar period, with over two hundred motion pictures. Among the best known are *Siete en la mira*, *Ni de aquí, ni de allá*, *Wetbacks/Mojados*, *Chicano*, *Soy chicano y mexicano*, *Raíces de sangre*, *Mojado power*, *Murieron a la mitad del río*, *Camelia la tejana*, and *La mafia de la frontera*. U.S. studios also mounted large-scale productions, starring some of Hollywood's biggest names—Jack Nicholson, Nick Nolte, Tom Cruise, Charles Bronson, María Conchita Alonso, and Shelley Long. Major films included *The Border*, *Borderline*, *Extreme Prejudice*, *Losing It*, *Viva Max*, *Born in East L.A.*, and *The Three Amigos*. *No Country for Old Men*, a 2007 film by the Cohen brothers that won four Academy Awards, was set in the west Texas desert and border and was based on the novel of the same name by Cormac McCarthy.

Mexican and U.S. movies about the border shared some similarities. They were almost all filmed for the same basic purpose, commercial success, a goal that influenced their treatment of border themes. Action took precedence over character study, plot development, and social content. Motion pictures dealing with immigration and crime were characterized by violence and sex. The plots were almost always set in the United States and tended to disregard Mexican issues. In the case of comedies, much humor was based on negative stereotypes of Mexicans, U.S. citizens, and border residents.

In both Mexico and the United States, filmmakers working outside the major studios have produced some of the most accurate and moving portrayals of border life. These movies concentrate on the lives, experiences, and perceptions of border residents to create documentaries and works of art that reflect a deep sensitivity toward the complexity of border reality. *Alambrista* (1977), *The Ballad of Gregorio Cortez* (1982), *El Norte* (1983), *Break of Dawn* (1988), *Like Water for Chocolate* (1992), *Traffic* (2000), and *The Three Burials of Melquiades Estrada* (2005) stand out among these productions.[57]

Literature of the border region blossomed after 1945, especially as the oral traditions, always typical of the area, were incorporated into more formal literary expressions. On the U.S. side, Chicano literature predominated, encompassing border life both thematically and spiritually. Many contemporary Mexican American writers—José Villarreal, Miguel Mendez, Alurista, Alejandro Morales, Arturo Islas, Margarita Cota Cárdenas, Ernesto Galarza, and Irene Beltrán Hernández—used the border as a setting and inspiration.[58] Equally impressive in quantity and quality was literary expression originating on the Mexican side of the border. An outpouring of anthologies, short story collections, poetry, plays, and essays made border literature one of the most dynamic and promising of Mexico's regional literatures.[59] In recent years, the border region also witnessed the development of unique currents in critical and feminist theory focusing on the particular problems of the interpretation of works of art produced in the multiethnic, multicultural border states.[60] Literature about the U.S.-Mexican border region provides valuable insights into the reality of this region and its place in the two nations.

In the 1960s the Mexican government attempted to make the border more culturally palatable to both Mexican and prospective U.S. tourists. The Programa Nacional Fronterizo (PRONAF), discussed in chapter 5, sought to rehabilitate the reputation of the border region and raise awareness of its cultural riches. Regional museums and cultural centers displayed native arts and crafts. Millions of pesos were invested in commercial and cultural facilities designed to improve the appearance of border cities and promote the sale of Mexican products. In Ciudad Juárez, officials built an attractive new entrance to the city, including a statue of Abraham Lincoln, a large shopping center complex, hotels, restaurants, an arts-and-crafts center, a museum of art and history, a convention building, a country club, a racetrack, and a *charro* (rodeo) ring. The U.S. recession of the early 1970s, among other factors, discouraged travel, however, and the program was only partially successful in drawing new tourists to the border.

The Tijuana Cultural Center (CECUT) was inaugurated in that city in 1982 to strengthen national identity and to attract U.S. tourists with cultural exhibits, an OMNIMAX theater, and a symphony hall. It was designed by prominent Mexico City architects and contained exhibits that reflected the culture of central Mexico. By 2000, control of the facility shifted to Baja California and a museum reflecting regional cultural history was installed. CECUT is a federal facility under Mexico's National Council for Culture at the Arts, which is part of the Secretariat of Education. In recent years CECUT in Tijuana has emerged as the leading cultural institution in the region, with strong roots in the local community and a rich schedule of meetings, concerts, opera, theater art expositions, and book presentations. It has also expanded its publication efforts to appeal to the binational regional community. For example, in 2014 CECUT published a history of Tijuana in English to appeal to the Hispanic population and others in nearby San Diego interested in regional history.[61]

The social profile of the postwar border area, which resulted primarily from a century of population movement from east to west and south to north, was clearly as complex as its economy. The social problems confronting the region have been many and diverse, including the health threats of environmental degradation, a spreading public-service crisis, and the widespread psychological and social stresses inherent in the border's multiethnic society. The cultural changes that accompanied the emergence of this new society left a unique imprint on the region. With all of these issues, life on the border has presented a unique challenge for scholars and policymakers who attempt to understand and guide the rapidly changing region.

NOTES

1. Octavio Paz, *Labyrinth of Solitude* (New York: Grove Press, 1961), 13.

2. Implicit compound rates.

3. For an excellent review of the enormous literature on the causes and consequences of Mexican migration, see Jorge Durand and Douglas S. Massey, "Mexican Migration to the United States: A Critical Review," *Latin American Research Review* 27, no. 2 (1992).

4. Ricardo Romero Aceves, *Baja California: Histórica y legendaria* (México, D.F.: Costa-Amic, 1983), 100; Héctor Lucero Antuna, *Evolución política constitucional de Baja California Sur* (México, D.F.: Universidad Nacional Autónoma de Mexico, Instituto de Investigaciones Jurídicas, 1979), 24.

5. Juan Ramón García, *Operation Wetback: The Mass Deportation of Mexican Undocumented Workers in 1954* (Westport, CT: Greenwood Press, 1980).

6. Linda C. Majka and Theo J. Majka, *Farm Workers, Agribusiness, and the State* (Philadelphia: Temple University Press, 1982), 158–66; Rodolfo Acuña, *Occupied America: A History of Chicanos* (New York: Harper & Row, 1988), 144–50; García, *Operation Wetback*, 45–57; Ellis W. Hawley, "The Politics of the Mexican Labor Issue, 1950–1965," *Agricultural History* 40 (1966): 157–76; Ernesto Galarza, *Merchants of Labor: The Mexican Bracero Story* (Charlotte, NC: McNally and Loftin, 1964), 183–98; California Senate, Committee on Labor and Welfare, *California's Farm Labor Problems* (Sacramento, CA: Senate of the State of California, 1961); Tony Dunbar and Linda Kravitz, *Hard Traveling: Migrant Farm Workers in America* (Cambridge, MA: Ballinger Publishing, 1976), 69–98; Miles Corwin, "The Grapes of Wrath Revisited," *Los Angeles Times*, September 9, 1991.

7. Oscar J. Martínez, *Border People: Life and Society in the U.S.-Mexico Borderlands* (Tucson: University of Arizona Press, 1994), 148–55.

8. Ted Conover, *Coyotes: A Journey through the Secret World of America's Illegal Aliens* (New York: Vintage Books, 1987).

9. Quoted in Richard C. Jones, *Ambivalent Journey: U.S. Migration and Economic Mobility in North-Central Mexico* (Tucson: University of Arizona Press, 1995), 100–107.

10. James D. Cockcroft, *Outlaws in the Promised Land: Mexican Immigrant Workers and America's Future* (New York: Grove Press, 1986), 109.

11. David E. Lorey, ed., *United States–Mexico Border Statistics since 1900* (Los Angeles: UCLA Latin American Center Publications, UCLA Program on Mexico, University of California, Los Angeles, 1990), table 1011; Rakesh Kochhar, Roberto Suro, and Sonya Tafoya, "The New Latino South: The Context and Consequences of Rapid Population Growth," Pew Hispanic Center, 2005, http://www.pewhispanic.org.

12. INEGI, 2010 Mexican census, http://www3.inegi.org.mx/sistemas/temas/default.aspx?s=est&c=17484.

13. See Oscar J. Martínez, *Border Boom Town: Ciudad Juárez since 1848* (Austin: University of Texas Press, 1978); Thurber D. Proffitt, "The Symbiotic Frontier: The Emergence of Tijuana since 1769" (PhD diss., University of California, Los Angeles, 1988).

14. U.S. International Trade Commission, *The Impact of Increased United States–Mexico Trade on Southwest Border Development* (Washington, D.C.: Government Printing Office, 1986); Paul Ganster, "Percepciones de la migración mexicana en el condado de San Diego," *Revista mexicana de sociología* 53 (1991): 259–90; Paul Ganster, "Impact of the Peso's Devaluation on Retail Sales in San Diego County," *San Diego Economic Bulletin* 33 (March 1985).

15. Niles M. Hansen, *The Border Economy: Regional Development in the Southwest* (Austin: University of Texas Press, 1981), 37. See also Mayo Murrieta and Alberto Hernando, *Puente México: La vecindad de Tijuana con California* (Tijuana: Colegio de la Frontera Norte, 1991). For Mexican commuter workers, see INEGI, "Encuesta nacional de empleo urbano," http://www.inegi.org.mx; for income estimates, see Serge Rey et al., "The San Diego–Tijuana Region," in *Integrating Cities and Regions: North America Faces Globalization*, ed. James W. Wilkie and Clint E. Smith (Los Angeles and Guadalajara: University of California, Los Angeles, Program on Mexico and the Universidad de Guadalajara, 1998, 105–64).

16. Martínez, *Border People*, 277–83.

17. For Mexican expenditures in U.S. border communities, see Suad Ghaddar and Cynthia J. Brown, "The Economic Impacts of Mexican Visitors along the U.S.-Mexico Border: A Research Synthesis," Center for Border Economic Studies, University of Texas–Pan American, December 2005. For expenditures by U.S. residents in Mexico's border zone, see "Viajeros internacionales en la zona fronteriza," based on Banco de México data and accessed on the Baja California Secretariat of Tourism website (http://www.descubrebajacalifornia.com).

18. See also Lorey, *United States–Mexico Border Statistics since 1900*, table 2010, which shows that per capita income in the Mexican border region was significantly higher than the national average in 1980.

19. Quoted in Martínez, *Border Boom Town*, 109.

20. Quoted in Martínez, *Border Boom Town*, 109.

21. See also Lorey, *United States–Mexico Border Statistics since 1900*, tables 315, 316.

22. Pan-American Health Organization (PAHO), *U.S.-Mexico Border Health Statistics*, 6th ed. (El Paso, TX: PAHO, 1990). Life expectancy estimates for Mexico are from CONAPO; those for the United States are from the U.S. Census. The 2012 data are from the World Bank. It should be noted that life expectancy estimates vary somewhat depending on the source used.

23. United Nations, *Evolución de la frontera norte*, 63.

24. Martín de la Rosa, *La presencia de grupos norteamericanos en Tijuana* (Tijuana: Colegio de la Frontera Norte, 1987), chap. 1; José Manuel Valenzuela Arce, *El movimiento urbano popular en Tijuana* (Tijuana: Colegio de la Frontera Norte, 1987), 13.

25. PAHO, *U.S.-Mexico Border Health Statistics*.

26. José Manuel Valenzuela Arce, *Empapados de sereno: El movimiento urbano popular en Baja California (1928–1988)* (Tijuana: Colegio de la Frontera Norte, 1991). Data for 2000 are from PAHO, *Basic Indicators 2003: Health Situation in the United States–Mexico Border* (El Paso, TX: Pan American Health Organization, 2003); 2009 data are from a presentation by the Border Environment Cooperation Commission at the March 2010 SCERP Border Institute.

27. Clare Ribando Seelke, "Mexico's 2012 Elections," Congressional Research Service, September 4, 2012, http://fas.org.

28. When interpreting the data in table 6.5, it is important to consider the fact that, because the categories employed to define Mexican-origin population differed in several census years, they are not strictly comparable from one year to another.

29. Paul Ganster and Alan Sweedler, "The United States–Mexico Border Region: Security and Interdependence," in Lorey, *United States–Mexico Border Statistics since 1900*, 423; U.S. Census 2000.

30. U.S. Bureau of the Census, "Detailed Languages Spoken at Home and Ability to Speak English for the Population 5 Years and Over for the United States: 2006–2008," April 2010, https://www.census.gov/hhes/socdemo/language.

31. See Mark Hugo Lopez and Ana Gonzalez-Barrera, "What Is the Future of Spanish in the United States?" Fact Tank: News in the Numbers, Pew Hispanic Research Center, September 5, 2013, http://www.pewresearch.org.

32. Martínez, *Border People*.

33. See Walter Fogel, *Mexican Americans in Southwest Labor Markets* (Los Angeles: Mexican-American Study Project, University of California, 1967), 7–21, 145–69; U.S. Department of Commerce, Bureau of the Census, *Current Population Reports—Demographic, Social, and Economic Profile of States: Spring 1976*, Series P-20, #334 (Washington, D.C.: Government Printing Office, 1979), 47; National Commission for

Employment Policy, *Hispanics and Jobs: Barriers to Progress* (Washington, D.C.: National Commission for Employment Policy, 1982), 45–56; California Department of Industrial Relations, *Californians of Spanish Surname* (San Francisco: California Department of Industrial Relations, 1964), 17–18, 33, 46–52.

34. See David E. Lorey, ed., *United States–Mexico Border Statistics since 1900: 1990 Update* (Los Angeles: University of California, Los Angeles, Latin American Center Publications, 1993), table 711.

35. "Latinos Lead Southern California's Economic Boom," *Statesman-Journal* (Oregon), July 18, 1997. The article was based on a *Washington Post* story. Also see National Association of Latino Elected Officials, Education Fund, Latino Election Profiles, California, March 2, 2004, http://www.naleo.org.

36. NALEO, *2008 General Election Profile: Latinos in Congress and State Legislatures after Election 2008: A State-by-State Summary*, http://www.naleo.org/08PostElec-Profile.pdf.

37. Douglas S. Massey, "March of Folly: U.S. Immigration Policy after NAFTA," *American Prospect* 9, no. 37 (March 1998): 16.

38. Jones, *Ambivalent Journey*, 95–96.

39. See J. Edward Taylor, "International-Migrant Remittances, Savings, and Development in Migrant-Sending Areas" (paper prepared for the International Migration at Century's End conference, Barcelona, Spain, May 7–10, 1997); Ricardo Sandoval, "Migrants Fueling Ventures in Mexico," *San Jose Mercury News*, June 29, 1998.

40. Jones, *Ambivalent Journey*, 105–6.

41. J. Edward Taylor, "Mexico-to-U.S. Migration and Rural Mexico: A Village Economy-wide Perspective," in *Immigration and Ethnic Communities: A Focus on Latinos*, ed. Refugio I. Rochín (East Lansing: Julian Samora Research Institute, Michigan State University, 1996), 59–66.

42. Rodolfo de la Garza et al., "Binational Impact of Latino Remittances" (policy brief of the Tomás Rivera Policy Institute, March 1997); *Informe sobre la inflación, octubre–diciembre 2005* and *Programa monetario para 2006*, Banco de México, January 2006; Roberto Coronado, "Workers' Remittances to Mexico," *Business Frontier* 1 (2004). Also see D'Vera Cohn, Ana Gonzalez-Barrera, and Danielle Cuddington, "Remittances to Latin America Recover—but Not to Mexico," Pew Research Center, November 2013, http://www.pewhispanic.org/2013/11/15/remittances-to-latin-america-recover-but-not-to-mexico.

43. See two excellent chapters in Stanley Robert Ross, ed., *Views across the Border: The United States and Mexico* (Albuquerque: University of New Mexico Press, 1978): Carlos Monsiváis, "The Culture of the Frontier: The Mexican Side," 50–67, and Américo Paredes, "The Problem of Identity in a Changing Culture: Popular Expressions of Culture Conflict along the Lower Rio Grande Border," 68–94. See also David R. Maciel and María Herrera-Sobek, eds., *Culture across Borders: Mexican Immigration and Popular Culture* (Tucson: University of Arizona Press, 1998); Jorge A. Bustamante, "Demystifying the United States–Mexico Border," *Journal of American History* 79 (1992): 485–90.

44. Kochhar, Suro, and Tofoya, "The New Latino South."

45. Miguel Tinker Salas, *In the Shadow of the Eagles: Sonora and the Transformation of the Border during the Porfiriato* (Berkeley: University of California Press, 1997), 149.

46. Salas, *In the Shadow of the Eagles*, 145, 258.

47. Salas, *In the Shadow of the Eagles*, 118.

48. Salas, *In the Shadow of the Eagles*, 150. See also Josiah McC. Heyman, "Imports and Standards of Justice on the Mexico–United States Border," in *The Allure of the Foreign: Imported Goods in Postcolonial Latin America*, ed. Benjamin Orlove (Ann Arbor: University of Michigan Press, 1997), 151–83.

49. World Bank International Tourism Receipts (http://data.worldbank.org/indicator).

50. See Paul Ganster, David Piñera Ramírez, and Antonio Padilla Corona, "A Reflection at 50 Years: 1964–2014," in *Tijuana 1964: A Photographic and Historic View/ Una visión fotográfica e histórica*, ed. Paul Ganster, 2nd ed. (Tijuana, Baja California, and San Diego: Centro Cultural Tijuana and San Diego State University Press, 2014), 63–71; Kristin Hill Maher and David Carruthers, "Urban Image Work: Official and Grassroots Responses to Crisis in Tijuana," Urban Affairs Review 50, no. 2 (March 2014): 244–68.

51. Salas, *In the Shadow of the Eagles*, 31.

52. Manuel Peña, "Música fronteriza/Border Music" (manuscript, n.p., n.d.).

53. See David Reyes and Tom Waldman, *Land of a Thousand Dances: Chicano Rock 'n' Roll from Southern California* (Albuquerque: University of New Mexico Press, 1998), and companion CD set *Brown-Eyed Soul* (Rhino Records); Steven Loza, *Barrio Rhythm: Mexican American Music in Los Angeles* (Urbana: University of Illinois Press, 1992); Américo Paredes, *A Texas-Mexican "Cancionero": Folksongs of the Lower Rio Grande Border* (Urbana: University of Illinois Press, 1976); Américo Paredes, "The Mexican Corrido: Its Rise and Fall," in *Madstones and Twisters*, ed. Moody C. Boatright (Dallas: Publications of the Texas Folklore Society, 1958), 91–105; Manuel Peña, *The Texas-Mexican Conjunto: History of a Working Class Music* (Austin: University of Texas Press, 1985); Manuel Peña, "Music for a Changing Community: Three Generations of a Chicano Family Orquesta," *Latin American Music Review* 8 (1987): 230–45.

54. Alejandro L. Madrid, *Nor-tec Rifa! Electronic Dance Music from Tijuana to the World* (Oxford: Oxford University Press, 2008); Gavin Mueller, "Review of Alejandro L. Madrid. 2008. Nor-tec Rifal [*sic*]: Electronic Dance Music from Tijuana to the World. Oxford: Oxford University Press," *Current Musicology* 90 (2010); José Manuel Valenzuela, *Paso del Nortec: This Is Tijuana* (México, D.F.: Trilce Ediciones, Consejo Nacional para la Cultura y las Artes, Editorial Océano de México, El Colegio de la Frontera Norte, and Universidad Nacional Autónoma de México, 2004).

55. See Jean Charlot, *Mexican Mural Renaissance* (New Haven, CT: Yale University Press, 1963); Eva Cockcroft, John Weber, and James Cockcroft, *Towards a People's Art: The Contemporary Mural Movement* (New York: E. P. Dutton, 1977); Jacinto Quirarte, "Chicano Murals in San Diego," in *Reglas del juego y juego sin reglas en la vida fronteriza/Rules of the Game and Games without Rules in Border Life*, ed. Mario Miranda and

James W. Wilkie (México, D.F.: Asociación Nacional de Universidades e Institutos de Enseñanza Superior, 1985), 229–54; Marcia Isabel Campillo López, "Transborder Public Art: Murals and Graffiti in the Imperial-Mexicali Valleys," in *Imperial-Mexicali Valleys: Development and Environment of the U.S. Mexican Border Region*, ed. Kimberly Collins and Paul Ganster (San Diego, CA: San Diego State University Press, 2004), 427–43. See also the excellent website about the Chicano Park murals (http://www.chicanoparksandiego.com).

56. David R. Maciel, "Braceros, Mayordomos, and Alambristas: Mexican Immigration to the United States in Contemporary Cinema," *Hispanic Journal of Behavioral Sciences* 8 (1986): 371–72.

57. Norma Iglesias, *Entre yerba, polvo y plomo: Lo fronterizo visto por el cine mexicano* (Tijuana: Colegio de la Frontera Norte, 1991); David R. Maciel, *El Norte: The U.S.-Mexican Border in Contemporary Cinema* (San Diego: Institute for Regional Studies of the Californias, San Diego State University, 1990); Carl J. Mora, *Mexican Cinema: Reflections of a Society, 1896–1980* (Berkeley: University of California Press, 1982); Allen L. Woll, *The Latin Image in American Film*, rev. ed. (Los Angeles: University of California, Los Angeles, Latin American Center Publications, 1980).

58. See, for example, Edward Simmen, ed., *North of the Rio Grande: The Mexican-American Experience in Short Fiction* (New York: Penguin, 1992).

59. See, for example, José Manuel Di-Bella, Sergio Gómez Montro, and Harry Polkinhorn, eds., *Literatura de la frontera México–Estados Unidos: Memoria del primer encuentro de escritores de las Californias/Mexican-American Border Writing: Proceedings of the First Conference of Writers from the Californias* (Mexicali/San Diego: Dirección de Asuntos Culturales de la Secretaría de Educación y Bienestar Social del Gobierno del Estado de Baja California/Institute for Regional Studies of the Californias, San Diego State University, 1987).

60. See, for example, Héctor Calderón and José David Saldívar, eds., *Criticism in the Borderlands: Studies in Chicano Literature, Culture, and Ideology* (Durham, NC: Duke University Press, 1991); José E. Limón, *Mexican Ballads, Chicano Poems: History and Influence in Mexican-American Social Poetry* (Berkeley: University of California Press, 1992); Gloria Anzaldúa, *Making Faces, Making Souls—Haciendo Caras: Creative and Critical Perspectives by Women of Color* (San Francisco: Aunt Lute Foundation Books, 1990). Claudia Sadowski-Smith, *Border Fictions: Globalization, Empire, and Writing at the Boundaries of the United States* (Charlottesville: University of Virginia Press, 2008), provides an excellent analysis of border literature and contemporary trends. Other useful studies include Núra Vilanova, *Writing Fiction from Northern Mexico* (San Diego, CA: San Diego State University Press, 2007), and Daniel A. Olivas, *Things We Do Not Talk About: Exploring Latino/a Literature through Essays and Interviews* (San Diego, CA: San Diego State University Press, 2014).

61. David Piñera Ramírez and Gabriel Rivera, *Tijuana in History: Just Crossing the Border* (Tijuana: Tijuana Cultural Center, 2013); Paul Ganster, ed., *Tijuana 1964: A Photographic and Historic View/Una visión fotográfica e histórica*, 2nd ed. (Tijuana: Tijuana Cultural Center, 2014).

7

BORDER ISSUES IN
U.S.-MEXICAN RELATIONS

Boundary, Environment, Health, and Native Americans

The economic and social trends that defined the border region in past centuries show all signs of continuing unbroken in the twenty-first. As the area evolves, it will continue to play an ever more important role in the social and economic lives of the people of Mexico and the United States. The border will also figure ever more prominently in the interactions between the two countries and their inhabitants. Indeed, issues in U.S.-Mexican relations—economic, social, environmental, political, and strategic—have often been most pronounced and most divisive along the boundary. This is also true for recently emerging issues such as the border and security and the wave of migrant children from Central America at the border in 2013, 2014, and 2015. At the border, domestic and international issues come face to face and exert a constant influence on one another. This chapter and the next present a consideration of present and likely future bilateral relations in the context of long-term historical changes in the border region since 1900, in the belief that the historical record explains present patterns and tensions while providing a portent of things to come.

THE ELUSIVE BOUNDARY

Relations between Mexico and the United States have often been directly concerned with the boundary that unites and divides the two countries. The U.S.-Mexican border was arbitrarily drawn in much of the natural terrain through which it cuts, a fact that has had a lasting impact on regional conflicts. Such natural resources as water and ecosystems and such environmental problems as air pollution, which have never paid much attention to the location of the international boundary, have become binational problems spanning the border. Tremendous population growth and expansion of urbanized areas of border cities have driven rapid environmental degradation.

The fact that the physical boundary was not only drawn in an arbitrary fashion but has also moved in the relatively recent past has generated serious tensions between Mexico and the United States. Beginning in the late nineteenth century, conflict between the United States and Mexico repeatedly came to a head over such issues as the natural shifting of the Rio Grande/Río Bravo main channel that marks the international boundary and the division of the waters of the Colorado River for irrigation on both sides of the border. Conceptions of the border have also changed over time. The maritime boundaries between the United States and Mexico at the border, for example, proved to be a continual source of friction in the 1980s and 1990s, as the Mexican fishing industry boomed and environmentalists raised concerns about dolphin kills, producing a U.S. embargo on Mexican tuna imports in 1990. Although an international agreement reduced the numbers of dolphins killed by the Mexican tuna boats and the United States lifted the embargo in 2000, environmentalists continue to be concerned.[1]

Among the most complex disputes over the physical boundary was that of the Chamizal, a six-hundred-acre tract of land adjacent to the Rio Grande in the vicinity of El Paso and Ciudad Juárez. At the time of the signing of the Treaty of Guadalupe Hidalgo in 1848, the Chamizal was south of the Rio Grande in Mexico. But flooding led to changes in the river's course, and by 1864 the tract was north of the river in the United States. For residents of Ciudad Juárez and the state of Chihuahua, the Chamizal remained national territory, and they denounced U.S. claims to jurisdiction over the area. Although the central government of Mexico formally protested in 1867, neither nation assigned the matter a high priority, and it remained unresolved—and frequently a thorn in international relations—until the mid-twentieth century. Not until 1963, when U.S.-Mexican relations reached a high-water mark fueled by U.S. concerns about the Cuban Revolution, was the Chamizal territory returned to Mexico.

The dispute over the Chamizal was not the only one caused by changes in the Rio Grande's course. Morteritos Island, near Roma, Texas, was part of Mexico until 1884, when Texans claimed jurisdiction because in 1848 the island had been on the U.S. side of the river. Additional disagreements arising from the shifting course of the Rio Grande prompted the United States and Mexico to sign a treaty in 1884 providing for negotiated settlements over lands transferred from one side of the border to the other in this way. Five years later the responsibility for administering the treaty was placed in the hands of the International Boundary Commission, which has managed the transfer of hundreds of acres of land along the Rio Grande/Río Bravo during the last century.

THE ENVIRONMENT UNDER SIEGE

In a region where water constitutes the lifeblood of both urban and rural existence, it is not surprising that the flows of major regional rivers and subsurface aquifers became a source of lasting conflict between Mexico and the United States. Toward the end of the nineteenth century, as population increased along the border and in the adjacent states, U.S. entrepreneurs began building irrigation works, which reduced the amount of water entering the Mexican border states from the Colorado River. In 1895, Mexico filed a $35 million claim with the International Boundary Commission. The commission urged the two countries to negotiate a comprehensive treaty regulating the use of water for irrigation. But settlement of the dispute would not come until 1922, when U.S. state representatives signed the Colorado River Compact, which divided the river into two basins, each with rights to half the water. Twenty-two years later, Mexico and the United States signed a treaty guaranteeing Mexico 1.5 million acre-feet per year.

Conflicts over the Colorado's water intensified in the 1940s and 1950s, as infrastructure investment in agricultural production soared in both countries.[2] The International Boundary and Water Commission was established in 1944 to continue the work of the International Boundary Commission and also to address water-quality issues. By the 1960s, due to water usage in both countries, water flowing to the delta in the Gulf of California—on the Mexican side of the border—had ceased entirely. Mexico filed complaints with the United States about both the amount and the quality of water it received. In 1973 the dispute over the Colorado was finally resolved through agreements on the amount of water that would be available to the Mexican side of the border and the levels of salinity that would be acceptable for the water delivered (the water-treatment plant called for in the agreements did not actually begin operations until years later).

Pressures on the binational relationship caused by claims to the precious flow of the Colorado are certain to continue. The Colorado now supplies water to seven U.S. states, ten U.S. Indian tribes, and two Mexican states for a total of some 40 million users.[3] In 1997, a new U.S. ruling divided the Colorado's water among the western states and allowed for the sale of excess stored water by some states to Nevada and California, which are always in need of more than their allocated share (both San Diego and Tijuana import

Satellite image of the fertile Imperial and Mexicali valleys, bisected by the international border. The image clearly shows different land-tenure arrangements, farming practices, agricultural infrastructure investment, and water availability on the two sides of the boundary.

*The All American Canal carries water from the Colorado River to the Imperial Valley.
Note the small side canals to capture seepage water to return to the main canal. By 2010
twenty-three miles of the canal had been lined with concrete to eliminate seepage. 2006.*

about 90 percent of their water). As Arizona, Utah, and Nevada expanded
their use of Colorado River water, California sought ways to assure water for
its burgeoning population and expanding cities. In 2003, San Diego reached
an agreement with the Imperial Irrigation District and the Metropolitan Water District of Southern California to line with concrete portions of the All
American Canal and Coachella Canal that transport water from the Colorado
River to the productive Imperial and Coachella agricultural valleys.[4] This
project reduced seepage by about 67,000 acre-feet per year, or enough water
for some 130,000 families. However, the leakage from the canal had charged
an aquifer and filled agricultural drains across the border in the Mexicali Valley that support irrigated agriculture on about three thousand acres and sustain
thousands of Mexican families. Despite the obvious impact on Mexicali farmers, the California authorities devised the plan without consultation with their
Mexican neighbors. The canal lining project and a water conservation and
transfer agreement with the Imperial Irrigation District provide an additional
eighty-thousand acre-feet per year for use in San Diego.[5]

Similar battles raged over the waters of the Rio Grande/Río Bravo,
which separates the U.S. border states of New Mexico and Texas both from
one another and from the Mexican states of Tamaulipas, Nuevo León, and
Coahuila. In 1938 a treaty was signed in the United States to apportion Rio

Grande water among U.S. border states. The 1944 water treaty with Mexico established rules for sharing the bounty of the lower Rio Grande, and two reservoirs—the Falcón and the Amistad—were built to control water flow. But as population grew in the postwar period, these agreements were no longer satisfactory for managing water in the region. The states of Tamaulipas and Nuevo León tangled over the thorny issue of urban and industrial water needs in Monterrey versus agricultural water needs in Tamaulipas. Texas and New Mexico found themselves with entirely different legal conceptions of water rights. In the 1990s, long-term drought in northeast Mexico and Texas, accompanied by inefficient irrigation methods in Mexico in the Conchos basin, a tributary of the Rio Grande, produced a long series of shortages of deliveries of water to Texas farmers. This created significant acrimony between the two countries. A combination of increased rainfall and irrigation efficiency investment in Mexico and Texas, funded by the North American Development Bank, eventually resolved the problem.[6]

U.S. and Mexican authorities have not been able to develop agreements to jointly manage the river basins, or watersheds, that lie across the international boundary. Water basins are natural systems defined by the stream courses that flow from the upper mountain ridges and join at a common outlet, whether to a marine body of water, lake, or large river. In order to assure their long-term ecological integrity and sustainable human exploitation, these basins need to be managed as complete natural units in order to protect water resources and habitat, prevent erosion and land degradation, and support the quality of life of the residents of the watershed. Although the 1944 treaty apportions surface water between U.S. and Mexican users, there are no arrangements for binational management of the watersheds to preserve water quality and quantity. All along the border, upstream water users take actions that hurt downstream users. California and the other U.S. states that share the water of the upper Colorado River basin use huge quantities of water to support growing urban populations and irrigated agriculture, leaving only about 10 percent of the Colorado River's poor-quality waters to reach Mexico and usually not even a trickle reaches the Gulf of California. The Colorado delta has been transformed from an enormously rich biological area into an ecosystem in crisis, without the minimum water needed to maintain important plant and animal systems. Farmers in the Conchos basin in Coahuila use excessive amounts of water, much of it wasted through inefficient irrigation practices, so that not enough water flows downstream into the Rio Grande, causing shortages and economic hardship for Texas farmers. On the western end of the border, the Tijuana River watershed empties into the Pacific through an important ecosystem, the Tijuana salt marsh estuary. This endangered habitat is impacted not only by contaminated runoff, renegade sewage flows, and sedimentation from nearby urban settlements in Tijuana but from land uses farther upstream such as cattle ranching, industry, agriculture, and sand mining.

Each country is now encouraging basin-wide planning and management approaches within its national territory, but the two federal governments have not developed a mechanism for binational planning and management of these important resources. In 2001, the Good Neighbor Environmental Board (GNEB), a federal advisory panel for border environmental issues, recommended that a border-wide watershed approach be initiated and institutionalized.[7] The following year, a consortium of U.S. and Mexican border universities reiterated the call for transborder water and watershed management at its annual policy forum, which included public- and private-sector participants as well as environmental organizations and academics.[8] In response to insufficient federal involvement, state governments, local governments, universities, and community members and organizations have seized the initiative. Particularly notable are efforts at the San Pedro River, which flows northward from Sonora into Arizona and is home to one of the richest ecosystems of the border, and at the Tijuana River, which is two-thirds in Baja California and one-third in California and one of the world's biological hotspots in terms of many endangered species. Local participants have formed a binational working group with assistance from the state of California, have developed a draft binational planning document, and have secured participation of federal agencies to work toward development of a more formal binational planning and management mechanism.[9] In 2012, the San Diego Regional Water Quality Control Board of the State of California Environmental Protection Agency released a strategy based on stakeholder consultations for protection and restoration of the Tijuana River valley in the U.S. part of the watershed. Recommended actions include specific projects to address sedimentation and trash problems that primarily impact the U.S. portion of the lower watershed. Initially driven primarily by San Diego agency stakeholders, the effort has made greater efforts to involve Mexican stakeholders in the process.[10]

In 2012, the U.S. and Mexican commissioners of the International Boundary and Water Commission responded to the many calls for improved binational management of shared watersheds by initiating discussions on a new minute to the 1944 U.S.-Mexico Water Treaty that would provide a framework for joint actions on management of the Tijuana River watershed. Discussions had advanced to the point that observers were optimistic that a new minute would be in place during 2015 to lay the basis for long-term watershed management along the border. Should this effort be successful, it will pave the way for more effective use of the border's shared resources.

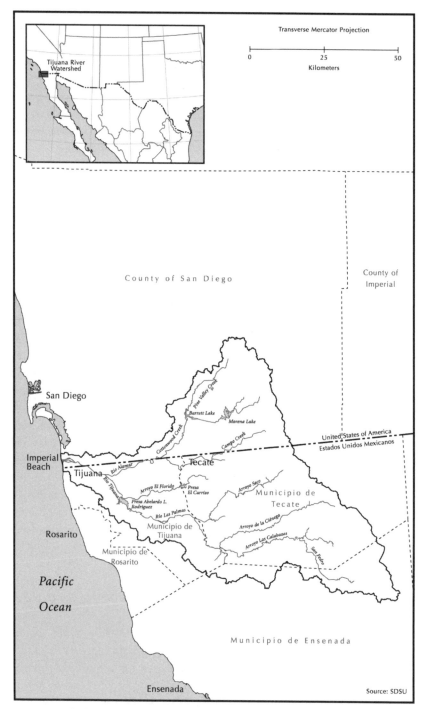

Map 13. *The binational Tijuana River watershed.*

According to recent reports from the Mexican government and multilateral organizations, Mexico's shortage of fresh water in the North was caused in large part by overexploitation of existing aquifers and a lack of adequate infrastructure for water treatment and distribution.[11] A 1997 World Bank report announced that almost one-third of Mexico's 258 aquifers were in danger of running dry. The threat of water shortages was greatest in sixteen states in northwestern, northern, and central Mexico. It was estimated that the aquifer underlying Ciudad Juárez–El Paso was being drained unsustainably at twenty times the rate of recharge; at that pace, the water supply would be exhausted by 2025.

The groundwater situation is not much better in the U.S. border region. Over the past century, the major groundwater resources of the U.S. border region have undergone significant depletion due to increasing human demands for urban areas and agriculture and largely uncontrolled pumping of these resources. In some areas, the level of the water table has fallen more than three hundred feet, which has caused surface subsidence of more than ten feet. Although Arizona, Texas, and New Mexico have some regulations for some years and in 2014 California added a weak regulatory program to balance extraction with recharge, these efforts have not been successful. The result is that everywhere in the U.S. border region, groundwater resources are poorly managed and deteriorating in quality and quantity.[12]

Conflicts over both surface and subsurface water show no sign of abating. As groundwater sources are depleted and as groundwater, inland surface waters, and coastal waters become more contaminated, water issues are more likely than ever to continue to plague U.S.-Mexican relations at the border. Although the two federal governments and the U.S. states have not been able to develop a transborder groundwater management agreement to protect border aquifers that are under threat, there has been some progress. By 2007, the U.S. and Mexican federal governments and the U.S. border states of Texas, Arizona, and New Mexico had launched a cooperative effort to study major border aquifers and lay the groundwork for eventual management of these critical water resources.[13]

A complicating factor for the water crisis, as well as for natural resources, human health, natural disasters, and other features of border life, is the effect of climate change on the U.S. Southwest and northern Mexico.[14] The National Climate Assessment, mandated by the U.S. Congress, and related independent work by hundreds of scientists provide a useful analysis of climate-change effects on the U.S.-Mexican border region largely due to increased concentrations of greenhouse gases produced by human activities. Observed recent climatic change in the border region includes a rise in average daily temperatures, fewer cold spells and more heat waves, unusually severe droughts, and decreased flows of the major river systems of the region—the Colorado and Rio Grande rivers.[15] Projections include increased average annual temperatures, increased heat waves, fewer frost-free days, increased seasonal temperatures, and earlier melting of the mountain snowpacks that feed the Colorado and Rio Grande systems. Coastal areas on the Pacific and Gulf coasts of the border will experience increased flooding due to sea-level rise, and everywhere in the border area, riparian and wetland ecosystems will be degraded, and wildfires will increase.

Adaptation to these impacts presents a challenge for the border region. State-level climate action plans produced by New Mexico, Arizona, California, Baja California, and Nuevo León mainly address reduction of greenhouse gas emissions. Some local governments along the border have also begun to address climate-change issues, looking at greenhouse gas reduction strategies in particular. San Diego released a draft comprehensive climate action plan in 2014 that addresses reducing emissions as well as the additional issues of adaptation and social equity.[16] While there has been sharing of information about climate-change plans across the border, no binational or coordinated integrated climate action plans have emerged.

Due to the cultural and institutional diversity along and across the border, as well as uneven economic development, the border population and ecosystems are exposed unevenly to the impacts of climate change.[17] Climate change will impact sensitive ecosystems that span the border, but institutional complexities at the border, along with different regulatory systems, make development of shared approaches for adaptation very challenging. The poorer regions of the border will be more vulnerable to increased temperatures and more extreme weather events, but the two distinct human systems that meet at the border hinder building adaptive capacity across it. Systems that provide water for urban, industrial, and agricultural uses in the border region will also be stressed. A 2010 study by the Bureau of Reclamation concluded that water supply in the Colorado River basin would decline over the next fifty years, and human uses would increase, leaving a shortfall of 3.2 million acre-feet by 2060.[18] The implications for water security in the border are significant for irrigated agriculture in the Imperial Valley in California, the Mexicali Valley in Baja California, and areas of Arizona. Moreover, Tijuana, Tecate, and Mexicali in Baja California are largely dependent on Colorado water for all urban uses, and U.S. border cities such as San Diego, Yuma, and Tucson rely on Colorado River water as a key component of their supply. Border cities such as Las Cruces, El Paso, and Ciudad Juárez in the Rio Grande river system face similar insecurities about long-term water supply.

The U.S.-Mexican border region contains natural areas with important and sometimes endangered plant and animal species that rely on unpredictable and oversubscribed water resources. Because of intense development, including urbanization and agriculture, many natural systems and species of native flora and fauna are under stress or threat of extinction. Much of the coastal zone of Southern California has been developed, and coastal wetlands have been paved over and coastal terraces covered with urban sprawl, nearly destroying critical habitats such as salt marshes and coastal sage scrub. Although important natural areas remain south of the border in Baja California, rapid urban and rural development is wreaking havoc with natural systems there. Elsewhere, threats such as declining amounts of water available for maintaining healthy natural systems have reduced surface water flows and lowered water tables, causing wetlands and riparian areas to dry up. Lack of water flowing down the Colorado River has severely impacted the formerly rich ecosystem of the Colorado delta and the upper Gulf of California. An agreement of the U.S. and Mexican sections of the International Boundary and Water Commission, Minute 319 to the 1944 U.S.-Mexico Water Treaty, provided, in a collaborative project with U.S. and Mexican environmental organizations, for release of a pulse flow of more than one hundred thousand acre-feet of water into the dry channel Colorado River at Morelos Dam, at the border with Mexico.[19] The goal of this effort is to acquire water rights and provide sufficient water to restore critical areas of the Colorado delta.

The riparian areas and lush cottonwood forest of the Santa Cruz River valley in southern Arizona survive only because treated sewage from the international treatment plant for the twin-city pair of Ambos Nogales is discharged into the river. But even this is threatened as new developments that rely on groundwater are springing up in the region and drawing down the level of local aquifers, which eventually will reduce water for the natural habitat. In other regions of the border, invasive plants that have been introduced are causing severe problems. Water hyacinth (*Eichornia crassipes*), hydrilla (*Hydralla verticallata*), giant reed (*Arundo donax*), and salt-cedar (*Tamarisk*) line large stretches of the Rio Grande, choking out natural vegetation and reducing the amount of water for native ecosystems or for human uses.[20]

Preservation of important natural habitats along the border depends on protection of water resources and also on conserving large, contiguous areas sufficient to permit key species of plants and animals to reproduce and thrive. Fortunately, large areas of the U.S. border region are federal or state lands that are protected to one degree or another. In a few areas these protected areas transcend the international boundary where U.S. and Mexican protected areas face each other across the border and constitute a de facto binational protected

New retirement communities and vacation homes near the Santa Cruz River at Rio Rico, Arizona, are extracting groundwater and threatening the important riparian vegetation. 2006.

area, although they are not managed jointly. Examples of these twin protected areas include Big Bend National Park in Texas and the Sierras del Carmen preserve in Mexico, as well as Organ Pipe National Monument and Cabeza Prieta Wildlife Preserve in southern Arizona and the Gran Desierto–Pinacate complex in adjoining Sonora, Mexico.[21]

One innovative effort to protect connected areas of habitat is in San Diego County, where the Multiple Species Conservation Program, negotiated among developers, land owners, environmentalists, and government officials, is in effect. There, protected areas and corridors of habitat that link the protected areas together are protected permanently from development. The challenge facing the region now is finding a way to manage these areas so that they link with protected areas that need to be established in Baja California. The ultimate goal is to create transborder conservation areas. Nongovernmental organizations, private citizens, and academic researchers are taking the lead, trying to develop new mechanisms to protect land in Mexico to complement protected areas across the border. Binational conservation and coordinated management of protected areas remains one of the great environmental challenges for the future along the U.S-Mexican border.[22]

An unexpected challenge to binational conservation was the emergence of border security as a high national priority in the United States due to the September 11, 2001, terrorist attacks, growing concern about the large number of undocumented aliens living in the United States, increasing drug trafficking along the border with Mexico, and growing violence in Mexican border cities. A primary response by the U.S. Congress and administration has been to fortify the border with Mexico, with some $2 billion expended by 2014 for the construction of a fence and related infrastructure such as multiple lines of fencing, new all-weather roads, stadium lighting, and sensor networks along the border in urban and many rural areas. These works have fragmented border habitats, caused erosion in many areas, and prevented migration of many small animals and larger species, including mountain lions and antelope, as well as of endangered and rare animals, such as ocelots, jaguars, and brown bears.[23] The barrier to migration reduces the genetic diversity of these species, and small numbers trapped on one side or the other of the border fence are more likely to disappear.

Contamination with toxic substances and water laden with salts and other suspended materials have increased the threat to border ecosystems. Untreated industrial and municipal wastes have been discharged into the waterways on both sides of the border, contaminating surface streams and aquifers throughout the region. The Salton Sea, the body of water lying just north of the international boundary in California, is an example of effects of water pollution and complexities involved in protecting and cleaning up water resources. Without drainage to the sea, the levels of contaminants in the Salton Sea—mostly caused by agricultural runoff containing both naturally occurring substances and fertilizer, herbicide, and pesticide residues from Mexico and the United States—have made the lake a toxic stew. The New River, actually a drainage ditch originating in Mexicali, adds human and industrial wastes to the Salton Sea. Huge numbers of migratory seabirds, including the endangered California brown pelican, died off in 1996 and 1997, and the threat to nearby human populations became increasingly serious. Declining amounts of water flowing into the Salton Sea also pose a threat to the health of this important ecosystem. In 2006, Mexicali built a new wastewater treatment plant that sent the treated effluent south toward the Gulf of California, and new power-generating plants in Mexicali that began operating in 2003 used water from the old Mexicali treatment plant for cooling, reducing the amount of discharge into the New River and the Salton Sea. Fallowing of land and less water use on Imperial Valley crops also reduced agricultural drainage flow into the Salton Sea.

According to the Pacific Institute, the Salton Sea "lies on the brink of catastrophic change."[24] Without major restoration efforts, the surface level of the sea will drop twenty feet over the next twenty years, tripling the salinity and exposing more than one hundred square miles of dusty lakebed to the desert winds. These changes will likely increase air pollution in the valley, causing alarming increases in asthma and other respiratory diseases and higher death rates among children and the elderly. The rich ecosystem of the sea will also decline as the increasing salinity kills most of the fish, which will eliminate much of the food supply for many species of migratory birds that rely on the water as a resting and breeding place. Many proposals have been made for restoration of the New River and the Salton Sea, but solutions are elusive and enormously expensive.[25]

Although water is perhaps the most critical natural resource issue facing the border, environmental degradation has also been a pervasive problem that involved various interrelated resources and social forces on both sides of the border. Industrial waste emerged as a significant issue in the discussions prior to approval of the North American Free Trade Agreement (NAFTA) in the United States, and after implementation of the accord began, U.S. and Mexican environmental groups and government regulators continued to raise the issue. Lack of data and control mechanisms exacerbated environmental problems at the border. Many maquiladoras had toxic-discharge problems, according to the Mexican government.[26] In the mid-1980s, it was estimated that forty-four tons of hazardous *maquila* waste per day went unaccounted for. In the 1990s the problem persisted: only 12 percent of maquiladoras were es-

The New River—often called the most polluted river of North America—at the point where it enters the United States near Calexico, California, from Mexicali, Baja California, flowing north to California's Salton Sea. 2006.

timated to achieve compliance with hazardous materials regulations requiring the return of substances to the United States for processing and disposal.[27] In 1994, the Mexican government shut down a lead smelter in Tijuana, Metales y Derivados, which was the Mexican subsidiary of a U.S. company.[28] The owners then abandoned the site and returned to the United States, leaving behind some six thousand metric tons of lead slag; waste piles and byproducts; sulfuric acid; and heavy metals. The abandoned site was not secured properly, and in 1998 a coalition of U.S. and Mexican environmental groups filed a submission with the trilateral Commission for Environmental Cooperation of North America (CEC), which was created as part of the NAFTA process, charging that the Mexican government had failed to enforce its environmental laws. After the CEC published its findings, the Mexican government, with the assistance of the U.S. Environmental Protection Agency (EPA), began to remove the hazardous waste from the site, which was fully cleaned up by 2008. While the Metales y Derivados case is the poster child for groups opposed to industrial development in the region, by 2000 many border maquiladoras had implemented modern environmental management systems and were in compliance with relevant governmental regulations. In 2004 and 2005, a joint California–Baja California government water-testing program revealed that there were very few unauthorized discharges of industrial waste in the sewage systems of Ensenada, Tecate, Tijuana, and Mexicali.[29] By the early 2000s, the greatest source of toxic materials reaching the Tijuana River and the Pacific Ocean was stormwater runoff from urban Tijuana that picked up contaminants from small businesses and households.[30]

Poor air quality emerged as an important health issue as twin cities increased in size. Foul air north and south of the boundary was generated by automobiles, smelting plants and other businesses, and agriculture (through smoke from burning fields and dust storms from overtilled soil). Exhaust from the vehicle fleet everywhere along the border was the primary cause of air pollution, although other factors contributed. Mexican border cities generally do not have programs for testing motor vehicles to ensure that the pollution control equipment is working properly. In addition, everywhere along the border, the sale of older, polluting vehicles from U.S. border cities to Mexican border cities is a common practice. One result is that the vehicle fleet of the Mexican twin city is older and in poorer condition and produces more contamination per vehicle than the vehicle fleet on the other side of the border. The mixing and movement of pollutants in air currents—stemming from different sources in Mexico and the United States—creates a region-wide problem, particularly severe in Ciudad Juárez–El Paso and in the Imperial Valley–Mexicali Valley regions. Both the El Paso area of Texas and the Imperial Valley of California were out of compliance with U.S. federal air-quality standards. Mexican border cities often failed to meet Mexican norms as well. Poor air quality was linked to high rates of asthma and other respiratory diseases, particularly in the vulnerable populations of the elderly and young children.[31] Fed up with dirty air, in 1993 business and community leaders in the El Paso–Ciudad Juárez

Public outcry forced the U.S. and Mexican governments to clean up the Metales y Derivados hazardous waste site in Tijuana. The sign warns not to enter the site because of the presence of materials that are hazardous to health. By 2009 the site had been cleaned up, and basketball courts and a paved soccer field were later installed. 2005.

region came together in a binational committee to work on the air pollution problems in a regional, transborder fashion. Formed under the auspices of the Texas Air Control Board with support from Environmental Defense, the Paso del Norte Air Quality Task Force had as an initial goal the establishment of a binational air-quality management district, similar to the South Coast Air Quality Management District in the Los Angeles area. In 1996, the two federal governments established a formal agreement and a committee, known as the Joint Advisory Committee on Air Quality for the Paso del Norte Region, made up of local, state, and federal officials as well as business leaders and environmental groups, to continue the work of this grassroots group.[32]

By 2015, progress on addressing border air pollution had been made. The close collaboration of agencies from both countries through the U.S.-Mexico Border Environmental Program had produced air-quality monitoring networks; cleaner fuels, newer vehicle fleets in border cities, and more paved roads had improved air quality. However, border urban growth, increased trade-related truck traffic, and long delays in crossing the border northbound all generated additional pollution. Scientists and regulators also began to examine previously overlooked types and sources of pollution, including traffic pollutants at border ports of entry.[33] Long lines of idling and slow-moving commercial and passenger vehicles waiting to cross into the United States regularly produce dangerously high levels of ozone and fine particles that are known to increase risk of cardiovascular illness and asthma. These levels of pollutants affect the health not only of car passengers and pedestrians waiting to cross the border but also of people in the surrounding, densely populated areas adjacent to the ports of entry. The nearby communities are largely Hispanic and low income, and these groups bear a disproportionate exposure to the localized air pollution, making this an environmental justice issue. Executive Order 12898 requires that environmental justice be considered in federal planning, but there is little evidence this has occurred along the border.[34]

Attempts to clean up the border environment or stop further degradation were erratic until the early 1990s. Although the 1983 La Paz agreement had created a mechanism led by the EPA and Mexico's environmental ministry to address border environmental problems and there were some successful efforts at cleanup, progress was very uneven. However, the pressing nature of environmental problems at the border attracted significant national U.S. attention in the discussions of the early 1990s that expedited the approval and signing of the North American Free Trade Agreement in 1993. In 1992, as part of the push for NAFTA, the administrations of President George H. W. Bush and President Carlos Salinas de Gortari formulated an Integrated Border Environmental Plan (IBEP) that was based on the general 1983 La Paz border environmental agreement. With this, the U.S. and Mexican governments initiated a series of bilateral programs and other measures to provide a comprehensive approach to the worsening border environmental problems. One effort consisted of a succession of border environmental plans, first the IBEP (1992–1994), then the Border XXI Program (1996–2000), the Border 2012 Plan (2002–2012), and, most recently, Border 2020 (2012–2020).[35] The U.S. Environmental Protection Agency and its Mexican counterpart environmental ministry led these plans and programs and together provided institutional continuity for the efforts. A second set of actions included the creation by Mexico and the United States of two totally new binational institutions to address the lack of adequate environmental infrastructure, especially for water, wastewater, and solid waste. The Border Environment Cooperation Commission (BECC) was established with headquarters in Ciudad Juárez to review proposed projects and to recommend them for funding. The North American

Development Bank (NADB), located in San Antonio, was to arrange funding packages for BECC-approved projects. Finally, the third part of these important actions was the creation of the trilateral Commission for Environmental Cooperation of North America, which was part of the NAFTA agreement, set up in Montreal. While the CEC was to promote harmonization of environmental laws among the three partners and to reduce environmental regulation barriers to trade, the commission did undertake a number of actions that were important to the U.S.-Mexican border region. The governments of the United States and Mexico hoped that these actions would not only begin to address border environmental problems in a comprehensive way but also reduce the strident opposition to NAFTA by environmental groups and many others in border communities.

The IBEP was not well received by the border community in 1992. It had been developed by the two federal governments with little input from local stakeholders; consequently, it neglected to address many important local issues. This plan was replaced in 1996 by Border XXI, a binational five-year program to address the most challenging border environmental issues through nine borderwide workgroups on specific issues such as air quality and hazardous waste management. As part of the process to develop Border XXI, more than forty public meetings seeking input about local priorities were held in the U.S. and Mexican border communities in 1995 and 1996. These meetings were somewhat historic in that officials from both governments were in the same room listening to environmental concerns from local governments and citizens. In the long run, this helped to increase dialogue between border residents and the federal governments, especially in Mexico. Successes of Border XXI included more transparency and stakeholder engagement, elaboration of emergency response plans for U.S. and Mexican twin cities, and development of air monitoring networks for several Mexican border cities, including Mexicali and Tijuana. A major shortcoming of Border XXI was the inability of the two governments to develop a workable system for tracking hazardous materials shipments across the border.[36]

Border XXI was succeeded in 2000 by Border 2012, a ten-year plan designed with specific environmental improvement goals and local workgroups that incorporate a range of stakeholders from local U.S. and Mexican communities. Along with the institutional lead provided by the EPA and its Mexican counterpart, Border 2012 also included as partners the U.S. and Mexican health secretariats, the governments of the ten border states, and U.S. border tribal governments.[37] Border 2012 incorporated specific goals for border environmental cleanup and established a series of measures to assess progress. Some indicators indirectly measured progress through counting numbers of administrative enforcement actions or tallying the number of sister-city emergency response plans in place. Others measured air and water quality and noted the number of new treatment plants. The EPA and its U.S. and Mexican partners published periodic reports on these indicators.[38] Border 2020 continues specific goals and adjusts approaches. Important changes include an eight-year implementation horizon, five new guiding principles, two-year action plans that account for resource and priority changes and consider the particular needs of a community or geographic area, the addition of indicators and communication committees, and updated goals and objectives.[39]

As part of its outreach efforts as the main U.S. agency lead for border environmental programs, the EPA established offices in San Diego and El Paso in 1994. These offices became very important in communicating between border communities and the EPA regional headquarters in San Francisco and Dallas and the national headquarters in Washington, D.C. These offices are of practical and symbolic importance to border communities. Not only do they provide an important conduit of information and help make the policy process transparent, but they also reflect the commitment of the agency to the task of addressing border environmental issues with input from local residents.

A side agreement between the United States and Mexico that was part of the NAFTA process created two new bilateral organizations, the BECC and the NADB, to address the environmental infrastructure needs of the border region. The two institutions were designed to be binational border institutions, with equal participation by the United States and Mexico, including in terms of management, boards of directors, and advisory boards. The BECC in particular was set up with mechanisms to facilitate citizen input; one result was adoption of sustainable development criteria for projects and binational citizen advisory panels for project review. There were no existing models for these two institutions; they had to be created from scratch.

Slow to approve and fund specific environmental infrastructure projects, the two institutions were severely criticized by both impatient border residents and the treasury departments of Mexico and the United States. However, a 2005–2006 attempt to disband NADB initiated by Mexico's treasury department and seconded by the U.S. Treasury Department was turned back through vigorous lobbying in the U.S. Congress by border leaders and their supporters.[40] Defenders of the BECC and NADB pointed out that the institutions had funded important new environmental infrastructure, directly improving the lives of millions of border residents. The new binational institutions had also significantly improved the capacity of border communities to plan, operate, and maintain water and wastewater infrastructure. Nevertheless, the two governments failed to correct the basic flaw in NADB that required funds to be loaned at commercial rates. Most border communities were accustomed to receiving grant funds for infrastructure projects, and poor U.S. and almost all Mexican communities lacked adequate revenue streams for loan repayment. Although NADB was able to use grant funds from EPA to lower the effective rate of the loans, the amount of support was inadequate to rectify the deficit of environmental infrastructure, particularly given the rapid growth rate of border communities, especially in Mexico. Through 2013, NADB had contracted almost $2.25 billion in financing for some 192 projects through loans and grants.[41] In addition, the two institutions had provided considerable training to agencies in small border communities in infrastructure project development and management. NADB also provided important infrastructure management training so that Mexican and U.S. border communities actually had qualified personnel to manage and operate infrastructure projects once they were built. In early 2015, the governing boards of these two binational institutions were considering a proposal to merge, primarily to increase operating efficiency.

A critical partner in the BECC and NADB work to improve border water and wastewater infrastructure has been the U.S. Environmental Protection Agency, which has provided grant monies through its Border Environment Infrastructure Fund (BEIF). These funds were allocated as direct grants or as part of loan packages to make borrowing affordable for poor border communities. In total, $601.2 million in BEIF grants supported 104 water and wastewater projects in the United States and Mexico. Initially, EPA was able to provide $100 million per year in BEIF funds, but from 2008 on, the support dwindled to $10 million per year.[42] The decline in BEIF funding was due to changing priorities in the U.S. congressional appropriations, which had shifted from development of border communities to huge investments in border security infrastructure and Department of Homeland Security expansion.

Another important environmental achievement of NAFTA was the creation of the trilateral Commission for Environmental Cooperation of North America, established in Montreal by the NAFTA partners to harmonize the environmental regulations of the three countries and to make sure that environmental regulations did not unnecessarily restrain trade. The CEC, with advisory boards for public and local government input, has focused considerable attention on the environmental problems of the border region, including transborder air pollution, hazardous waste, and the need for an environmental review process that transcends the border. An interesting feature of the CEC's structure allows citizens of the NAFTA region to file complaints against governments that fail to enforce their own environmental laws and regulations, enabling the public to play an active whistle-blower role. After review, the CEC may investigate the matter and publish its findings, which are not enforceable but bring considerable pressure to bear on a government that is lax with its enforcement efforts. By 2006, submissions and published findings in the border region concerned matters such as a battery recycling plant in Tijuana, a smelter in Sonora, and municipal governments in Sonora discharging wastewater into rivers. Current submissions under consideration are complaints about the failure of municipal and state governments in Sonora to stop industrial pollution, the failure of the Mexican federal government to enforce environmental laws in the Gulf of California, and the Mexican government's permitting development of a regasification plant offshore of Tijuana and adjacent to the Coronado Islands and the location of critical habitat for important bird species.[43]

Another institution that emerged during the NAFTA period is the Good Neighbor Environmental Board, created by the Enterprise for the Americas Act in 1992. This federal panel advises the president and Congress about border environmental concerns and policy options through yearly reports and occasional comment letters. The board has members from the relevant federal agencies as well as border-state and local governments, environmental organizations, academia, border tribes, and the private sector. The GNEB interacts with national agency personnel and elected representatives through an annual meeting in Washington, D.C., and with border stakeholders through meetings held in border communities each year. Recent GNEB reports have addressed environmental health issues of children, transportation and air pollution, impacts on natural and cultural resources, watershed management, and other important border environmental issues.[44]

While the three governments were establishing new institutions and programs to address the growing border environmental issues, academic research on border environmental matters increased significantly. In 1989, Congress authorized the formation of a consortium of border universities to address the region's environmental problems. The Southwest Consortium for Environmental Research and Policy (SCERP), with university members in the U.S. and Mexican border states, conducted more than four hundred applied research projects through an annual appropriation in the EPA budget. Headquartered in San Diego, SCERP published research findings, translated scientific research into forms more accessible to border, regional, and national stakeholders, and improved build capacity in border communities through training along with undergraduate and graduate education. SCERP held annual technical meetings and a policy forum with practitioners and researchers from both countries to focus on key issues and to develop policy options. The consortium issued sixteen volumes of reports on border environmental issues, and its researchers published hundreds of articles in scientific journals. SCERP ended operations in 2013 as congressional funding priorities migrated to supporting university-based research on border security issues through the Department of Homeland Security.[45]

The 1990s saw growing awareness of the border's environmental problems, which had been building for decades and were exacerbated by exploding populations, urbanization, and international trade and industry. The two decades following NAFTA saw a remarkable set of actions by government and communities to address the key border environmental issues in a comprehensive and consistent fashion. The bilateral and trilateral border environmental programs, including Border 2020 and its predecessors under the La Paz agreement, the BECC and NADB, and the CEC, brought significant attention to the environmental issues of the border region. The federal efforts brought focus to border environmental programs and facilitated involvement of the public and state and local governments in reviewing projects and helping to define policy priorities. Border 2020 and BECC project review processes brought new levels of transparency and citizen participation in border environmental matters. By establishing priorities and indicators, Border 2020 brought promise of evaluation of progress, or lack of progress, on the most critical border environmental problems. The U.S.-Mexico Border Environmental Program led by EPA and its Mexican counterpart agency provided critical continuity and institutional attention to border environmental concerns and community engagement. Border 2020 and the NAFTA environmental institutions brought hope to border residents and raised expectations that have not yet been fully met.

By 2006 the programs had accomplished a great deal. But due to rapid population and trade growth, the problems were growing—at times faster than mitigation efforts. After NAFTA was passed and implementation had begun, U.S. congressional attention to many border issues began to wane and the funding necessary to implement the projects and programs defined by the NAFTA environmental institutions was not forthcoming. Engagement in Iraq and the response to the September 11, 2001, terrorist attacks on New York and Washington, D.C., served to refocus national attention regarding the border on security matters and not on the quality of life of the region's residents. Ironically, just as the capacity to address binational border environmental issues was increasing, federal resources for the effort were decreasing.

PUBLIC HEALTH ISSUES

Public health issues constitute an important set of challenges along the U.S.-Mexican border for a number of reasons. The border region is the poorest area of the United States, and there is a clear relationship between poverty and health problems. According to a 2006 analysis by the U.S.-Mexico Borders County Coalition, if the U.S. border region, comprising the counties along the international boundary, were the fifty-first state, it would rank[46]

- Last in access to health care
- Second in death rates due to hepatitis
- Third in deaths related to diabetes
- Last in per capita income
- First in the number of school children living in poverty
- First in the number of children who do not have health insurance

Inhabitants of the U.S. border states suffer from higher rates of many diseases and worse mortality rates than the rest of the nation. Although Mexico's northern border is better off in terms of health characteristics than the Mexican national average, it still lags behind the United States. The significant migration into the border region from central and southern Mexico and across the border into the United States has introduced disease into the area, including dengue and cholera, while diseases such as HIV/AIDS have flowed from the United States across the border into Mexico. In the Texas *colonias*, or unauthorized housing subdivisions without basic infrastructure, along the Rio Grande, hepatitis occurred at several times the national average.[47] A mysterious epidemic of spina bifida and anencephaly, both neural-tube defects, swept the Texas border counties between 1988 and 1992, affecting children at more than twice the average U.S. rate. Although many observers suspected toxic chemical exposure related to maquiladora employment was responsible, the link was not proven.[48]

Water pollution from industrial and urban development plagued the border, which led to health problems for border residents. One high-profile case was the untreated sewage that flowed north from Tijuana to San Diego. Not until 1997 did an international joint sewage treatment plant on the California side of the border begin operations to reduce the cross-border flow of contaminated water. The capacity of this new plant was quickly reached, while an existing plant in Tijuana was able to treat only about half of the waste it received and provided only minimal, or primary, treatment of sewage. Tijuana began to upgrade its sewage treatment system in 2002 and developed a twenty-year master plan for potable water and wastewater; by 2005 it was implementing parts of the master plan with an infrastructure loan from Japan. Despite these significant efforts on the part of authorities in Tijuana, keeping up with the needs of the rapidly growing urban population was daunting.

The international border has also exacerbated some other health problems. Tuberculosis was brought to the region by migrants from the south. Often infected individuals were diagnosed at clinics and hospitals in the United States, where they began a course of treatment. However, undocumented migratory status and the international border often interrupted the full course of treatment. As a result, a drug-resistant strain of tuberculosis emerged in the border region. Public health officials responded with a binational program to provide follow-up on both sides of the border. This instance illustrates the complexity of problems in the border zone and the need for transborder cooperation to address issues that spill across the international boundary.[49]

Many border residents have become accustomed to accessing health services on both sides of the international boundary. The high cost of health care in the United States drives many people south of the border in search of dental services, pharmaceutical drugs at a fraction of their cost in the United States, and other medical services, including cosmetic surgery, eye surgery, primary health care, and alternative cancer therapies not available in the United States.[50] Mexican border cities catered to people across the border, attracting new clients as health-care costs escalated in the United States during the 1990s and early 2000s. Border cities such as Algodones in Baja California began by providing low-cost dental service to winter residents of the nearby Imperial Valley and Yuma region. By 2000, these "snowbirds," often on fixed incomes, were able to find not only dentists in Algodones but optometrists, dozens of pharmacies, and even primary care physicians—all advertising their services on English-language flyers and signage.[51] Sometimes Spanish-speaking residents of U.S. border cities prefer to cross into Mexico for health-care services delivered in their native language. Although these health services are less costly than those available across the border in the United States, they provide a lucrative living for many Mexican border residents. Employers in the U.S. border cities recognized the realities of transborder health services, and by the late 1990s some were offering binational health-care plans so that workers and their families could access health care in either the U.S. or Mexican twin city. In San Diego, for example, many companies have workers who reside in Tijuana with their families, and the transborder health coverage provides better service to the families and savings to the company.

Public health officials on both sides of the border, aware for many decades that disease and public health issues flow back and forth across the international border, have been cooperating to address these issues. The Pan American Health Organization established a field office in El Paso in 1942 as part of the cooperative effort for World War II, and the following year the U.S.-Mexico Border Health Association was formed. By 2014, both organiza-

Even small Mexican border towns such as Tecate, Baja California, sell medical services to clients from across the border. In this case, a dentist advertises that English is spoken and cosmetic dentistry is available. 2002.

tions had ended operations, but for decades they provided critical communication for addressing the evolving health issues that the U.S.-Mexican border faces.[52] As part of the increased levels of cooperation between the United States and Mexico with the development and implementation of NAFTA, the U.S. Congress authorized the president of the United States to reach an agreement with Mexico to establish a binational commission to address the unique and severe health problems of the border region, and in 1997 Congress authorized funding for a new commission. Not until 2000, however, was the U.S.-Mexico Border Health Commission created by the signing of an agreement by the U.S. secretary of health and human services and the secretary of health of Mexico. Although the commission is not adequately funded, it does bring U.S. and Mexican federal health authorities together with the health departments of the ten border states and local entities to address critical health issues of the border region.[53]

For the last several decades, U.S. and Mexican health authorities have devoted more attention to communicable diseases at the border, an area particularly vulnerable because of enormous flows of people back and forth on a daily basis, as well as underserved populations in both countries. The outbreak of the H1N1 influenza pandemic, commonly called swine flu, in Mexico in March and April 2009 and its rapid spread to the border and other locations in the United States highlighted the need for close cooperation of Mexican and U.S. authorities at the border. Disease-resistant tuberculosis and measles are communicable diseases that have been the focus of concern recently in this very dynamic region.

NATIVE AMERICANS AND THE BORDER

The Native American tribal peoples who occupy portions of ancestral lands or reservations in the border region are a small but important component of the border's population.[54] Currently there are some twenty-six federally recognized tribes in the immediate border zone in the United States, with a total population on the reservations in 2000 of 26,810 residents. The four U.S. border states have 149 federally recognized tribes with a total population on the reservations in 2000 of 370,931, while the total American Indian population for those states was over 1.3 million. In 2010, the four border states had a total Native American population of just over 1.6 million. Approximately 30 percent of the Native American population of the border states lives on reservation land. The federally recognized tribes are sovereign nations, with powers somewhat similar to those of the U.S. states. Mexican traditional indigenous peoples of the immediate Mexican border zone are located primarily in Baja California and Sonora and consist of seven tribal groups and approximately one thousand people. The Mexican border states have fourteen indigenous groups native to the region, with a 2000 population of 157,576. In addition to the people native to the borderlands, the great migratory flows, from southern Mexico to the northern border and into the United States, have established new groups of indigenous peoples in the region. In some areas, such as Baja California and Sonora, these new groups now outnumber the local tribes. Mixtec people from the Oaxaca region of southern Mexico were first brought to the northwest of Mexico by labor contractors to work on the tomato and fresh vegetable harvests. Many who arrived to work in the Mexicali Valley and in San Quintín on the coast south of Ensenada remained and settled in the fast-growing cities of Tijuana and Mexicali and moved across the border to central and Southern California, first as agricultural laborers and then as permanent residents.[55] As a result of this migratory flow, Tijuana now has bilingual Mixtec-Spanish schools, and border universities are introducing language courses in Mixtec and Zapotec.

The boundary established by Mexico and the United States partitioned the traditional lands utilized by a number of tribal peoples. The new international boundary separated scattered settlements from each other and separated plant and animal resources from those who had traditionally utilized these for food and to produce the materials and tools necessary for daily life. Two groups that are especially affected by the border are the Tohono O'odham of the Arizona-Sonora region and the Kumeyaay of the California–Baja California area. Increasing migration controls at the border in the 1980s and 1990s and intensified border security in the wake of the September 11, 2001, terrorist attacks on New York and Washington, D.C., have made it much more difficult for Mexican and U.S. tribal members to interact across the border. Most Kumeyaay of Baja California, for example, lack regular employment and bank accounts, as well as Mexican passports, which are required for a visa to visit the United States; the ability of U.S. consulates to provide visas for such special cases was practically eliminated due to growing concern about border security. However, through the diligent work of the Kumeyaay in California, a census of Baja California Kumeyaay was produced, enabling these people to obtain border-crossing permits to visit relatives and take part in tribal activities, although not to reside north of the border or to work. While members of the Tohono O'odham are still able to cross at informal gates since the tribal lands share some sixty miles of the border with Mexico, increased drug trafficking, human smuggling, and Border Patrol enforcement activities on the reservation have produced a climate of fear among residents who live in isolated houses. At the same time, off-road vehicles used by smugglers and human foot traffic have caused significant damage to archaeological and cultural sites and have destroyed flora and fauna of the fragile desert ecosystem.[56]

Native Americans on both sides of the border are among the poorest residents of the region. They are characterized by low incomes, low levels of education, substandard housing and services, and social and health problems. The Mexican border tribes are particularly threatened. Lacking the legal protections and minimal government services accorded their counterparts in the United States, they often must seek employment in urban areas well away from their traditional homes. They also must constantly fight to retain their traditional lands, particularly those near expanding urban areas. Most of the traditional languages spoken by Mexican border tribes, eight in total, are on the list of twenty languages identified by Mexico's National Commission for the Development of Indian Peoples as being at risk of disappearing.[57]

Examples of Native American economic development efforts. Wind turbine project and Golden Acorn Casino, both projects of the Campo Kumeyaay nation in eastern San Diego County. Mexico can be seen in the backgrounds of both photographs. 2006.

U.S. border tribes are making significant efforts to develop economically and to raise the standard of living of tribal members by creating economic enterprises and jobs on the reservation. The most usual mechanism used is establishment of gambling activities such as bingo halls, card rooms, and casinos. Some tribes have successfully diversified through establishment of resorts, truck stops, RV parks, golf courses, outlet malls, banks, and wind-power alternative-energy projects. A recent study of tribal government gaming in California demonstrated that the average per capita income of gaming tribes in the state increased 55 percent between 1990 and 2000 as opposed to 15 percent on nongaming reservations. Although gaming helped reduce the poverty of families of gaming tribes from 36 percent in 1990 to 26 percent in 2000, this is still well above the national average of about 10 percent. The economic development brought by gaming helped the population on California reservations grow 6 percent annually between 1990 and 2000 as tribal members returned to work on the reservations.[58] Mexican border tribes, however, do not have this option and have focused economic development on establishing nature and cultural tourism enterprises in an attempt to develop jobs that are appropriate to their traditions and that enable families to remain in the rural areas.

Tribes located near the border have been affected strongly by the rapid growth of security personnel and infrastructure since the 1990s, especially after September 11, 2001. As border security was enhanced and immigration requirements became stricter, U.S. border indigenous peoples such as the Kumeyaay in San Diego County and the Tohono O'odham in Arizona were isolated from their relatives south of the border. The ability of these peoples to pass back and forth was made more difficult, especially for natives living on the Mexican side of the international boundary. Often of low income and lacking even a Mexican passport, they found obtaining a visa to cross north to visit relatives or to participate in ancient traditional cultural ceremonies very difficult. Eventually, U.S. authorities developed special arrangements with border tribal members that did not require a formal U.S. visa for entrance into the United States.

More disturbing for U.S. border tribal peoples was the increase in numbers of unauthorized migrants crossing their rural and isolated lands, which included professional smugglers and eventually incorporated transportation of illegal drugs as part of the illicit activities. By 2009, the Tohono O'odham reservation was a major entry point for narcotics along the U.S.-Mexican border; that year tribal police seized 319,000 pounds of marijuana as well as quantities of cocaine, methamphetamines, and heroin.[59] Violence grew on the reservation as traffickers intimidated local residents, and assaults associated with drug smuggling increased. Many young tribal members were sucked into the easy money of human and drug trafficking, increasing drug addiction on the reservation and leading to the incarceration of many of these individuals. The buildup of Border Patrol presence on the reservation also worried many tribal members as the former tranquility of this isolated region was destroyed. Not only did traffickers destroy the landscape by blazing new roads through the desert, but increased road construction by the Border Patrol had a deleterious effect. Smugglers and unauthorized migrants also leave significant quantities of trash when crossing the border. One study from 2005 estimated that every day more than a ton of trash was left on the Tohono O'odham reservation in Arizona.[60]

NOTES

1. See Faye Fiore, "Activists Alarmed by Bid to Reverse Dolphin-Safety Law," *Los Angeles Times*, September 9, 1995; Dick Russell, "Tuna-Dolphin Wars," *Defenders: The Conservation Magazine of Defenders of Wildlife* (summer 2002).

2. Norris Hundley Jr., *The Great Thirst: Californians and Water—a History*, rev. ed. (Berkeley: University of California Press, 2001), provides a detailed analysis of competition for Colorado River water among the seven basin states and Mexico.

3. U.S. Bureau of Reclamation (USBR), "Colorado River Basin Water Supply and Demand Study," USBR, 2012, http://www.usbr.gov/lc/region/programs/crbstudy/finalreport/index.html.

4. Sandra Dibble, "Mexican Opposition to Canal Lining Grows," *San Diego Union-Tribune*, December 19, 2004; Sandra Dibble, "Worries over Water: Mexicali Valley Farmers Fear Groundwater Loss When U.S. Lines Canal," *San Diego Union-Tribune*, July 6, 2005; Vicente Sánchez Munguía, ed., *The U.S.-Mexican Border Environment: Lining the All-American Canal: Competition or Cooperation for Water in the U.S.-Mexican Border*, SCERP Monograph Series 13 (San Diego, CA: San Diego State University Press, 2006).

5. San Diego's effort to expand the sources of its water supply as well as its reliability are outlined at San Diego County Water Authority, "Enhancing Water Supply Reliability," http://www.sdcwa.org/enhancing-water-supply-reliability.

6. For information on the Texas-Mexico water conflict, see Mary E. Kelly, *The Río Conchos: A Preliminary Overview* (Austin: Texas Center for Policy Studies, 2001); J. Schmandt et al., *Water and Sustainable Development in the Binational Lower Rio Grande/Río Bravo Basin* (The Woodlands, TX: Houston Advanced Research Center and the Instituto Tecnológico y de Estudios Superiores de Monterrey, 2000).

7. Good Neighbor Environmental Board, *Fourth Report of the Good Neighbor Environmental Board to the Congress and the President* (Washington, D.C.: U.S. EPA, September 2001).

8. Southwest Center for Environmental Research and Policy, "Binational Water Management Planning: Opportunities, Costs, Benefits, and Unintended Consequences: Secure and Sustainable Water by 2020" (summary of Border Institute IV, May 2002), http://trw.sdsu.edu/English/Characteristics/Docs/BI-IVeng.pdf.

9. The website of the Udall Center for Studies in Public Policy at the University of Arizona (http://udallcenter.arizona.edu/publications/epp.php#2007) lists activities in that watershed. Tijuana River watershed efforts are discussed in Paul Ganster, "Transborder Management for the Tijuana River Watershed," *Southwest Hydrology* 4, no. 5 (September/October 2005): 24–25, and Richard Wright and Rafael Vela, eds., *Tijuana River Watershed Atlas/Atlas de la cuenca del Río Tijuana* (San Diego: San Diego State University Press and Institute for Regional Studies of the Californias, 2005).

10. The website of the San Diego Regional Water Quality Control Board includes the recovery strategy document as well as other information about the initiative. See "Tijuana River Valley Recovery Strategy," San Diego Regional Water Quality Control Board, http://www.waterboards.ca.gov/sandiego/water_issues/tijuana_river_valley_strategy/index.shtml.

11. Mexico's national water commission, CONAGUA, reported in 2011 that aquifers in northeastern Baja California, along the coast of Sonora, and in the Rio Grande watershed are overdrafted, and those on the coasts of Baja California and Sonora are affected by saltwater intrusion from excessive pumping. See M. Wilder et al., "Climate Change and U.S.-Mexico Border Communities," in *Assessment of Climate Change in the Southwest United States: A Report Prepared for the National Climate Assessment*, ed. G. Garfin et al. (Washington, D.C.: Island Press, 2013), 365–66.

12. See, for example, Leonard F. Konikow, "Groundwater Depletion in the United States (1900–2008)," U.S. Geological Survey (USGS) Scientific Investigations Report 2013-5079, USGS, 2013, http://pubs.usgs.gov/sir/2013/5079; Zack Guido, "Groundwater in the Arid Southwest," Southwest Climate Change Network, September 15, 2008, http://www.southwestclimatechange.org/impacts/water/groundwater.

13. W. M. Alley, ed., "Five-Year Interim Report of the United States–Mexico Transboundary Aquifer Assessment Program: 2007–2012," U.S. Geological Survey (USGS) Open-File Report 2013-1059, USGS, 2013, http://pubs.usgs.gov/of/2013/1059.

14. Wilder et al., "Climate Change and U.S.-Mexico Border Communities." Also see the full National Climate Assessment released in 2014: http://nca2014.globalchange.gov.

15. Garfin et al., *Assessment of Climate Change in the Southwest United States*, 3.

16. City of San Diego, "Climate Action Plan Working Draft," February 2014, http://www.sandiego.gov/planning/genplan/cap.

17. Wilder et al., "Climate Change and U.S.-Mexico Border Communities," addresses socioeconomic features of the border in light of climate change.

18. U.S. Bureau of Reclamation (USBR), "Colorado River Basin Water Supply and Demand Study," USBR, 2010, http://www.usbr.gov/lc/region/programs/crbstudy/finalreport.

19. Rowan Jacobson, "The Day We Set the Colorado River Free," *Outside Magazine* (July 2014), is a useful journalistic account of this pulse flow and the effort to restore parts of the delta. For the text of Minute 319, see "Minute no. 319," International Boundary and Water Commission, http://www.ibwc.gov/Files/Minutes/Minute_319.pdf.

20. See the comment letter by the Good Neighbor Environmental Board, October 20, 2004, on the GNEB website: http://www.epa.gov/ocem/gneb.

21. The April 2004 Border Institute VI of the Southwest Consortium for Environmental Research and Policy explored the challenges of binational ecosystem conservation; D. Rick Van Schoik, "Proceedings of Border Institute VI: Transboundary Ecosystem Management," in *Connecting Mountain Islands and Desert Seas: Biodiversity and Management of the Madrean Archipelago II*, comp. Gerald J. Gottfried et al. Proceedings RMRS-P-36 (Fort Collins, CO: U.S. Department of Agriculture, Forest Service, Rocky Mountain Research Station, 2004), 380–83.

22. For the Big Bend region and adjacent areas in Mexico, see Kris Axtman, "Big Bend's Big Problems," *Christian Science Monitor*, November 18, 2003; Mary E. Kelly and Héctor M. Arias Rojo, "River Restoration in the Chihuahuan Desert: The Río Conchos and the Forgotten River Stretch of the Rio Grande," Border Institute VI, Southwest Consortium for Environmental Research and Policy, April 13, 2004, www.scerp.org; for the San Diego–Baja California border area, see "Las Californias Binational Conservation Initiative: A Vision for Habitat Conservation in the Border Region of California and Baja California" (prepared by the Conservation Biology Institute, September 2004), http://www.consbio.org.

23. Laura López-Hoffman et al., eds., *Conservation of Shared Environments: Learning from the United States and Mexico* (Tucson: University of Arizona Press, 2009). Also see Ana Córdova and Carlos de la Parra, eds., *A Barrier to Our Shared Environment: The Border Fence between the United States and Mexico* (Mexico City: Secretariat of Environment and Natural Resources, 2007).

24. Michael J. Cohen and Karen H. Hyun, "Hazard: The Future of the Salton Sea with No Restoration Project," Pacific Institute, May 1, 2006, http://pacinst.org/publication/restoration-project-critical-to-salton-seas-future.

25. See, for example, New River Improvement Project Technical Advisory Committee, *Strategic Plan: New River Improvement Project, December 2011*, CalEPA, http://www.calepa.ca.gov.

26. On the environment of the border in general, see Paul Ganster and Hartmut Walter, eds., *Environmental Hazards and Bioresource Management in the United States–Mexico Borderlands* (Los Angeles: University of California, Los Angeles, Latin American Center Publications, 1990); Paul Ganster, ed., *The U.S.-Mexican Border Environment: A Road Map to a Sustainable 2020*, SCERP Monograph Series 1 (San Diego, CA: San Diego State University Press, 2000). The SCERP Monograph Series (http://www.scerp.org) provides recent information on air and water, hazardous waste, environmental management, and other aspects of the border environment. The website of the

U.S.-Mexico Border 2020 Program (http://www.epa.gov/usmexicoborder) is also a very rich source of information on the border environment.

27. Joseph Newman, "Maquiladoras Achieve Only 12 Percent Hazmat Compliance," *EnviroMexico* 9 (November 1996): 1–2.

28. Commission on Environmental Cooperation, "Metales y Derivados Final Factual Record," *North American Environmental and Law and Policy* 8 (2002), is the CEC's report on the case.

29. Claudia Villacorta and Ricardo Martinez, "Dispelling a Myth of Industrial Wastewater Pollution in Tijuana," *Southwest Hydrology* 4, no. 5 (September/October 2005): 30–31.

30. Richard M. Gersberg et al., "Quality of Urban Runoff in the Tijuana River Watershed," in *The U.S.-Mexican Border Environment: Water Issues along the U.S.-Mexican Border*, ed. Paul Westerhoff, SCERP Monograph Series 3 (San Diego, CA: San Diego State University Press, 2000).

31. Kimberly Collins, *Understanding Air Pollution and Health in the Binational Airshed of the Imperial and Mexicali Valleys*, rev. ed. (Calexico, CA: California Center for Border and Regional Economic Studies, San Diego State University, Calexico, 2003); Alan Sweedler, ed., *The U.S.-Mexican Border: Air Quality Issues along the U.S.-Mexican Border*, SCERP Monograph Series 6 (San Diego, CA: San Diego State University Press, 2003); Ross Pumfrey, ed., *The U.S.-Mexican Border Environment: Binational Air Quality Management*, SCERP Monograph Series 14 (San Diego, CA: San Diego State University Press, 2006).

32. See the website for the Joint Advisory Committee (http://www.jac-ccc.org). Important recommendations of the committee have been implemented, including use of oxygenated gasoline in El Paso and Ciudad Juárez to reduce ozone, development of an air-quality plan for Ciudad Juárez, and a vehicle inspection program for Ciudad Juárez.

33. Penelope J. E. Quintana et al., "Risky Borders: Air Pollution and Health Effects at U.S.-Mexican Ports of Entry," *Journal of Borderlands Studies* (forthcoming, 2015).

34. U.S. Government, "Federal Actions to Address Environmental Justice in Minority Populations and Low-Income Populations," 1994; David V. Carruthers, ed., *Environmental Justice in Latin America: Problems, Promise, and Practice* (Cambridge, MA: MIT Press, 2008); Quintana et al., "Risky Borders."

35. Paul Ganster, "Evolving Environmental Management and Community Engagement at the U.S.-Mexican Border," *Eurasia Border Review* 5, no. 1 (spring 2014): 19–40; U.S.-Mexico Border 2020 Program (http://www2.epa.gov/border2020).

36. See *The U.S.-Mexico Border XXI Program: Progress Report 1996–2000* (Washington, D.C.: U.S. Environmental Protection Agency and Mexican Secretariat of Environment, Natural Resources, and Fisheries, 2000).

37. Information on Border 2012 and the many activities associated with the program can be found at http://www.epa.gov/border2012.

38. See Border 2012, *U.S.-Mexico Environmental Program, Indicators Report 2005* (final draft, April 19, 2006), available at http://www.epa.gov/border2012.

39. "What Is Border 2020?" U.S. Environmental Protection Agency, http://www2.epa.gov/border2020/what-border-2020.

40. See the letter sent by the Good Neighbor Environmental Board of April 16, 2006, to the president and Congress in support of NADB (http://www.epa.gov/ocem/gneb). The Border Trade Alliance (http://www.thebta.org), a grassroots advocacy organization that supports expanded trade with Canada, Mexico, and the Americas, lobbied heavily in Washington, D.C., to retain and enhance NADB.

41. An excellent summary of BECC-NADB accomplishments is BECC-NADB, "Quarterly Status Report, June 30, 2014," BECC, http://www.becc.org/uploads/files/06-30-14_becc-nadb_sr_final_eng.pdf.

42. BECC-NADB, "Quarterly Status Report, June 30, 2014."

43. For additional information on these filings and the activities of the Commission for Environmental Cooperation, see the CEC website (http://www.cec.org).

44. GNEB reports are available at http://www.epa.gov/ocem/gneb.

45. See, for example, the National Center for Border Security and Immigration—Borders, with headquarters at the University of Arizona (http://www.borders.arizona.edu); Paul Ganster, ed., *SCERP Monograph Series: The U.S.-Mexican Border Environment*, 16 vols. (San Diego, CA: San Diego State University Press, 2000–2012).

46. Health Resources and Services Administration, as referenced on the United States–Mexico Border Health Commission website (http://www.borderhealth.org); Dennis L. Soden, "At the Cross Roads: US/Mexico Border Counties in Transition," IPED Technical Reports, Paper 27, March 2006, http://digitalcommons.utep.edu/iped_techrep/27.

47. Bruce Selcraig, "Poisonous Flows the Rio Grande," *Los Angeles Times*, October 25, 1992.

48. A study published by the *American Journal of Epidemiology* found that men who worked with certain chemicals were at least two times more likely than the average male to father an anencephalic child. See Danielle Knight, "Birth Defects Continue in U.S.-Mexico Border Areas," study produced by Interpress Service (PeaceNet), June 19, 1998.

49. See Teresa N. Quitugua et al., "Transmission of Drug-Resistant Tuberculosis in Texas and Mexico," *Journal of Clinical Microbiology* 40, no. 2 (August 2002): 2716–24; the *2005 Annual Report* of the United States–Mexico Border Health Commission provides details on the TB and other border programs (http://www.borderhealth.org/reports.php?curr=about_us#J2005).

50. Jorge Augusto Arredondo Vega, "Trade in Health Services in the Mexico-U.S. Border Area" (paper presented at the World Health Organization Meeting on International Trade in Health Services, Geneva, June 1997); Michelle Weinberg et al., "The U.S.-Mexico Border Infectious Disease Surveillance Project: Establishing Binational Border Surveillance," *Emerging Infectious Disease* 19, no. 1 (January 2003).

51. For the case of Alogodones, see Alex P. Oberle and Daniel D. Arreola, "Mexican Medical Border Towns: A Case Study of Algodones, Baja California," *Journal of Borderlands Studies* 19, no. 2 (2004): 27–44.

52. The website of the Pan American Health Organization (PAHO) discusses the reasons for closing the El Paso Field Office. See "PAHO/WHO's US-Mexico Border Field Office to Conclude Mission after Seven Decades of Service," PAHO, http://www.paho.org/hq/index.php?option=com_content&view=article&id=9286&Itemid=1926&lang=en.

53. The website of the United States–Mexico Border Health Commission (http://www.borderhealth.org) includes useful information on border health problems and the work of the commission.

54. The U.S. census counts residents on the reservations of border tribes, and often these figures include Native Americans who are not members of the reservation's tribe, as well as non–Native Americans residing on the reservation. In addition, most U.S. border tribes have many tribal members who do not reside on the reservation, and it is likely that not all tribal members responded to the census. The 2000 Mexican census provides data on Mexican border and border state tribes.

55. Felipe López and David Runsten, "Mixtecs and Zapotecs Working in California: Rural and Urban Experiences" (paper presented at the conference Indígenas Mexicanos Migrantes en Estados Unidos: Construyendo Puentes entre Investigadors y Líderes Comunitarios, University of California, Santa Cruz, October 11–12, 2002).

56. Good Neighbor Environmental Board, *U.S.-Mexican Border Environment: Air Quality and Transportation & Cultural and Natural Resources: Ninth Report of the Good Neighbor Environmental Board to the President and Congress of the United States* (Washington, D.C.: U.S. Environmental Protection Agency, March 2006), available at http://www.epa.gov/ocem/gneb.

57. Comisión Nacional para el Desarrollo de los Pueblos Indígenas, "Indicadores socioeconómicos de los pueblos indígenas de México," 2002, http://www.cdi.gob.mx/index.

58. Center for California Native Nations, University of California at Riverside, "An Impact Analysis of Tribal Government Gaming in California, January 2006," available at http://www.cnn.ucr.edu.

59. Asa Revels and Janet Cummings, "The Impact of Drug Trafficking on American Indian Reservations with International Boundaries," *American Indian Quarterly* 38, no. 3 (summer 2014).

60. Good Neighbor Environmental Board, *A Blueprint for Action on the U.S.-Mexico Border. Thirteenth Report of the Good Neighbor Environmental Board to the President and Congress of the United States* (Washington, D.C.: U.S. Environmental Protection Agency, 2010).

8

BORDER ISSUES IN
U.S.-MEXICAN RELATIONS

Drug Trafficking, Security, Migration,
NAFTA, and Transborder Cooperation

DRUG TRAFFICKING

Beginning in the 1980s and continuing into the next century, drug trafficking emerged as a pressing issue in border life, broadly affecting U.S.-Mexican relations as well as the regional economy and society. The United States blamed Mexico for its role as the source of the illegal drugs and for its failure to prevent the drugs from being transshipped through the border region to the United States. Indeed, Mexico had clearly come to supplant Colombia in the U.S.–Latin American drug trade; Andean countries controlled the production of cocaine and Colombia controlled the refining, but Mexican drug lords dominated distribution to and marketing within the United States. One analyst estimated that, in 1984, Mexico was the source of 36 percent of the heroin, 30 percent of the cocaine, and 9 percent of the marijuana sold in the United States. By 2006, the President's Office of National Drug Control Strategy reported that 65 percent of the narcotics sold in the U.S. market entered across the southwestern border.[1] Mexico countered such charges by arguing that its extensive drug interdiction programs could not change the fact that the U.S. market represented the principal stimulant to drug trafficking. U.S. consumers continued to spend billions of dollars per year on illegal drugs. The U.S. government estimates that Mexican traffickers receive more than $13.8 billion in revenue from illicit drug sales to the United States; 61 percent of that revenue, or $8.5 billion, is directly tied to marijuana export sales. Some 8.1 percent of the total population aged twelve and older in the United States had used illegal drugs in 2005. Drug addiction in Mexico was also a growing problem that intensified during the 1990s. Domestic production of marijuana in California, Kentucky, and Tennessee probably accounted for one-half of U.S. consumption of that substance.

As border drug smuggling interdiction efforts increased, drug traffickers showed considerable ingenuity. As the border between San Diego and Baja California became more controlled, Mexican drug traffickers moved marijuana cultivation efforts across the border to San Diego County. In 2005 law enforcement seized more domestically cultivated marijuana in the San Diego region than they seized crossing the San Diego region's border points of entry.[2] It should be remembered that cross-border drug smuggling is very dynamic; as border controls in one region of the border are tightened, smuggling shifts elsewhere. When the San Diego sector was flooded with Border Patrol officers and the triple fence was installed, smugglers turned to tunneling under the fences or going around in open boats. Recently, narcotics have been launched across the fence with catapults and potato guns, and small drones have been used for small quantities of drugs.[3] The heated exchanges between U.S. and Mexican spokespeople on the drug issue were reminiscent of the Prohibition years, when illegal substances had similarly shaped border life and affected international relations.

Just as during Prohibition, the trade in illegal substances was both a boon and a bane for border communities. It brought benefits to some individuals and to some local communities, providing jobs and investment capital and stimulating local markets for a broad array of legal as well as illegal goods and services. Infusion of large amounts of cash into the border region stimulated in some regions an exuberant style of architecture that was often referred to as "narcoarchitecture."[4] But regional social costs—violence abetted by high-tech weaponry, organized crime, corruption of local officials, addiction, and health problems (including HIV/AIDS infection) from Los Angeles to Mexico City—far outweighed the benefits. The drug malaise spread like a cancer from the border nexus. Gangs involved in the trade and its associated service industries routinely crossed the border to engage in illegal activities and escape detection and prosecution. The total cost of illicit drug use in the United States—in lost productivity, increased crime, and other impacts—was estimated to be $180.9 billion in 2002; by 2007 it was more than 198.0 billion.[5]

By the late 1980s the concern over the trade in illegal drugs led the United States to station the National Guard at the international boundary; by the 1990s there was widespread fear that the border would be militarized in order to control the flow of drugs and migrants. In 1997 the U.S. Department of Defense, responding to an outcry against the use of the military in drug-trafficking assignments along the U.S.-Mexican border, ordered U.S. ground-troop units to halt foot patrols in the region. The action was a clear result of the heavy criticism from citizens and officials in Texas and Mexico following an incident in which a U.S. marine shot an eighteen-year-old high school student along the Texas border. The two hundred or so soldiers and marines supporting overall U.S. antidrug efforts at the border were withdrawn, although the National Guard continues to serve in support roles for the immigration and customs authorities along the southern border.[6]

From the 1990s on, fierce competition among Mexican drug-trafficking gangs and families produced an ongoing series of drug wars in a number of border cities, producing assassinations of rival gang members and the murders of government officials, public safety officers, and reporters. In September 2006, U.S. ambassador to Mexico Tony Garza issued an advisory message to Americans, citing rising violence in Mexico related to drug trafficking. He noted that "drug cartels, aided by corrupt officials, reign unchecked in many towns along our common border" and that 1,500 Mexicans had lost their lives to narco-violence during the year.[7] In 2005, there were 182 murders in the border town of Nuevo Laredo, Tamaulipas, and the Arellano-Felix drug cartel, operating out of Tijuana, was responsible for some 500 murders over several years, most in Mexico but some in the United States. Mexican authorities reported that there were 295 homicides in Tijuana in 2003, most related to the drug wars.[8] By the dawn of the twenty-first century, it was clear to Mexican federal and border leaders that the drug problem had become a national Mexican problem, impacting all levels of society. According to estimates, by 2010 3 to 4 percent of Mexico's gross domestic product (GDP) derived from the drug trade, which employed some 450,000 people.[9]

Mexico installed its first democratically elected president from an opposition party in 2000, Vicente Fox of the Partido Acción Nacional (PAN), but his administration continued the traditional accommodation of drug-trafficking organizations and did little to stem the mounting violence and corruption related to drugs. Fox's successor, President Felipe Calderón, who took office in 2006, met the problem head-on through deployment of tens of thousands of troops to staff check points, replacement or shadowing of local law enforcement, implementation of street patrols, and oversight of law enforcement in states with high levels of drug violence. This strategy may have backfired; the fragmentation of the structure of the drug cartels increased violence, and Mexico in 2010 had some eleven thousand drug-related murders, with twenty-seven hundred homicides in Ciudad Juárez.[10] Calderón's successor, Enrique Peña Nieto, who took office in 2012, modified the strategy of confronting the drug cartels directly with the military, implementing a policy with an emphasis on economic development and reform. However, this approach did not quell the violence, and by early 2015 Peña Nieto faced increasing criticism by Mexican public opinion.

Border Patrol vehicle near border fence in the mountains east of San Diego. The three tires are dragged behind the vehicle to smooth the road so that later undocumented crossers will leave footprints. 2004.

During the 1990s, drug trafficking became more closely linked with efforts to control the movement of people as the United States stepped up efforts to enforce its smuggling laws at the border. Programs by the Border Patrol such as Operation Hold the Line (1993) in El Paso, Operation Gatekeeper (1994) in the San Diego sector, and Operation Safeguard (1994) in Nogales, Arizona, increased the number of agents on the border, especially near major border cities. These efforts were accompanied by the addition or extension of high steel fences, new unpaved roads for law enforcement activities, sensors, video cameras, lighting at night, and aerial surveillance. Because these actions, for example, made it very difficult for migrants to cross in the San Diego area, the flow of migrants was deflected eastward, first to the mountains of Southern California and northern Baja California, then to the deserts of the Imperial Valley region, and finally to the desert region of southern Arizona. Eventually, the migrant stream also turned toward the Texas border, another border area with an arid climate and extreme summer temperatures and thus quite hazardous for people crossing on foot. Due to extreme temperature and weather conditions in the mountains and deserts in these areas, the number of migrants who died from exposure skyrocketed. Also, as enforcement increased, the

Increased enforcement, including fences and patrols, have forced undocumented border crossers away from coastal San Diego and into the desert to the east. Summer temperatures can reach 127 degrees in the Imperial Valley where U.S. volunteers, including the Border Angels, provide emergency watering stations for migrants. The mountains in the background are in Mexico. 2006.

number of accidents involving overloaded vehicles carrying undocumented migrants increased as well. The toll in human lives along the border was terrible. From 1998 to 2012 the number of migrant deaths each year increased from 263 to 477 per year, although the number of apprehensions of persons attempting to cross the border declined during that same period by a factor of four, from 1,555,776 to 364,768.[11]

SECURITY

After the September 11, 2001, terrorist attacks on New York and Washington, D.C., the border with Mexico became the object of security concern among U.S. policymakers. Immediately, security checks were tightened along the border. Vehicles and pedestrians wanting to cross into the United States faced long waits, often of two hours or more. This disrupted the lives of many border residents, particularly those who lived in Mexico and worked in the neighboring U.S. twin city. In the post-9/11 months, stories of queuing up

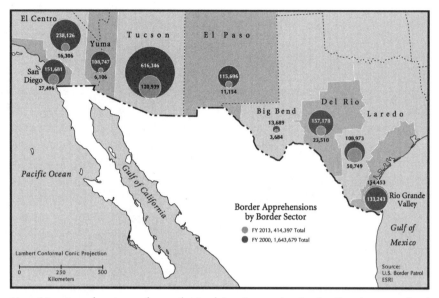

Map 14. *Apprehensions of unauthorized immigrants by Border Patrol sector, fiscal years 2000 and 2013. During this period, total apprehensions declined, as did those on the western half of the border. The eastern part of the border saw an increase in apprehensions.*

at 3 a.m. in order to get to work by 8 a.m. or staying in the U.S. city during the workweek and returning home to Mexico only on weekends were common everywhere along the border. Even nearly a decade and a half after the terrorist attacks, long lines and unpredictable waiting times to cross the border are common, particularly in the large twin cities of San Diego–Tijuana and El Paso–Ciudad Juárez. Security was also tightened for commercial vehicle crossings into the United States. X-ray technology was installed to scan each entering truck for unauthorized cargo, larger numbers of cargo trailers were unloaded, and paperwork was more closely scrutinized. These efforts translated into longer waiting times for trucks, which raised costs for shippers and also increased congestion at ports of entry, with idling trucks adding considerably to local air pollution problems. A 2005 analysis of the costs of increased waiting times for commercial crossings and personal travel at the border between San Diego and Tijuana produced surprising results. In this one border region, border delays cost the U.S. and Mexican economies an estimated $7.2 billion in gross output in 2007, resulting in 60,000 jobs lost or not created.[12] Studies from other ports of entry along the border indicate equivalent costs due to long waits for northbound crossing. In total these delays cost many

Truck being scanned by gamma ray technology that reveals undeclared cargo. Otay Mesa Port of Entry, San Diego, 2006.

billions of dollars, amounting to an enormous "security tax" on border residents and companies.

Washington, D.C., policymakers and many residents in the U.S. border region view border security in terms of enhancing border controls to prevent the unauthorized entrance of people or materials that might be used in terrorist attacks. The refrain "Secure the southern border" is ubiquitous in national politics in the United States, uttered with great regularity and without thought by elected officials and the administration. Residents of the Mexican side of the border, however, tend to view security in terms of personal safety and public order. The 1990s saw growing levels of crime throughout Mexico and in the border region, including high-profile drug killings and kidnapping of business executives and family members of the wealthy. This ongoing crime wave is compounded by low levels of confidence among border Mexicans in the local, state, and federal police; nationally only one in five crimes is reported, and few of those are solved. The result is that most border Mexicans do not feel safe from crime. A survey of major urban areas of Mexico conducted in 2005 documents this perception of a lack of personal safety, with 84 percent in Ciudad Juárez, 80 percent in Nuevo Laredo, 75 percent in Tijuana, and 48 percent in Mexicali reporting that they feel unsafe. Baja California leads the nation in crime, with more than 2.5 times as many crimes per capita as the national average for the period from 1990 to 2005. Tijuana and Mexicali were among Mexico's most dangerous cities.[13] By 2014, security had improved in the Baja California border region, although Ciudad Juárez and the Mexican cities along the lower Rio Grande had not made much progress in restoring security or reducing homicides and other crimes.[14] The border was a paradox in terms of personal security, however. While Mexican border cities had high murder and crime rates, U.S. border cities such as San Diego and El Paso were among the safest in the nation.

Ciudad Juárez has also been plagued by crime for the past decade and a half. Particularly shocking has been the number of women who have been murdered and whose bodies have been dumped by the roadside or buried in shallow graves in the desert. Even though the homicide rate for women (per 100,000 inhabitants) was higher in Toluca (4.4), Tecate (3.0), and Acapulco (2.6) than in Ciudad Juárez (2.4), for the period from 1998 to 2004, many of the Ciudad Juárez murders were particularly gruesome. In 84 of the 373 murders of women between 1990 and 2004, the victims had suffered humiliating, painful, and cruel deaths, with their bodies showing visible signs of torture. The murders continued at high levels through 2014. The heinous nature of these murders, along with the alleged incompetence and indifference of law enforcement and political authorities, attracted the attention of Mexican and U.S. human rights organizations, scholars, and community leaders. Recently, Hollywood celebrities have added their voices to the growing outcry.

Theories abound regarding both the perpetrators and their victims. The victims in Ciudad Juárez are of similar age, marital status, and education level to those in other Mexican cities. Some recent research also suggests that high femicide rates may not be restricted to Ciudad Juárez but may be consistent with rates in nonborder Mexican cities and even a few U.S. cities.[15] One difference, however, is that many of the Ciudad Juárez victims worked in maquiladoras and apparently disappeared on their way to or from work. Some observers believe the Ciudad Juárez murders to be part of what is referred to as "situational violence"—domestic violence as well as drug, gang, and robbery activities. Others suggest that responsibility lies with an organized group linked to wealthy businessmen, police, drug traffickers, and politicians involved in organized prostitution, pornography, and the like. Still other commentators suspect serial copycat killers or a broad unorganized reaction by unconnected men against changing social roles sparked by globalization and the growing independence of women in border towns. Although much is unknown in regard to these terrible murders, there is agreement in several areas. First, the police and prosecuting authorities have not properly investigated these cases and brought those responsible to justice. Second, it is likely that most of the victims did not know the perpetrators and that the women were killed because they were women.[16]

MIGRATION

Migration has been one of the most enduring and sensitive border issues for Mexico and the United States. A host of concerns raised by legal and undocumented immigration to the United States from Mexico and the status and treatment of legal and unauthorized residents of the border region have time and again been at the center of conflict between the two countries. The migration debate has pitted citizens of Mexico against citizens of the United States and citizens of the United States against one another.

The immigration "problem" is a creation of the twentieth century. From 1848 until the end of the nineteenth century, the border was not patrolled, and migration across it concerned few people. Early U.S. immigration legislation (in 1917 and 1924) generally made exceptions for Mexican migrants; only in 1929 did it become a violation of the law to enter the United States from Mexico without documentation.

The tensions caused by the migration issue, as we now think of it, emerged in the 1940s with the institutionalized flow of Mexican temporary workers under the Bracero Program, as U.S. farmers sought Mexican labor during the peak of the wartime economic boom. One unforeseen result of the program was the emergence of a network throughout Mexico, at the border, and in the United States that both stimulated and facilitated migration for seasonal or permanent employment in the United States. U.S. economic expansion in the postwar period was concentrated in the states where migrant networks were most ingrained. Jobs in cities—and in services—became more common, and this employment was generally not seasonal in nature. As a result, migration became more permanent and increasingly characterized by the movement of families rather than of individual males. The flow of migrants became dizzyingly diverse, consisting of many groups moving for many different reasons.

Once a network was established and family members were in place to provide communications and assistance, the migrant flow could not simply be shut off whenever the U.S. economy cooled down. The fact that migrant populations from Mexico had historically been recognized and accepted as U.S. citizens after a period of work and acculturation, regardless of reforms in U.S. immigration laws, reinforced migration networks and migrant lore.[17]

The northward flow of workers increasingly became considered illegal as U.S. immigration law changed. In other words, even as the number of migrants in relation to the populations of the sending and receiving nations remained fairly steady, changes in U.S. immigration law caused an increasing number of Mexican migrants to fall into a different legal status than those who had preceded them. For example, the 1965 amendments to the Immigration and Nationality Act eliminated national-origin quotas. Coming as it did at the end of the Bracero Program, this reform (and further modifications of the law in 1976) had the effect of converting, almost overnight, the status of a large portion of the long-established Mexican migrant flow from legal to illegal. Ironically, with these changes in immigration law, the debate in the United States over migrant labor switched from a traditional focus on quotas for legal immigrants to concerns about illegal, or unauthorized, immigrants.

The fate of the much debated Immigration Reform and Control Act of 1986 (IRCA) has proven that the immigration dilemma cannot easily be solved. After a brief three-year period during which the promulgation of the act seemed to slow border crossings, migration climbed to its previous levels. The act also sent mixed signals to potential migrants by creating a framework for the legalization of the status of millions of unauthorized Mexicans who had been living in the United States; by the fall of 1988 some 3.1 million had applied for amnesty.[18] In 2006, one of IRCA's authors, former senator Alan Simpson, acknowledged that a failure of the legislation was that it lacked adequate provisions to prevent employers from hiring undocumented workers.[19] Thus, the act did not fundamentally change the demand for unauthorized immigrant laborers.

Several findings of recent literature on immigration refute widely held beliefs about the causes, consequences, social characteristics, and costs of migration from Mexico to the United States.[20] Migration from Mexico, for example, correlates much more strongly with U.S. employment needs than with Mexican unemployment. And the principal benefit to employers of migrant labor was not its low cost but its flexibility. Many recent studies do not detect any statistically significant difference between the characteristics of legal and undocumented migrants: age, family status, education, English proficiency, and income were more important than legal status in determining how Mexican migrants affected the U.S. economy, whether they stayed, how well they assimilated, and how they fared economically.[21] Counter to the prevailing popular view, the assimilation of new arrivals from Mexico was considerably faster than that of other historical migrant groups to the United States: 90 percent of first-generation Hispanics born in California had native fluency in English; in the second generation only 50 percent still spoke Spanish.[22] Hispanics also enter into mixed marriages more often than other cultural or ethnic groups. The 2000 U.S. Census revealed large numbers of interracial partnering of Hispanics with whites and other groups in all the U.S. border states; this was even more pronounced in the 2010 census, with 17 percent in Texas, 16 percent in Arizona, 18 percent in California, and 22 percent in New Mexico.[23]

A large body of recent research conducted by experts on migration issues indicates that both Mexico and the United States probably gained more than they lost from the northward flow of Mexican people in the period between 1940 and 1995.[24] Some immigrants were clearly net beneficiaries of certain U.S. public services (notably primary and middle school education), but in general those costs were more than recouped in the form of benefits to hundreds of thousands of employers (who profited from paying low wages) as well as to millions of consumers (who benefited from paying low prices). Although some states, such as California and Texas, and gateway cities, such as Los Angeles and New York, incurred substantial net fiscal costs for migration, the national advantage outweighed the difference. This situation, however, rendered the allocation of tax resources a major source of conflict between state and local governments, on the one hand, and the federal government, on the other. Local governments incur most of the costs for services provided to unauthorized immigrants, but the federal government, which receives significant tax payments from undocumented workers, does not reimburse local entities for these expenses. For the Mexican economy, immigrants' remittances to family members became one of the major sources of foreign exchange and in 2006 reached an annual total of about $30 billion. Due to the 2008–2009 U.S. recession and other factors, remittances declined to $22 billion in 2013, which was still more that the 2013 tourism receipts of $13.9 billion and second only to petroleum exports.[25]

The causes of migration proved to be much more complex than previously believed. Far more important for migrants than the simple push-and-pull factors of wage differentials were larger, global issues of market consolidation (including North American integration), the process of learning that accrues to migrants (sometimes called human capital), and the networks created by migration (sometimes referred to as social capital). Consequently, migrants generally came not from poor, isolated communities disconnected from international markets but from areas undergoing rapid change as the result of insertion into global production networks. Migrants sought not income but investment capital and insurance against risk in their communities of origin.[26]

The problems with migration, according to new studies, primarily concerned its contribution to continuing poverty. Migrants tended to depress the

wages of low-skilled U.S. workers, for example, particularly the 10 percent of
the U.S. workforce with fewer than twelve years of education. And migrants
themselves—again, those with the least schooling—sometimes remained mired
in poverty, forcing them to rely on public assistance in the United States.[27] In
times of economic downturn, migrants suffered the brunt of concerns over
scarce jobs. In California during the early 1990s, for example, voters passed a
series of laws to exclude unauthorized migrants from public benefits. Migrant
life also remained insecure: in 1996 and 1997, changes in U.S. enforcement
led to a series of deaths, as migrants were compelled to reroute their journeys
northward and cross through less hospitable border terrain.

Many migration experts supported alternative approaches to the largely
ineffectual, periodic policy tightening and border-crossing enforcement on
the part of the United States. Such established policies generally had not been
logical responses to the deep-level causes and consequences of migration but
rather short-term reactions driven by political debates that were locked in
outdated understandings of the phenomenon. In general, the experts believed,
U.S. policies based in efforts to drive up the cost of migrating actually lowered
the odds of repatriation and increased the numbers of permanent undocumented residents, converting a circular movement into a unidirectional flow.[28]
Some specialists believed that annual quotas or formal guest worker programs
would be more successful solutions to what was seen as a likely permanent
immigration reality.

Regardless of scholarly assessments of the meanings and impacts of migration from Mexico, the flow of workers from Mexico to the United States
has historically been accompanied by acrimonious debate over both its short-
term and long-term economic and social effects. In the United States many
agribusiness, manufacturing, and service employers of migrants—legal and
unauthorized—argued for easy access to inexpensive Mexican labor. Organized labor, in contrast, argued that low wage rates put U.S. workers out of
jobs. Many residents of the United States felt that by allowing or implicitly
encouraging Mexican migration, the United States was losing control of its
borders and thus of its sovereignty. Further complicating the picture was
the importance of the migration "safety valve" to Mexican political stability,
which was a prime concern for U.S. national security. Both Mexican and
U.S. analysts understand that the ongoing outflow of discontented, motivated
individuals from Mexican communities to jobs in the United States, coupled
with the flow back of remittances to those same regions, facilitated Mexican
political stability.

Adding to the difficulty of understanding illegal immigration to the
United States from Mexico is the inability to measure the flow accurately.[29]

Problems in Immigration and Naturalization Service (INS) data collection—such as the fact that the same individuals were sometimes counted repeatedly and the number of aliens seized rose when the INS and the Border Patrol received increased funding—kept policymakers in the dark about the real dimensions of migration. And the changing dynamics and scale of migration, which might have had a major impact on policy, were little understood—migrants increasingly came from urban rather than rural areas, they more often sought manufacturing and service employment instead of agricultural work, they more frequently came to the U.S. border states intending to stay permanently, and more women and families joined the flow.

The continuing flow of immigrants across the porous boundary and into the border region was from time to time accompanied by hostility and heightened tensions in the bilateral relationship. Periodic bouts of violence against immigrants at the hands of the U.S. Border Patrol, proven or alleged, received much media attention and led Mexico to lodge formal complaints with the United States and to include the issue in discussions between Mexican and U.S. presidents.[30] With each attempt to crack down on migrants—for example, the mid-1990s initiatives known as Operation Hold the Line in El Paso and Operation Gatekeeper in the San Diego region—U.S.-Mexican relations suffered. Mexico charged that its citizens were physically mistreated, deprived of food and water, kept in crowded jail cells, and denied first aid after apprehension by the Border Patrol. These measures disrupted local economies but seemed to have little effect on long-distance migrants, who simply crossed the border at other places. Ironically, stepped-up enforcement discouraged migrants from returning to Mexico and encouraged them to remain permanently in the United States.

Available data clearly suggest that the United States will be unable to stop the movement of people northward as long as North American economic integration continues, migrant networks exist to direct the flow and allocate jobs, and the communities sending migrants need their remittances for investment and insurance purposes. It is not clear that immigration law reforms in 1986 and 1996 or militarization of the border have succeeded in appreciably slowing the flow; in fact they have sometimes encouraged migrants to stay in the United States. It seems safe to predict that migration will continue to haunt U.S.-Mexican relations and debate over the issue will continue to shape life in the border region.

In the first decade and a half of the twenty-first century, the contentious political debate about immigration continued as the nature of the flow of unauthorized migrants evolved. As awareness emerged that many U.S. regions had large numbers of unauthorized immigrants deeply embedded in the economy and society, the debate became national, and decisions were often made in Congress by elected officials who did not understand the realities of the border region with Mexico. By 2000, there were 8.6 million unauthorized immigrants, increasingly spread throughout the country beyond the border region, in the South, the Midwest, and Northeast. As these numbers increased to 12.2 million in 2007, the level of acrimonious political debate increased. The perception prevailed that these undocumented people were mainly from Mexico and had entered across the southern border; however, in 2012 only 52 percent were from Mexico.[31] When George W. Bush assumed office early in 2001, one of his goals was to address the problem of undocumented immigration. However, political support for reform evaporated with the September 11, 2001, terrorist attacks on New York and Washington, D.C., and attention shifted to homeland security and controlling, or hardening, the southern border. The U.S. recession that began in 2007 and emerged full-blown in 2008 likewise eliminated widespread political support for immigration reform. President Barack Obama faced a divided and dysfunctional Congress, and no progress on immigration was made until he began to alter immigration policy through executive action in 2014. These efforts coincided with those of several U.S. states, including California, which began to address concerns about undocumented residents through actions such as issuing driver's licenses and legitimizing study in public universities.

The flow of migration across the border between Mexico and the United States is a complex and dynamic phenomenon, influenced by recessions and growth in the U.S. economy, the state of the Mexican economy, border enforcement, enforcement of U.S. labor laws, and other factors. For example, hardening the border to prevent unauthorized immigrants from entering the country encouraged more family members to migrate to the United States to stay with working mothers and fathers. This enabled families to remain together and to avoid both trips to Mexico and incurring the risks and expense of crossing back into the United States. In fiscal year (FY) 2014, for the first time more non-Mexicans (252,600) than Mexicans (226,771) were apprehended at the border with Mexico; apprehensions were last that low in 1970, with 219,000 apprehensions.[32]

For decades, some migrants detained at the border were unaccompanied minors, age seventeen and under, attempting to reconnect with their families in the United States. These children had to be housed separately from adult detainees and provided with schooling and other services; eventually most were released to a relative in the United States as they could not be deported like adults. From FY 2009 through FY 2014, the yearly number of Mexican unaccompanied minors averaged fewer than 15,000. In FY 2012, the numbers of children from Central America surged, and by FY 2014 the numbers totaled

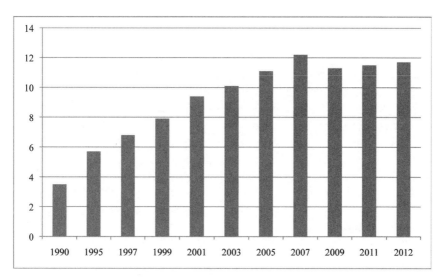

U.S. unauthorized immigrant population in millions, 1990–2012. (Jeffrey S. Passel, D'Vera Cohn, and Ana Gonzalez-Barrera, "Population Decline of Unauthorized Immigrants Stalls, May Have Reversed," Washington, D.C.: Pew Research Center, September 23, 2013)

67,339. Mexican children made up 83 percent in FY 2009, a figure that declined to just 23 percent in FY 2014. High rates of poverty, gang violence, and drug trafficking had driven these children to flee Honduras, El Salvador, and Guatemala.[33] Ironically, some part of that violence in Central America can be attributed to deportation of gang leaders from the Los Angeles area and other parts of the United States in the 1990s. When these hardened criminals arrived in El Salvador and other Central American countries, they proceeded to apply locally the lessons learned in the United States, leading to greater criminality and instability in local societies.[34]

In 2005 and 2006, the intersection of drug-trafficking concerns, efforts to slow unauthorized migrants at the border, and fears of terrorists using the border created a political storm that resulted in another flare-up of the national debate about immigration. In the period since the last debate and policy reaction (the IRCA in 1986), however, the nature of migration from Mexico had again changed in important ways. By the early twenty-first century, for example, undocumented immigrants had moved far beyond the border region and could be found throughout the nation. Immigration thus became a national issue in a way it had never been before. New realizations also shaped the debate: a large number of undocumented immigrants had U.S. citizen children, who shared with all other U.S. citizens the protections guaranteed by the Constitution, and undocumented migrants and their children were proudly serving in the U.S. armed services, significantly in Afghanistan and Iraq. Proposals in the House and Senate variously included provisions to criminalize unauthorized status, fortify the border, enhance enforcement of employer sanctions, provide a path to citizenship, and create a guest worker program. The debate produced massive public protests in the spring of 2006 by immigrants—undocumented and legal, recent and long-time—and their supporters that surprised all parties to the rancorous debate. Undocumented immigration continued to inspire discussions about providing a path to citizenship and modifying deportation policies so as not to separate undocumented parents from their U.S. citizen children or undocumented children who had arrived at a young age and grown up as Americans.

TRADE AND THE 1994 NORTH AMERICAN FREE TRADE AGREEMENT

By the 1990s the economies above and below the international boundary had become more closely intertwined than at any earlier time. Awareness of this economic integration was greatly enhanced by the debate over the North American Free Trade Agreement (NAFTA) and its passage by the U.S. Congress in November 1993, followed by implementation beginning in 1994. Ironically—given the spirited debate that preceded the congressional vote—the agreement introduced no fundamental changes to the U.S.-Mexican relationship; the border is the best proof of this fact. NAFTA did establish a framework to facilitate and regulate future commercial and financial flows in North America.[35]

Free trade was the economic policy in Mexico that brought the reforms of Carlos Salinas de Gortari (during his presidency from 1988 to 1994) to the attention of the international community. By spearheading NAFTA, Salinas went forward with the opening of the Mexican economy begun during the administration of Miguel de la Madrid Hurtado (1982–1988) as a response to the economic crisis of the 1980s. The Mexican government's approach to reactivating the economy—which had been hit by a sharp decline in the price of oil and peaking interest rates—was to privatize state-owned companies and facilitate foreign competition and investment in the country. From the mid-1980s, Mexico substantially reduced its tariff rates, amending its laws and its constitution to spur foreign investment. Tariffs that averaged 24 percent in 1984 dropped to 11 percent by 1990. In a 1986 policy shift as important as the

U.S. citizens and extended immigrant families march on May 1, 2006, to protest strict immigration proposals in the U.S. Congress and to advocate for legislation to provide amnesty for undocumented immigrants. San Ysidro (San Diego), 2006.

signing of NAFTA, Mexico committed itself to freer world trade by joining the General Agreement on Tariffs and Trade (GATT). In his pursuit of free trade with the United States, Salinas was responding to the desperate need for investment in a context in which neither oil nor loans could be counted on to fuel Mexican development. Mexican domestic economic policy drove the free trade initiative.

Debate over the establishment of a formal free trade area raged for the three years between 1990 and 1993, after which there was still a long wait to see what NAFTA would mean. Nevertheless, the interdependence of the U.S. and Mexican economies had been a historical fact for at least a century. As already shown, the pace of economic integration of the two countries had increased markedly after World War II until, by the 1980s, Mexico had become the third-largest trading partner of the United States. The border region was particularly closely incorporated into the binational economy as investments, trade, cross-border shopping for goods and services, and labor flows grew across the border. There were several areas in which scholars agreed substantially on the meaning of freer trade for the border region. First was the issue of job creation, loss, and transfer. There was widespread fear that NAFTA would spur a massive relocation of U.S. factory jobs to Mexico. But this concern was based on a gross exaggeration of the role of labor in production costs and location decisions and an underestimation of the expense involved in building new factories and training new workers in Mexico. As many economists pointed out, jobs would be created by the volume and vigor of overall trade; if commerce grew in a balanced way on both sides (which freer trade made more likely), employment would increase in both countries.

Trends after 1994 bore out these assessments. The focus on manufacturing was the central flaw in the argument that free trade would be followed by a general relocation of industrial jobs from the United States to Mexico. The attention on jobs in such industries as steel, autos, textiles, and appliances was generally misplaced. The real action was certain to be in the service sector, which was more important to all three NAFTA-related North American economies (U.S., Mexican, and Canadian) than agriculture and manufacturing combined. Sure enough, the biggest growth areas in the first few years of NAFTA were such services as retailing, banking, communications, transportation, insurance, publishing, tourism, film distribution, education, civil engineering, software design, and natural gas and electric power distribution. Because these industries provided services and products within the Mexican economy and were previously off limits to U.S. capital, such new investments in Mexico implied few if any lost jobs in the United States. While there was great concern expressed in the United States about the effects of relocation of jobs to Mexico, researchers have noted that Mexican operations have enabled many U.S. manufacturing firms to remain competitive in the face of global competition and to add jobs to their domestic operations. It has also been pointed out that typical *maquila* products get about 40 percent of their components from the United States, whereas for products from China sold in the United States, only about 5 percent are of U.S. origin.[36]

A second fear about NAFTA involved wages: $1-per-hour wages in Mexico would surely take jobs from U.S. workers, who were paid much more. But there were many questionable assumptions behind this concern. The commonly cited $1-per-hour pay scales, for example, were atypical in Mexican manufacturing; the infamous 10:1 wage figures were derived from misleading GDP per capita comparisons. Economists pointed out that a better measure would be GDP per industrial worker. There the ratio was 2:1, and it represented the average difference between Mexican and U.S. productivity in advanced industrial installations, which, of course, wages can be expected to reflect. U.S. firms might be able to pay employees half as much, but the workers would then only produce about half as much in the same time. Mexican productivity was low because of poor education, obsolete technology, and inefficient management. Many economists also pointed out that low wages were not the key to future Mexican industrial strength. Mexico's future manufacturing success would depend instead on a whole host of factors, in particular the ability to develop and adapt new technologies and design new products as well as to increase the productivity of its workforce. In modern manufacturing, labor costs generally represent a low proportion of the total value added.

A central issue often overlooked in the jobs-and-wages debate was infrastructure. Even with low wages it frequently cost much more to produce goods in Mexico than in the United States. Electricity was less reliable; railroads were less efficient; roads and ports were in disrepair. And additional costs of production—such as benefits, training, and turnover rates—were at least as important as wages in influencing location decisions. The fact that there was no great rush to move manufacturing jobs to Mexico after NAFTA went into effect indicates that firms were aware of these issues and accustomed to taking them into account in their decision making.

Other fears about NAFTA revolved around migration. Some supporters believed that NAFTA would eventually attract U.S. industry to Mexico, revitalizing Mexico's economy and putting its people to work at home rather than forcing them to seek employment in the United States. This idea, however, was anathema to U.S. organized labor, already distraught because of declining influence and membership (which had fallen from a high of 18.1 million members in 1973 to 16.7 million by 1990 and to 15.7 million in 2005[37]) and worried that U.S. industries would leave the country and Mexican migrants would drive wages down. These fears, although widespread, were not borne out by data on the first several years under NAFTA.[38] Even after ten years of NAFTA and unprecedented levels of Mexican migration to the United States, the link between migration and NAFTA policies is difficult to document. Most likely, imports of inexpensive grains, primarily corn from the United States, caused dislocation among the many small farmers in central and southern Mexico, resulting in their migration out of Mexico in search of economic opportunity. Beyond this case, it is apparent that migration was entrenched in patterns of U.S.-Mexican interdependence going back half a century and fluctuated normally according to economic and other conditions.

Recent research on NAFTA trade outcomes made some observers' early fears appear overblown. Total bilateral trade in goods soared to $266.6 billion per year in 2004 from the $100.3 billion pace of 1994. By 2012, total bilateral trade in goods was $493.5 billion, and Mexico was the number two trading partner after Canada, ahead of Japan and China.[39] Although the recession of 2008 produced a dip in bilateral trade in 2009, the total trade in goods in 2014 was still almost five times the total in 1994 at the beginning of NAFTA. These changes had a direct impact on the border region. With the number

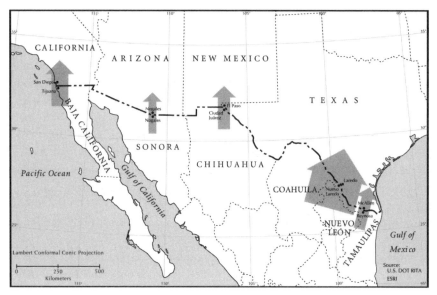

Map 15.   Five leading border freight ports of entry, loaded truck and rail containers, 2013.

of freight cars that made the Piedras Negras–Eagle Pass crossing tripling from 50,000 to 150,000 in the first three years, the twin city challenged Laredo–Nuevo Laredo (which accounted for 60 percent of rail traffic) for first place. In 2004, 69 percent of the value of the bilateral NAFTA merchandise trade with Mexico was carried by truck, and another 12.7 percent was carried by rail.[40] From 1995 through 2004, the number of trucks crossing into the U.S. border states increased 167 percent for California, 109 percent for Arizona, 1,378 percent for New Mexico, and 160 percent for Texas. The chart on the next page shows U.S. imports and exports with Mexico for the first twenty years of NAFTA. Map 15 shows the northbound flow in 2013 of loaded truck and rail containers through the five leading ports of entry along the U.S.-Mexican border. Much of the trade between the two neighbors took place across the land border and through these five ports of entry.

The main turn of events in the early NAFTA period was an increase in intra-industry trade—that is, the exchange of goods within manufacturing sectors and within firms. Such items as electrical machinery, electricity-distribution equipment, telecommunications equipment, office machinery parts, furniture, and automatic data-processing machinery topped the list of goods shipped to and from both countries. NAFTA clearly intensified the integration of the two economies rather than distancing them. Although it was tempt-

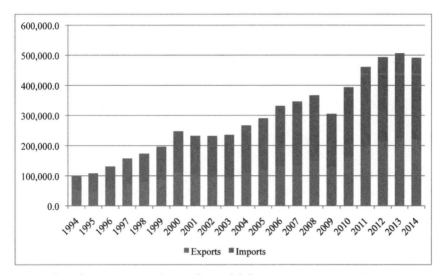

U.S. trade with Mexico in goods, in millions of dollars, 1994–2014. (U.S. Census Bureau, U.S. International Trade Data. Note: *Millions of dollars on a nominal basis, not adjusted for inflation)*

ing to attribute all post-1994 changes to NAFTA, post-NAFTA trade clearly followed significant earlier increases that came on the heels of Mexico's entry into GATT in 1986 and the influence of the Salinas years.

As for employment, while union studies documented 96,000 jobs that moved to Mexico between 1980 and 1995, that number was less than the average monthly fluctuation in the size of the U.S. workforce. In 1997, *Newsweek* reported that 38,148 jobs were lost at 286 firms as a result of NAFTA but noted that 3 million had been created in the United States in the same period. The NAFTA–Transitional Adjustment Assistance Program, created as part of NAFTA legislation, certified that as of 2002 about 525,000 workers total, or about 58,000 per year, had been adversely affected by job shifts to or trade with Mexico or Canada.[41] About 100,000 of the job losses were in the apparel industry, but the total numbers are very small in the context of the overall U.S. economy. While border cities such as El Paso lost apparel manufacturing jobs as those operations were moved to Ciudad Juárez, many of the jobs soon were moved to even lower-wage regions in Central America or Asia. In other words, even without NAFTA, these jobs would have eventually moved offshore. It should be noted that data are not available regarding jobs created in the United States as a result of NAFTA-related activities. However, U.S. unemployment reached a historical low of 4.0 percent, with 3.4 million jobs created in 2000 alone.[42]

The most serious problems under NAFTA had existed long before 1994. Much of the effect of the trade agreement was symbolic: Mexico appeared to be a more secure investment site; that is, tying Mexico to the United States appeared to lower the risk of Mexican investments. As was revealed during the 1994–1995 Mexican economic crisis, however, appearances of stability could be deceiving. Nonetheless, NAFTA stimulated a significant increase in foreign direct investment (FDI) in Mexico, growing 3.6 times from 1994 to 2003. After ten years of NAFTA, FDI in Mexico showed signs of slowing down due to competition from China and Mexican business-climate problems such as corruption, personal-safety issues, poor highways, a looming energy shortage, and the lack of a stable legal framework.[43] Employers could and did threaten to move to Mexico to obtain labor concessions for favorable tax treatment by local governments—even if they had no intention of doing so. And labor problems persisted throughout the Mexican border states. Sexual harassment was a problem in the *maquilas*, where male supervisors sometimes exploited their positions to extort sexual favors from female employees and where pregnant women were sometimes fired.[44] *Maquila* workers found it difficult to form independent labor unions. When they were successful, such efforts were generally greeted by official hostility and usually lasted only a short time.[45]

On the positive side, with the increasing presence of large transnational corporations in the Mexican border region, these companies tended to impose worldwide corporate policies regarding labor and environmental practices that often exceeded local standards. Greater political openness in Mexico since NAFTA has translated into some opportunities for organized labor. The old state-supported unions have declined somewhat, and independent unions and confederations have increased. Tentative cooperation between U.S. and Mexican organized labor groups has also moved forward.[46] While real wages in the maquiladoras remained the same or improved slightly during the first years of NAFTA from 1993 to 2003, real wages in Mexico's non-*maquila* manufacturing industries fell slightly.[47]

Looking at specific border-area impacts of NAFTA reveals winners and losers in the agreement. In general, businesses that benefited from freer trade were those that were already competitive—that is, industries that were operating with great efficiency and were active in the global marketplace. The losers were enterprises that were highly protected under Mexico's postwar development model; these operations were either driven out of business or forced to become competitive.

In terms of trade specifically (ironically, trade was frequently overlooked in discussions of the agreement), at first glance it would appear that the border region achieved what it was after. Border merchants in Mexico had long fought to import goods duty-free from the United States for sale in their shops. But national producers and central-government officials frequently argued that special treatment would stifle domestic production. With NAFTA, tensions between producers and consumers were sometimes aggravated by the new rules. For example, in 1995 a supermarket chain in Tijuana began to import milk from a dairy in Yuma, Arizona. Local producers and the only pasteurizing plant in the region immediately complained, saying that the local facility produced enough milk and that the Mexican milk industry would suffer and Mexican jobs would be lost if the U.S. product was sold in Tijuana. Local Baja California officials from the Ministry of Agriculture ordered a ban on milk products from the United States, and U.S. officials protested that the action was a violation of NAFTA. The Mexican federal government eventually intervened to resume U.S. milk sales.

Some observers argued that NAFTA would lead to the demise of *maquila* production; others argued that the whole country would become one giant maquiladora. It is true that the trade advantage of the maquiladoras ceased under NAFTA, and by 2007 the maquiladora regulations had been replaced by new rules for export-oriented industry, the Program for Temporary Imports to Promote Exports (PITEX) and Maquiladora Manufacturing Industry and Export Services (IMMEX). But the comparative advantage of the far northern region of Mexico was certain to continue into the foreseeable future. The position of plants close to the U.S. market, their role in coproduction, and their wage rates were all still attractions for locating facilities in the Mexican border region. Although the maquiladoras have been merged with domestic industry, the manufacturing sector in Mexico's border region is dynamic and evolving.

In agriculture, inefficient producers on the border and in both countries were increasingly unable to compete. The basic-grains sector of Mexico is one example. At the end of 1992, Mexican corn cost $240 per ton, while Iowa corn bought at the border went for $110 per ton. Under NAFTA, Mexico gradually increased import quotas and eventually replaced all but residual subsistence production of corn in Mexico. The ten-year phase-in period under NAFTA was a response to social and political realities in Mexico: the years after the 1980s had proved devastating for Mexico's 2.7 million corn producers. Dislocation of these small producers likely contributed to the growing northward migration to Mexican border cities and to U.S. destinations in the 1990s and beyond.[48]

The main impact of the agricultural terms of NAFTA was felt by vegetable growers who catered to the U.S. winter market. NAFTA did not fundamentally change access, which had been expanding rapidly in the 1980s and early 1990s. It did, however, create a more stable environment for investment in export agriculture. Mexican producers on or near the border challenged the market dominance of the U.S. states of California and Florida. Conflicts over tomatoes, avocados, green peppers, oranges, strawberries, grapes, raisins, broccoli, and other crops joined long-standing disagreements over more traditional Mexican exports such as cattle and cotton.

U.S. producers employed various means—sanitary regulations, for example—to stem the flow of less expensive Mexican crops across the border. Tomatoes emerged as a focal point of dissension. As Mexican growers captured 63 percent of the U.S. winter tomato market in 1995–1996, U.S. producers—long threatened by Mexico's seasonal advantage—lodged two formal complaints with the International Trade Commission, petitioning for relief from competition across the border. In October 1996 Mexican growers relented, agreeing to sell their tomatoes at or above the reference price desired by Florida farmers. Ironically, consumers were left holding the bag, forced to pay higher prices that constituted a windfall for producers in both countries.[49] A similar battle was played out with avocado production.

In effect, NAFTA introduced few new factors into the equation of U.S.-Mexican economic relations. Two circumstances in particular combined to ensure this outcome. First, trade between the United States and Mexico had been relatively free before NAFTA was signed in 1994. Mexico had unilaterally lowered its tariffs and opened its economy to U.S. imports after 1985. Notwithstanding the distortions masked by average figures, in 1993 Mexican tariffs stood at roughly 5 percent, and U.S. tariffs stood at twice that amount.[50] Additionally, about 45 percent of Mexican exports to the United States entered duty-free under the General System of Preferences. Second—and perhaps the most important overlooked context for discussions of free trade in North America—NAFTA did not change the difference in size between the two economies. The U.S. economy towered over its Mexican counterpart; the much ballyhooed "world's biggest and richest market of $6.2 trillion [1994 dollars]" was made up of the United States' $6 trillion and Mexico's $0.2 trillion markets. Mexico's GDP was roughly the size of the gross product of Los Angeles County (which had one-tenth of Mexico's population); the U.S. trade deficit with Mexico was 0.1 percent of the U.S. economy. Given this basic asymmetry of proportion, most scholars agreed that NAFTA would affect Mexico much more profoundly than it would affect the United States.

It is important to note also that, as of 2015, NAFTA has not brought free trade—that is, a complete elimination of tariffs and quantitative controls—to North America; instead it provides thousands of pages of trade regulations. And, in addition to the mandated ten- to fifteen-year phase-ins, there have been successful attempts in both the United States and Mexico to brake the forward motion of the free trade train. In 1995 and 1996, for example, the Bill Clinton administration delayed the implementation of NAFTA with respect to both the movement of Mexican trucks across the border and throughout the United States and the importation of Mexican tomatoes. Between 1996 and 1999 U.S. and Mexican truckers were to have the freedom to carry cargo inside the states on the U.S.-Mexican border; in 2000 complete cross-border access was to be granted. Citing concerns about the safety of Mexican trucks, the lack of insurance coverage, and the problem of drug trafficking, the U.S. government implemented a fourteen-month delay in opening U.S. roads to Mexican truckers beyond a twenty-mile-wide border trade zone; the act was clearly a concession to the Teamsters Union. As election time neared, the Clinton administration also appeased vegetable growers in Florida by pressuring Mexico to stop the shipment of $800 million worth of low-price tomatoes into the United States. As the White House noted, Florida had twenty-five electoral votes; Mexico had none.

Mexico responded to the failure of the United States to permit Mexican long-haul trucking with billions of dollars in retaliatory tariffs on U.S. products. In 2011, the two countries signed an agreement for the U.S. Department of Transportation to conduct a three-year study of the safety of Mexican trucks. The results were released early in 2015 and concluded that "Mexico-domiciled motor carriers operating beyond the commercial zones had safety records that were equal to or better than the national average for U.S. and Canadian motor carriers operating in the United States."[51] While this may not definitively resolve the trucking issue, it does show that the NAFTA process has been helpful in addressing large and small trade disputes between the two countries.

It seems clear that the primary NAFTA goals of reducing investment and trade barriers were achieved quite successfully. Through increased competition, North American companies became more efficient and productive. Economic growth and job creation also received a boost as a result of the pact, although Mexico lagged behind. On the downside, there were regional and sector-specific negative impacts, including on U.S. textile workers and Mexican corn farmers, and neither country provided adequate mitigation strategies. While Mexico reduced overall poverty somewhat, income inequality remained very high. Income distribution in the United States remained a problem as well. The benefits of free trade were concentrated in the upper income groups; NAFTA did not bring the wide prosperity and quality-of-life improvement promised by some of its supporters.

NAFTA, over its first two decades, had notable effects in the border region. Due to increased maquiladora employment, expanded trade passing through the region, and greater foreign investment, economic expansion and job creation remained strong in the border zone. Although the receiving area for much internal migration that resulted in rapid urbanization and chronic urban services and infrastructure deficits, Mexican border cities were among the most prosperous of the nation, as were their residents. Basic indicators such as health characteristics, per capita income, and education levels placed the northern border in the top tier of Mexico's regions, along with the Federal District, Guadalajara, and Monterrey.

While the U.S. border region remained more prosperous than the Mexican border zone, it continued to lag behind the rest of the United States, and NAFTA did not change this. Although U.S. border cities experienced significant employment increases due to the explosion of international trade and services, much of the job creation was in low-paying, entry-level positions. By the late 1990s, business leaders in El Paso began to note that the promised NAFTA prosperity was elusive. There, the well-paying jobs in the clothing industry were lost as production shifted offshore, first to Mexico and then to China and elsewhere. The biggest job gains were in lower-paying positions related to commerce, trade, warehousing, and the service sector. Even in San Diego, the wealthiest of the U.S. border cities, much of the job growth was in the service sector, and service workers could not afford housing in the local market. The benefits of NAFTA-led growth in the U.S. border region, then, were not spread widely enough across the income groups for most residents to see an improvement in quality of life.

NAFTA did not create free trade for consumers in the border region. To some extent, the opposite occurred. With the implementation of NAFTA, Mexican border merchants and Mexican manufacturing interests, fearing an onslaught of competition, were successful in convincing Mexican customs to tighten enforcement of import regulations at the border for private individuals, particularly around the holiday season when Mexican border residents were accustomed to shopping in the U.S. border cities. For Mexican shoppers, this simply meant more trips across the border to shop. Perhaps the most visible sign of NAFTA in Mexican border communities was the immediate appearance of U.S. fast food and other franchises and, over a decade, of large U.S.-based retailers such as Walmart, Office Depot, and Home Depot. Although Mexican telephone service improved considerably with privatization and some internal competition, the Mexican telecommunications industry was not fully opened up by NAFTA, and the companies retained a stranglehold on border consumers. In the border area, calling a friend or neighbor just a few miles away across the border remained as expensive as an international call, even though it took place within the same transborder community. It is still less costly for most U.S. border residents to call, text, or tweet Hawaii than locations within sight across the border in Mexico.

TRANSBORDER COOPERATION

We have seen that myriad bilateral border issues have certain traits in common. As urbanization and development advance in the area adjacent to the international boundary, problems spill over from one side to the other and are binational concerns. These include air pollution, water supply shortages, natural resource conservation challenges, water pollution and sedimentation, infectious disease, drug addiction, public transportation and transportation infrastructure deficits, inefficient and saturated ports of entry, natural disasters, social problems, crime, and security issues. At the same time, many opportunities involve both sides of the border, such as regional economic development and investment, cultural opportunities, education, tourism, and recreation. Addressing the binational challenges and taking advantage of the opportunities can be most efficiently accomplished collaboratively by Mexican and U.S. stakeholders. The nature of the border—long, porous, unmarked, unguarded in some areas, and heavily militarized for growing sections of its length—creates complex problems that are particularly difficult to solve. The fact that the border region bridges two legal systems and two governance systems makes transboundary collaborative resolution of matters difficult. Different levels of economic development and resources available to solve border issues, linguistic and cultural differences, bureaucratic inertia with the silo approach of agencies, and elected officials with constituents only on one side of the border all are barriers to effective binational problem resolution. As well, the history of the two countries at times impedes collaboration. Many in the United States, knowingly or not, subscribe to aspects of American exceptionalism— the belief that the way things are done domestically is superior and should be applied across the border. Many Mexicans, with a strong sense of nationalism and suspicion of U.S. unilateralism, push back against suggestions from the north and advocate for their own approaches. The reality is that each side has something to offer the other, but getting to the point where they can do so is not often easy.

The geographical isolation of the U.S. and Mexican border states from the centers of political power—Washington, D.C., and Mexico City—complicates the resolution of problems stemming from domestic trends and bilateral relations. Residents of the border region have felt neglected and misunderstood by federal officials and policymakers. In the 1980s, however, the area attracted increasing attention in both national capitals: an Office of Border Affairs was created in the U.S. Department of State, and U.S. congressional groups meet regularly to discuss border issues. Similar units exist within the Mexican administration and legislative branch. In Mexico, El Colegio de la Frontera Norte, founded with government support as a branch of the prestigious El Colegio de México, serves as the northern border's graduate-level think tank. Regional public universities have emerged more recently in major Mexican border cities, offering undergraduate, graduate, and professional degrees.

At the same time, since the 1950s, mechanisms for dealing with problems as they arise have been developing through the initiative of local authorities. At many points along the boundary, local officials have worked out bilateral agreements and informal arrangements on such issues as pollution, tourism, transportation, emergency response, public health, and economic development. Governors of the ten border states meet regularly, and over time they have addressed substantive matters of common concern to area inhabitants. The Arizona-Sonora Commission has a long history of convening public- and private-sector representatives to work on joint opportunities and address border challenges. Representatives of the three legislatures of California, Baja California, and Baja California Sur for many years met regularly as the Commission of the Californias on matters of importance to the border region. The Border Legislative Conference brings border-state legislators together to work on issues of mutual concern, including trade facilitation, border energy, immigration, economic development, and border security.[52] While often producing positive results, these mechanisms are largely ad hoc and lack ongoing institutional and financial support, which limits their ability to address many border challenges and opportunities.

Such regional political processes, along with local initiatives, may be crucial for managing the bilateral border relationship into the twenty-first century. In the past, U.S. and Mexican leaders at the highest levels have chosen the boundary area as the site for key meetings and acts of state. Both Ronald Reagan and George H. W. Bush chose to meet with their Mexican counterparts at the border to discuss issues of regional, national, and bilateral significance. And in his first official meeting with a foreign leader after his election in 1992, President Bill Clinton joined President Salinas in San Antonio, Texas. Presidents George W. Bush and Vicente Fox both had high expectations for the U.S.-Mexican bilateral agenda upon taking office. However, U.S. involvement in Afghanistan and Iraq and preoccupation with national security after the 9/11 terrorist attacks derailed significant progress on bilateral and border issues at the level of the national administrations.

A well-known observer of U.S.-Mexican relations has stated that the bilateral relationship is fundamentally structured by three characteristics: "proximity, interpenetration, and asymmetry."[53] These traits are most pronounced at the U.S.-Mexican border, where the two societies meet and intermingle. All three of these qualities, as they are expressed in the U.S.-Mexican border region, have been transformed over the course of the century. Simple proximity has given way to a complex overlapping and integration; interpenetration has increasingly become interdependence. But disparities in economic might and political power, which have great potential to undermine bilateral attempts at problem solving, have changed the least.

The signing of NAFTA and bilateral agreements with Mexico on border environmental matters energized border cooperation.[54] The creation of new bilateral and trilateral border institutions coincided with trends in the United States and Mexico toward decentralization of administrative functions and increased public participation in policy formulation at the local level. As trade and investment flows grew, Mexican companies invested in the United States, and American franchises and investments flourished in Mexico, transborder cooperation was facilitated at the state and local levels. The two federal governments encouraged these efforts through the Border Liaison Mechanism, the environmental Border XXI, Border 2012, and Border 2020 processes, and the bilateral Border Environment Cooperation Commission and the North American Development Bank. The Border Legislative Conference and Border Governors Conference took new initiatives in developing and implementing state-to-state border programs, particularly in the areas of economic development and environmental cooperation. Local cooperation across the border was also helped by federal and state support for environmental and public health programs. Federal and state programs likewise encouraged university-to-university cooperation on education and research across the border. Border area leaders felt that the border had come to occupy a more important place in the bilateral U.S.-Mexican agenda and perceived that increasingly Washington, D.C., and Mexico City were responsive to initiatives and concerns originating in the border region and articulated by border people. Many border people had come to feel that they had a stronger voice.

The response to the events of 9/11 and preoccupation of the U.S. federal authorities with wars in the Middle East had consequences for the border region. U.S. strategic thinking did not contemplate forming a common external border with harmonized policies with its NAFTA partners. Instead the United States moved to harden its own sea, air, and land borders and to design and implement a series of measures in the border region, largely without local discussions or input. Nor were adequate consultations held with Mexico. Border leaders found themselves once again in the position of having to react to measures from Washington, D.C.; these often had unintended negative consequences for the border region that were not mitigated through federal programs and spending. It was clear that national security measures trumped local border concerns and perceptions. Border leaders had to scramble, for example, to turn back proposed agricultural policies that would have left fresh produce rotting before crossing the border and visa exit inspections that would have brought the border to a standstill, impacting hundreds of thousands of border residents. Border leaders also had to rebuff federal attempts to eliminate the North American Development Bank, and despite their best efforts, funds for border water and sewage infrastructure channeled through a congressional appropriation were halved and then cut even further. While funds became available to expand the size of the Border Patrol and to install high-tech surveillance equipment along the border, resources for roads, ports of entry, water and sewer projects, and other local priorities dried up. Resources flowed to the border security-industrial complex and away from needed border infrastructure and other programs.

Despite lingering asymmetries and conflicts over land, water, migration, the environment, and other issues, the society of the border has been remarkable in its adaptation to rapid change and in its capacity to receive migrants seeking new opportunities. Enlightened people on both sides increasingly see their problems as shared challenges and recognize that confronting them will require cooperation across the international boundary and throughout the border region.

NOTES

1. J. Cockroft, *Outlaws in the Promised Land: Mexican Immigrant Workers and America's Future* (New York: Grove Press, 1986), 107; Office of National Drug Control Policy (https://www.whitehouse.gov/ondcp).

2. M. Delal Baer, "Misreading Mexico," *Foreign Policy* (fall 1997): 146; also see the President's National Drug Control Strategy, February 2006: Office of National Drug Control Policy (https://www.whitehouse.gov/ondcp).

3. Ryan Parker, "Drone Loaded with Meth Crashes Near Mexico-California Border," *Los Angeles Times*, January 23, 2015.

4. See the interview with Tijuana architect Jorge Ozorno in Lawrence A. Herzog, *From Aztec to High Tech: Architecture and Landscape across the Mexico–United States Border* (Baltimore: Johns Hopkins University Press, 1999), 181–82.

5. Office of National Drug Control Policy, *The Economic Costs of Drug Abuse in the United States, 1992–2002.* Publication No. 207303 (Washington, D.C.: Executive Office of the President, 2004); National Drug Intelligence Center, *The Economic Impact of Illicit Drug Use on American Society* (Washington, D.C.: U.S. Department of Justice, 2011).

6. See William O. Walker, *Drugs in the Western Hemisphere: An Odyssey of Cultures in Conflict* (Wilmington, DE: Scholarly Resources, 1996); Timothy J. Dunn, *The Militarization of the U.S.-Mexico Border, 1978–1992* (Austin, TX: CMAS Books, 1996), which discusses use of federal troops for drug interdiction along the border.

7. "U.S. Ambassador Issues Advisory Message to Americans Regarding Increased Violence in Mexico," U.S. Embassy, Mexico, http://mexico.usembassy.gov.

8. For the Nuevo Laredo murders, see Centro de Estudios Fronterizos y de Promoción de los Derechos Humanos A.C. (http://www.derechoshumanosenmexico.org); for Tijuana, see Robert J. Caldwell, "U.S. Law Enforcement Captures the Head of Mexico's Most Violent Drug Cartel, the Arellano Félix Organization," *San Diego Union-Tribune,* August 20, 2006; Jorge Morales Almada, "Los cartels se disputan la frontera. Narcotraficantes de Tijuana y Sinaloa pugnan por el control de la zona limítofe México-EU," *La Opinión,* February 2, 2004.

9. David A. Shirk, *The Drug War in Mexico: Confronting a Shared Threat* (New York: Council on Foreign Relations, 2011).

10. Shirk, *The Drug War in Mexico.*

11. See Government Accountability Office, *Illegal Immigration: Border-Crossing Deaths Have Doubled since 1995; Border Patrol's Efforts to Prevent Deaths Have Not Been Fully Evaluated,* GOA-06-770 (Washington, D.C.: Government Accountability Office, August 2006); also see http://www.cbp.gov for Border Patrol statistics.

12. San Diego Association of Governments (SANDAG) and California Department of Transportation District 11, "Economic Impacts of Wait Times at the San Diego–Baja California Border," SANDAG, January 19, 2006, at http://www.sandag.cog.ca.us; "Economic Impacts of Wait Times in the San Diego–Baja California Border Region Fact Sheet (2007 Update)," SANDAG, http://www.sandag.org/uploads/publicationid/publicationid_1181_18568.pdf; a summary of wait times for other border cities is in Christopher E. Wilson, et al., *The State of the Border Report: A Comprehensive Analysis of the U.S.-Mexico Border* (Washington, D.C.: Woodrow Wilson International Center for Scholars, 2013), 70.

13. See Instituto Ciudadano de Estudios sobre la Inseguridad, "Cuarta encuesta sobre inseguridad" (México, D.F., 2006), at http://www.icesi.org.mx. The national average is 72.5 percent. For Baja California crime, see Rafael Ruiz Harrell, "Baja California," *Reforma* (February 13, 2006), which is also available on http://www.icesi.org.mx.

14. For a discussion of perceptions about insecurity, see Guadalupe Correa-Cabrera and Terence M. Garrett, "The Phenomenology of Perception and Fear: Security and the Reality of the US-Mexico Border," *Journal of Borderlands Studies* 29, no. 2 (2014): 243–55.

15. Pedro H. Albuquerque and Prasad R. Vemala, "Femicide Rates in Mexican Cities along the US-Mexico Border: Do the Maquiladora Industries Play a Role?" *Social Science Research Network*, June 3, 2014, http://ssrn.com/abstract=1112308.

16. For a comparison of Ciudad Juárez and Toluca female homicide rates, see Rafael Ruiz Harrell, "Toluca y Juárez: Los femicidios," cited in Natalia Ix-Chel Vázquez González, "Media Violence: A Study Case," *Convergencia, Revista de ciencias sociales* 47 (May–August 2008): 93 (http://convergencia.uaemex.mx/rev47/english/4_Natalia.pdf). While there is some scholarly research on these murders, much of the information is available through newspaper and other media accounts. Scholarly articles include Melissa W. Wright, "From Protests to Politics: Sex Work, Women's Worth, and Ciudad Juárez Modernity," *Annals of the Association of American Geographers* 94, no. 2 (2004): 369–86; Stanley Bailey et al., "Death at the Border," *International Migration Review* 33, no. 2 (1999): 430–34; and Mark Ensalaco, "Murder in Ciudad Juárez: A Parable of Women's Struggle for Human Rights," *Violence against Women* 12, no. 5 (2006): 417–40. News articles include Ginger Thompson, "In Mexico's Murders, Fury Is Aimed at Officials," *New York Times*, September 26, 2005; "Police Identify Teenager Killed in Mexican Border City," *Associated Press Worldstream*, March 15, 2005; Bob Herbert, "Punished for Being Female," *New York Times*, November 2, 2006; "Crime without Punishment in Mexico," *Economist*, June 4, 2005; Pat Broeske, "400 Dead Women: Now Hollywood Is Intrigued," *New York Times*, May 21, 2006.

17. Jorge Durand and Douglas S. Massey, "Mexican Migration to the United States: A Critical Review," *Latin American Research Review* 27, no. 2 (1992).

18. David M. Heer, *Undocumented Mexicans in the United States* (New York: Cambridge University Press, 1990); Susan Gonzalez Baker, *The Cautious Welcome: The Legalization Programs of the Immigration Reform and Control Act* (Santa Monica, CA, and Washington, D.C.: RAND Corporation/Urban Institute, 1990); Charles B. Keely, "Population and Immigration Policy: State and Federal Roles," in *Mexican and Central American Population and U.S. Immigration Policy*, ed. Frank D. Bean, Jurgen Schmandt, and Sidney Weintraub (Austin: University of Texas Press, 1989); Michael C. Lemay, "U.S. Immigration Policy and Politics," in *The Gatekeepers: Comparative Immigration Policy*, ed. Michael C. Lemay (New York: Praeger, 1989); Michael D. Hoefer, "Background of U.S. Immigration Policy Reform," in *U.S. Immigration Policy Reform in the 1980s: A Preliminary Assessment*, ed. Francisco L. Rivera-Batiz, Selig L. Sechzer, and Ira N. Gang (New York: Praeger, 1991); Barry R. Chiswick, "Illegal Immigration and Immigration Control," in Rivera-Batiz, Sechzer, and Gang, *U.S. Immigration Policy Reform*. See also Peter L. Reich, "Jurisprudential Tradition and Undocumented Alien Entitlements," *Georgetown Immigration Law Journal* 6, no. 1 (March 1992): 1–25; Peter L. Reich, "Public Benefits for Undocumented Aliens: State Law into the Breach Once More," *New Mexico Law Review* 21 (spring 1991): 219–49. For regional impacts of IRCA in Mexican sending regions, see Jesús Arroyo Alejandre, "Algunos impactos de la Ley de Reforma y Control de Imigración (IRCA) en una region de Jalisco de fuerte emigración hacia Estados Unidos de Norteamérica," in *Estados*

Unidos y el occidente de México, ed. Adrían de León Arias (Guadalajara: Universidad de Guadalajara, 1992).

19. See interview with Senator Alan Simpson, "Q&A: Alan Simpson; 1986 Immigration Reform Legislation," *San Diego Union-Tribune*, May 28, 2006.

20. Frank D. Bean, Jurgen Schmandt, and Sidney Weintraub, *Mexican and Central American Population and U.S. Immigration Policy* (Austin: University of Texas, Center for Mexican American Studies, 1989); Frank D. Bean et al., *At the Crossroads: Mexico and U.S. Immigration Policy* (Lanham, MD: Rowman & Littlefield, 1997); James P. Smith and Barry Edmonston, eds., *The New Americans: Economic, Demographic, and Fiscal Effects of Immigration* (Washington, D.C.: National Academy Press, 1997).

21. See Kevin F. McCarthy and Georges Vernez, *Immigration in a Changing Economy: California's Experience* (Santa Monica, CA: RAND Corporation, 1997); "[USC] Study Finds Immigrants' Economic Effect Mixed," *Los Angeles Times*, January 23, 1997; "Immigrants Not Lured by Aid, [Public Policy Institute of California] Study Says," *Los Angeles Times*, January 29, 1997; "Immigrants a Net Economic Plus, [National Research Council] Study Says," *Los Angeles Times*, May 18, 1997; "U.S.-Mexico Study Sees Exaggeration of Immigration Data," *New York Times*, August 31, 1997.

22. K. Anthony Appiah, "The Multiculturalist Misunderstanding," *New York Review of Books*, October 9, 1997.

23. William D. Frey, "Fresh Census Numbers," *Milken Institute Review* (Third Quarter, 2003); U.S. Census 2010.

24. See, for example, the study completed for the official Commission on U.S. Immigration Reform: Smith and Edmundson, *The New Americans*, 15–19. See also Mexican Ministry of Foreign Affairs/U.S. Commission on Immigration Reform, *Migration between Mexico and the United States: Binational Study/La migración entre México y Estados Unidos: Estudio binacional* (Mexico City/Washington, D.C.: Mexican Ministry of Foreign Affairs/U.S. Commission on Immigration Reform, 1998). Two recent examples are reports issued by the U.S./Mexico Border Counties Coalition: *Medical Emergency: Costs of Uncompensated Care in Southwest Border Counties* (2002) and *Illegal Immigrants in U.S./Mexico Border Counties: The Costs of Law Enforcement, Criminal Justice, and Emergency Medical Services* (2001). Both reports are available on the coalition's website at http://www.bordercounties.org.

25. D'Vera Cohn, Ana Gonzalez-Barrera, and Danielle Cuddington, "Remittances to Latin America Recover—but Not to Mexico," Pew Research Center, November 2013, http://www.pewhispanic.org. See Banco de México data for tourism receipts for 2013 as reported by the Secretaría de Turismo: "Resultados de la actividad turística: Enero–diciembre 2013," http://consulmex.sre.gob.mx/montreal/images/Consulado/Comunicado/rat2013_18feb14.pdf.

26. See Douglas S. Massey, "March of Folly: U.S. Immigration Policy after NAFTA," *American Prospect* 9, no. 37 (March 1998): 22–33.

27. Georges Vernez and Kevin F. McCarthy, *The Costs of Immigration to Taxpayers: Analytical and Policy Issues* (Santa Monica: RAND Corporation, 1997); Steven A.

Camarota, "The Labor Market Impact of Immigration: A Review of Recent Studies," *Center for Immigration Studies Backgrounder*, no. 1-98 (May 1998).

28. See Massey, "March of Folly"; Smith and Edmundson, *The New Americans*," where old models are critiqued and new ones proposed.

29. See Sam Fulwood III, "Uncountable Problem at the Border," *Los Angeles Times*, May 17, 1990. For data on border patrol salaries, ethnic makeup, and other issues, see Sebastian Rotella and Patrick J. McDonnell, "A Seemingly Futile Job Can Breed Abuses by Agents," *Los Angeles Times*, April 23, 1993.

30. See, for example, Marjorie Miller and Patrick McDonnell, "Rise in Violence along Border Brings Call for Action," *Los Angeles Times*, December 9, 1990; Gloria J. Romero and Antonio H. Rodríguez, "A Thousand Points of Xenophobia," *Los Angeles Times*, May 25, 1990; Sebastian Rotella and Patrick J. McDonnell, "When Agents Cross over the Borderline," *Los Angeles Times*, April 22, 1993.

31. Jeffrey S. Passel, D'Vera Cohn, and Ana Gonzalez-Barrera, *Population Decline of Unauthorized Immigrants Stalls, May Have Reversed* (Washington, D.C.: Pew Research Center, 2013).

32. Jens Manuel Krogstad and Jeffrey S. Passel, *U.S. Border Apprehensions of Mexicans Fall to Historic Lows* (Washington, D.C.: Pew Research Center, December 30, 2014).

33. U.S. Customs and Border Protection, Newsroom, "Southwest Border Unaccompanied Alien Children," January 2015, http://www.cbp.gov/newsroom/stats/southwest-border-unaccompanied-children; also see Jens Manuel Krogstad, Ana Gonzalez-Barrera, and Mark Hugo Lopez, "Children 12 and Under Are Fastest Growing Group of Unaccompanied Minors at U.S. Border," Pew Research Center, FactTank, July 22, 2014, http://www.pewresearch.org.

34. José Miguel Cruz, "Central American Maras: From Youth Street Gangs to Transnational Protection Rackets," *Global Crime* 11, no. 4 (2010): 379–98.

35. The best and most balanced studies in a largely polemic literature on free trade and NAFTA are Gary Clyde Hufbauer and Jeffrey J. Schott, *NAFTA Revisited: Achievements and Challenges* (Washington, D.C.: Institute for International Economics, 2005); William A. Orme Jr., *Understanding NAFTA: Mexico, Free Trade, and the New North America* (Austin: University of Texas Press, 1996); Sidney Weintraub, *NAFTA at Three: A Progress Report* (Washington, D.C.: Center for Strategic and International Studies, 1997).

36. This point is made by Shannon K. O'Neil, *Two Nations Indivisible: Mexico, the United States, and the Road Ahead* (New York and Oxford: Oxford University Press, 2013).

37. Barry T. Hirsch, "Union Membership and Coverage Database from the Current Population Survey: Note," *Industrial and Labor Relations Review* 56, no. 2 (January 2003): 349–54.

38. M. Delal Baer and Guy F. Erb, eds., *Strategic Sectors in Mexican-U.S. Free Trade* (Washington, D.C.: Center for Strategic and International Studies, 1995); Rogelio Ramírez de la O, "A Mexican Vision of North American Economic

Integration," in *Continental Accord: North American Economic Integration*, ed. Steven Globerman (Vancouver: Fraser Institute, 1995), 5–30. For a general overview, see Paul Ganster and Eugenio O. Valenciano, eds., *The Mexican-U.S. Border Region and the Free Trade Agreement* (San Diego: Institute for Regional Studies of the Californias, San Diego State University, 1992). An excellent, recent evaluation of NAFTA is Hufbauer and Schott, *NAFTA Revisited*. Other important recent studies are Daniel Lederman, William F. Maloney, and Luis Servén, *Lessons from NAFTA for Latin America and the Caribbean Countries: A Summary of Research Findings* (Washington, D.C.: World Bank, 2003); Demetrios Papademetriou et al., *NAFTA's Promise and Reality: Lessons from Mexico for the Hemisphere* (Washington, D.C.: Carnegie Endowment, 2003).

39. Office of the United States Trade Representative, "Mexico," https://ustr.gov.

40. See U.S. Department of Transportation, Research and Innovative Technology Administration, Bureau of Transportation Statistics (BTS) for transborder freight data: "Border Crossing/Entry Data: Query Detailed Statistics," BTS, http://transborder.bts.gov/programs/international/transborder/TBDR_BC/TBDR_BCQ.html.

41. Hufbauer and Schott, *NAFTA Revisited*, 83.

42. Baer, "Misreading Mexico," 544.

43. Hufbauer and Schott, *NAFTA Revisited*, 30, 33.

44. Sam Dillon, "Sex Bias at Border Plants in Mexico Reported by U.S.," *New York Times*, January 13, 1998. See also the story of Irma Leticia López Manzano in Oscar J. Martínez, *Border People: Life and Society in the U.S.-Mexico Borderlands* (Tucson: University of Arizona Press, 1994), 186–89.

45. See, for example, "Mexico Overturns Independent Union Victory at Border Factory," *San Francisco Chronicle*, November 15, 1997; Sam Dillon, "Bias Said to Hurt Independent Mexican Unions," *New York Times*, April 30, 1998; David Bacon, "Strike Closes Trailblazing Mexico Plant," *San Francisco Chronicle*, June 2, 1998; "Justice for Mexican Workers," *San Francisco Chronicle*, June 5, 1998. See also Edward J. Williams and John T. Passe-Smith, *The Unionization of the Maquiladora Industry: The Tamaulipan Case in National Context* (San Diego: Institute for Regional Studies of the Californias, San Diego State University, 1992).

46. Hufbauer and Schott, *NAFTA Revisited*, 105–8.

47. Hufbauer and Schott, *NAFTA Revisited*, 44.

48. See Hufbauer and Schott, *NAFTA Revisited*, 328.

49. Stephen Baker and S. Lynne Walker, "Mexico: The Salad Bowl of North America?" *Business Week*, February 25, 1995, 70–75; Bruce F. Johnston et al., eds., *U.S.-Mexican Relations: Agriculture and Rural Development* (Stanford, CA: Stanford University Press, 1987); Armand B. Peschard-Sverdrup, "The U.S.-Mexico Fresh Winter Tomato Trade Dispute: The Broader Implications," *CSIS Policy Paper on the Americas* 7, no. 4 (September 1996).

50. Many goods were not included in the General System of Preferences, and some high tariffs (on some seasonal tomatoes, for example) were hidden by average figures. See Orme, *Understanding NAFTA*, 71.

51. U.S. Department of Transportation, Federal Motor Carrier Safety Administration, "United States–Mexico Cross-Border Long-Haul Trucking Pilot Program Report to Congress," January 2015, http://www.fmcsa.dot.gov.

52. See the Border Legislative Conference website (http://www.csgwest.org); for an overview of cross-border cooperation in the San Diego–Tijuana region, see Paul Ganster, "Transborder Linkages in the San Diego–Tijuana Region," in *San Diego–Tijuana in Transition: A Regional Analysis*, ed. Norris C. Clement and Eduardo Zepeda Miramontes (San Diego: Institute for Regional Studies of the Californias, 1993), 109–27.

53. Abraham Lowenthal, *Partners in Conflict: The United States and Latin America* (Baltimore: Johns Hopkins University Press, 1987), 77.

54. Paul Ganster, "Evolving Environmental Management and Community Engagement at the U.S.-Mexican Border," *Eurasia Border Review* 5, no. 1 (spring 2014): 19–40.

SUGGESTED READINGS

These suggested readings include books, a few articles, and some reports published in English. The endnotes for each chapter also indicate many other sources in English that are available online as well as in printed form. The published literature in Spanish on many aspects of the U.S.-Mexican border, particularly related to Mexico's northern border region, is diverse and rich.

THE BORDERLANDS TO 1910

Benjamin, Thomas, and William McNellie, eds. *Other Mexicos: Essays on Regional Mexican History, 1876–1911*. Albuquerque: University of New Mexico Press, 1984.

Brear, Holly. *Inherit the Alamo: Myth and Ritual at an American Shrine*. Austin: University of Texas Press, 1995.

Crosby, Harry W. *Antigua California: Mission and Colony on the Peninsular Frontier*. Albuquerque: University of New Mexico Press, 1994.

French, William E. *A Peaceful and Working People: Manners, Morals, and Class Formation in Northern Mexico*. Albuquerque: University of New Mexico Press, 1996.

Moisés, Rosalio, J. H. Kelley, and W. C. Holden. *The Tall Candle: The Personal Chronicle of a Yaqui Indian*. Lincoln: University of Nebraska Press, 1971.

Montejano, David. *Anglos and Mexicans in the Making of Texas, 1836–1986*. Austin: University of Texas Press, 1987.

Piñera, David. *American and English Influence on the Early Development of Ensenada, Baja California, Mexico*. San Diego: Institute for Regional Studies of the Californias, San Diego State University, 1995.

Ruíz, Ramón Eduardo. *The People of Sonora and Yankee Capitalists*. Tucson: University of Arizona Press, 1988.

Sheridan, Thomas E. *Landscapes of Fraud: Mission Tumacácori, the Baca Float, and the Betrayal of the O'odham*. Tucson: University of Arizona Press, 2008.

Spicer, Edward H. *Cycles of Conquest: The Impact of Spain, Mexico, and the United States on the Indians of the Southwest, 1533–1960.* Tucson: University of Arizona Press, 1962.

Voss, Stuart F. *On the Periphery of Nineteenth-Century Mexico: Sonora and Sinaloa, 1810–1877.* Tucson: University of Arizona Press, 1982.

Wasserman, Mark. *Capitalists, Caciques, and Revolution: Chihuahua, Mexico, 1854–1911.* Chapel Hill: University of North Carolina Press, 1984.

Weber, David J. *The Mexican Frontier, 1821–1846: The American Southwest under Mexico.* Albuquerque: University of New Mexico Press, 1982.

———. *Myth and the History of the Hispanic Southwest: Essays.* Albuquerque: University of New Mexico Press, 1988.

———. *The Spanish Frontier in North America.* New Haven, CT: Yale University Press, 1992.

THE REVOLUTION, 1910–1929

Benjamin, Thomas, and Mark Wasserman, eds. *Provinces of the Revolution: Essays on Regional Mexican History.* Albuquerque: University of New Mexico Press, 1990.

Cardoso, Lawrence A. *Mexican Emigration to the United States, 1897–1931: Socioeconomic Patterns.* Tucson: University of Arizona Press, 1980.

Cumberland, Charles. "The Sonora Chinese and the Mexican Revolution." *Hispanic American Historical Review* 40 (1960): 191–211.

Deutsch, Sarah. *No Separate Refuge: Culture, Class, and Gender on an Anglo-Hispanic Frontier in the American Southwest, 1880–1940.* New York: Oxford University Press, 1987.

Hall, Linda B., and Don M. Coerver. *Revolution on the Border: The United States and Mexico, 1910–1920.* Albuquerque: University of New Mexico Press, 1988.

Harris, Charles H., and Louis R. Sadler. *The Border and the Revolution.* Las Cruces: Center for Latin American Studies/Joint Border Research Institute, New Mexico State University, 1988.

Justice, Glenn. *Revolution on the Rio Grande: Mexican Raids and Army Pursuits, 1916–1919.* El Paso: Texas Western Press, University of Texas, El Paso, 1992.

Katz, Friedrich. "Pancho Villa: Reform Governor of Chihuahua." In *Essays on the Mexican Revolution: Revisionist Views of the Leaders,* edited by William H. Beezley. Austin: University of Texas Press, 1979.

Raat, W. Dirk. *Revoltosos: Mexico's Rebels in the United States, 1903–1923.* College Station: Texas A&M University Press, 1981.

Sandos, James A. *Rebellion in the Borderlands: Anarchism and the Plan of San Diego, 1904–1923.* Norman: University of Oklahoma Press, 1992.

Vanderwood, Paul J., and Frank N. Samponaro. *Border Fury: A Picture Postcard Record of Mexico's Revolution and U.S. War Preparedness, 1910–1917.* Albuquerque: University of New Mexico Press, 1988.

Zamora, Emilio. *The World of the Mexican Worker in Texas.* College Station: Texas A&M University Press, 1993.

BORDER TOWNS

Arreola, Daniel D., and James R. Curtis. *The Mexican Border Cities: Landscape Anatomy and Place Personality.* Tucson: University of Arizona Press, 1993.

Camarillo, Albert. *Chicanos in a Changing Society: From Mexican Pueblos to American Barrios in Santa Barbara and Southern California, 1848–1930.* Cambridge, MA: Harvard University Press, 1996.

Clement, Norris C., and Eduardo Zepeda Miramontes, eds. *San Diego–Tijuana in Transition: A Regional Analysis.* San Diego: Institute for Regional Studies of the Californias, San Diego State University, 1993.

Collins, Kimberly, Paul Ganster, Cheryl Mason, Eduardo Sánchez López, and Magarito Quintero-Núñez, eds. *Imperial-Mexicali Valleys: Development and Environment of the U.S.-Mexican Border Region.* San Diego, CA: San Diego State University Press, 2004.

D'Antonio, William V., and William H. Form. *Influentials in Two Border Cities.* Notre Dame, IN: University of Notre Dame Press, 1965.

De León, Arnoldo. *The Tejano Community, 1836–1900.* Dallas, TX: Southern Methodist University Press, 1997.

Ganster, Paul, ed. *Tijuana 1964: A Photographic and Historic View/Una visión fotográfica e histórica.* 2nd ed. Tijuana, Baja California, and San Diego, CA: Centro Cultural Tijuana and San Diego State University Press, 2014.

Ganster, Paul, Felipe Cuamea Velázquez, José Luis Castro Ruíz, and Angélica Villegas, eds. *Tecate, Baja California: Realities and Challenges in a Mexican Border Community.* San Diego, CA: San Diego State University Press, 2002.

García, Mario T. *Desert Immigrants: The Mexicans of El Paso, 1880–1920.* New Haven, CT: Yale University Press, 1981.

Hinojosa, Gilberto Miguel. *A Borderlands Town in Transition: Laredo, 1755–1870.* College Station: Texas A&M University Press, 1983.

Katsulis, Yasmina. *Sex Work and the City: The Social Geography of Health and Safety in Tijuana, Mexico.* Austin: University of Texas Press, 2008.

Kearney, Milo, and Anthony Knopp. *Boom and Bust: The Historical Cycles of Matamoros and Brownsville.* Austin, TX: Eakin Press, 1991.

———. *Border Cuates: A History of the U.S.-Mexican Twin Cities.* Austin, TX: Eakin Press, 1995.

Klein, Alan M. *Baseball on the Border: A Tale of Two Laredos.* Princeton, NJ: Princeton University Press, 1997.

Kun, Josh, and Fiamma Montezemolo. *Tijuana Dreaming: Life and Art at the Global Border.* Durham, NC: Duke University Press, 2012.

Lister, Florence C., and Robert H. Lister. *Chihuahua: Storehouse of Storms.* Albuquerque: University of New Mexico Press, 1966.

Madrid, Alejandro L. *Nor-tec Rifa! Electronic Dance Music from Tijuana to the World.* Oxford: Oxford University Press, 2008.

Maher, Kristin Hill, and David Carruthers. "Urban Image Work: Official and Grass-roots Responses to Crisis in Tijuana." *Urban Affairs Review* 50 (March 2014): 244–68.

Martínez, Oscar J. *Border Boom Town: Ciudad Juárez since 1848.* Austin: University of Texas Press, 1978.

Meléndez-Ocasio, Marcel. "Mexican Urban History: The Case of Tampico, Tamaulipas, 1876–1924." PhD diss., Michigan State University, 1988.

Oberle, Alex P., and Daniel D. Arreola. "Mexican Medical Border Towns: A Case Study of Algodones, Baja California." *Journal of Borderlands Studies* 19, no. 2 (2004): 27–44.

Piñera Ramírez, David, and Gabriel Rivera. *Tijuana in History: Just Crossing the Border.* Tijuana, Baja California: Tijuana Cultural Center, 2013.

Price, John A. *Tijuana: Urbanization in a Border Culture.* Notre Dame, IN: University of Notre Dame Press, 1973.

Proffitt, T. D. *Tijuana: The History of a Mexican Metropolis.* San Diego, CA: San Diego State University Press, 1994.

Romo, Ricardo. *East Los Angeles: History of a Barrio.* Austin: University of Texas Press, 1983.

Saragoza, Alex M. *The Monterrey Elite and the Mexican State, 1880–1940.* Austin: University of Texas Press, 1988.

Sheridan, Thomas E. *Los Tucsonenses: The Mexican Community in Tucson, 1854–1941.* Tucson: University of Arizona Press, 1986.

Timmons, W. H. *El Paso: A Borderlands History.* El Paso: Texas Western Press, University of Texas, El Paso, 2003.

Valenzuela, José Manuel. *Paso del Nortec: This Is Tijuana.* México, D.F.: Trilce Ediciones, Consejo Nacional para la Cultura y las Artes, Editoríal Océano de México, El Colegio de la Frontera Norte, and Universidad Nacional Autónoma de México, 2004.

Vanderwood, Paul J. *Satan's Playground: Mobsters and Movie Stars at America's Greatest Gaming Resort.* Durham, NC: Duke University Press, 2010.

Young, Gay, ed. *The Social Ecology and Economic Development of Ciudad Juárez.* Boulder, CO: Westview Press, 1986.

MIGRATION

Akers Chacon, Justin, and Mike Davis. *No One Is Illegal: Fighting Racism and State Violence on the U.S.-Mexico Border.* Chicago: Haymarket Books, 2006.

Alvarez, Robert R. *Familia: Migration and Adaptation in Baja and Alta California, 1800–1975.* Berkeley: University of California Press, 1987.

Bean, Frank D., Rodolfo O. de la Garza, Bryan R. Roberts, and Sidney Weintraub. *At the Crossroads: Mexico and U.S. Immigration Policy*. Lanham, MD: Rowman & Littlefield, 1997.

Camarota, Steven A. "The Labor Market Impact of Immigration: A Review of Recent Studies." *Center for Immigration Studies Backgrounder*, no. 1-98 (May 1998).

Cardoso, Lawrence A. *Mexican Emigration to the United States, 1897–1931: Socioeconomic Patterns*. Tucson: University of Arizona Press, 1980.

Chavez, Leo R. *Shadowed Lives: Undocumented Immigrants in American Society*. Fort Worth, TX: Harcourt Brace College Publishers, 1998.

Doty, Roxanne. *The Law into Their Own Hands: Immigration and the Politics of Exceptionalism*. Tucson: University of Arizona Press, 2009.

Durand, Jorge, and Douglas S. Massey. "Mexican Migration to the United States: A Critical Review." *Latin American Research Review* 27, no. 2 (1992): 3–42.

Eastman, Cari Lee Skogberg. *Shaping the Immigration Debate: Contending Civil Societies on the US-Mexico Border*. Boulder, CO: First Forum Press, 2012.

Gamboa, Erasmo. *Mexican Labor and World War II: Braceros in the Pacific Northwest, 1942–1947*. Austin: University of Texas Press, 1990.

Gamio, Manuel. *The Mexican Immigrant: His Life Story*. Chicago: University of Chicago Press, 1931.

García, Juan R. *Mexicans in the Midwest, 1900–1932*. Tucson: University of Arizona Press, 1996.

Guerin-Gonzales, Camille. *Mexican Workers and American Dreams: Immigration, Repatriation, and California Farm Labor, 1900–1939*. New Brunswick, NJ: Rutgers University Press, 1994.

Gutiérrez, David G. *Between Two Worlds: Mexican Immigrants in the United States*. Wilmington, DE: Scholarly Resources, 1996.

Jones, Richard C. *Ambivalent Journey: U.S. Migration and Economic Mobility in North-Central Mexico*. Tucson: University of Arizona Press, 1995.

Lozano Ascencio, Fernando. *Bringing It Back Home: Remittances to Mexico from Migrant Workers*. La Jolla: Center for U.S.-Mexican Studies, University of California, San Diego, 1993.

Massey, Douglas S. "March of Folly: U.S. Immigration Policy after NAFTA." *American Prospect* 9, no. 37 (March 1998): 22–33.

———. *Return to Aztlán: The Social Process of International Migration from Western Mexico*. Berkeley: University of California Press, 1987.

Massey, Douglas S., Jorge Durand, and Nolan J. Malone. *Beyond Smoke and Mirrors: Mexican Immigration in an Era of Economic Integration*. New York: Russell Sage Foundation, 2003.

McCarthy, Kevin F., and Georges Vernez. *Immigration in a Changing Economy: California's Experience*. Santa Monica: RAND Corporation, 1997.

Mexican Ministry of Foreign Affairs/U.S. Commission on Immigration Reform. *Migration between Mexico and the United States: Binational Study/La migración entre México y*

Estados Unidos: Estudio binacional. Mexico City/Washington, D.C.: Mexican Ministry of Foreign Affairs/U.S. Commission on Immigration Reform, 1998.

Passel, Jeffrey S. "The Size and Characteristics of the Unauthorized Migrant Population in the U.S." Pew Hispanic Center Research Report, March 7, 2006.

Smith, James P., and Barry Edmonston, eds. *The New Americans: Economic, Demographic, and Fiscal Effects of Immigration.* Washington, D.C.: National Academy Press, 1997.

Vernez, Georges, and Kevin F. McCarthy. *The Costs of Immigration to Taxpayers: Analytical and Policy Issues.* Santa Monica: RAND Corporation, 1997.

MAQUILADORAS

Cañas, Jesus, and Roberto Coronado. "Maquiladora Industry: Past, Present, and Future." *Business Frontier* 2 (2002).

Cañas, Jesus, and Robert W. Gilmer. "Mexico Regulatory Change Redefines Maquiladora." *Crossroads, Economic Trends in the Desert Southwest* 1 (2007).

Carrillo, Jorge, and Alfredo Hualde. "Third Generation Maquiladoras? The Delphi–General Motors Case." *Journal of Borderlands Studies* 13 (spring 1988): 79–98.

Fatemi, Khosrow, ed. *The Maquiladora Industry: Economic Solution or Problem?* New York: Praeger, 1990.

Fernández-Kelly, María Patricia. *For We Are Sold, I and My People: Women and Industry in Mexico's Frontier.* Albany: State University of New York Press, 1983.

Iglesias Prieto, Norma. *Beautiful Flowers of the Maquiladora: Life Histories of Women Workers in Tijuana.* Austin: University of Texas Press, 1997.

Lugo, Alejandro. *Fragmented Lives, Assembled Parts: Culture, Capitalism, and Conquest at the U.S.-Mexico Border.* Austin: University of Texas Press, 2008.

Sklair, Leslie. *Assembling for Development: The Maquila Industry in Mexico and the United States.* San Diego: Center for U.S.-Mexican Studies, University of California, 1993.

Stoddard, Ellwyn R. *Maquila: Assembly Plants in Northern Mexico.* El Paso: Texas Western Press, University of Texas, El Paso, 1987.

Tiano, Susan. *Patriarchy on the Line: Labor, Gender, and Ideology in the Mexican Maquila Industry.* Philadelphia: Temple University Press, 1994.

Williams, Edward J., and John T. Passe-Smith. *The Unionization of the Maquiladora Industry: The Tamaulipan Case in National Context.* San Diego: Institute for Regional Studies of the Californias, San Diego State University, 1992.

Wilson, Patricia Ann. *Exports and Local Development: Mexico's New Maquiladoras.* Austin: University of Texas Press, 1992.

CONTEMPORARY ISSUES

Anderson, Joan B., and James Gerber. *Fifty Years of Change on the U.S.-Mexico Border: Growth, Development, and Quality of Life.* Austin: University of Texas Press, 2008.

Andreas, Peter. *Border Games: Policing the U.S.-Mexico Divide.* 2nd ed. Ithaca, NY: Cornell University Press, 2009.

Andreas, Peter, and Thomas J. Biersteker, eds. *The Rebordering of North America: Integration and Exclusion in a New Security Context.* New York: Routledge, 2003.

Andrés, Benny J., Jr. *Power and Control in the Imperial Valley: Nature, Agribusiness, and Workers on the California Borderland, 1900–1940.* College Station: Texas A&M University Press, 2015.

Annerino, John. *Dead in Their Tracks: Crossing America's Desert Borderlands.* New York: Four Walls Eight Windows, 1999.

Arreola, Daniel. *Tejano South Texas: A Mexican American Cultural Province.* Austin: University of Texas Press, 2002.

Balderrama, Francisco E., and Raymond Rodríguez. *Decade of Betrayal: Mexican Repatriation in the 1930s.* Albuquerque: University of New Mexico Press, 1995.

Barry, Tom, Harry Browne, and Beth Sims. *Crossing the Line: Immigrants, Economic Integration, and Drug Enforcement on the U.S.-Mexico Border.* Albuquerque: Resource Center Press, 1994.

Betts, Dianne C., Daniel J. Slottje, and Jesus Vargas-Garcia. *Crisis on the Rio Grande: Poverty, Unemployment, and Economic Development on the Texas-Mexico Border.* Boulder, CO: Westview Press, 1994.

Carruthers, David V., ed. *Environmental Justice in Latin America: Problems, Promise, and Practice.* Cambridge, MA: MIT Press, 2008.

Casey, Edward S., and Mary Watkins. *Up against the Wall: Re-imagining the U.S.-Mexico Border.* Austin: University of Texas Press, 2014.

Córdova, Ana, and Carlos de la Parra, eds. *A Barrier to Our Shared Environment: The Border Fence between the United States and Mexico.* Mexico City: Secretariat of Environment and Natural Resources, 2007.

Danelo, David J. *The Border: Exploring the U.S.-Mexican Divide.* Mechanicsburg, PA: Stackpole Books, 2008.

Dear, Michael. *Why Walls Won't Work: Repairing the US-Mexico Divide.* New York: Oxford University Press, 2013.

Dear, Michael, and Gustavo Leclerc, eds. *Postborder City: Cultural Spaces of Bajalta California.* New York: Routledge, 2003.

Domínguez-Ruvalcaba, Héctor, and Ignacio Corona. *Gender Violence at the U.S.-Mexico Border: Media Representation and Public Response.* Tucson: University of Arizona Press, 2010.

Dunn, Timothy J. *The Militarization of the U.S.-Mexico Border, 1978–1992.* Austin, TX: CMAS Books, 1996.

Esparza, Adrian X., and Angela J. Donelson. *Colonias in Arizona and New Mexico: Border Poverty and Community Development Solutions.* Tucson: University of Arizona Press, 2008.

Fernandez, Linda, and Richard T. Carson, eds. *Both Sides of the Border: Transboundary Environmental Management Issues Facing Mexico and the United States.* Boston: Kluwer Academic Publishers, 2002.

Fox, Claire, F. *The Fence and the River: Culture and Politics at the U.S.-Mexico Border.* Minneapolis: University of Minnesota Press, 1999.

Ganster, Paul. "Evolving Environmental Management and Community Engagement at the U.S.-Mexican Border." *Eurasia Border Review* 5, no. 1 (spring 2014): 19–40.

———, ed. *SCERP Monograph Series: The U.S.-Mexican Border Environment.* 16 vols. San Diego, CA: San Diego State University Press, 2000–2012. SCERP Monograph Series is available through Google Books: https://books.google.com.

———, ed. *The U.S.-Mexican Border Environment: A Road Map to a Sustainable 2020.* SCERP Monograph Series 1. San Diego, CA: San Diego State University Press, 2000. SCERP Monograph Series is available through Google Books: https://books. google.com.

Good Neighbor Environmental Board. *A Blueprint for Action on the U.S.-Mexico Border. Thirteenth Report of the Good Neighbor Environmental Board to the President and Congress of the United States.* Washington, D.C.: U.S. Environmental Protection Agency, 2010.

———. *U.S.-Mexican Border Environment: Air Quality and Transportation & Cultural and Natural Resources: Ninth Report of the Good Neighbor Environmental Board to the President and Congress of the United States.* Washington, D.C.: U.S. Environmental Protection Agency, 2006.

Grayson, George W. *The Cartels: The Story of Mexico's Most Dangerous Criminal Organizations and Their Impact on U.S. Security.* Santa Barbara, CA: Praeger, 2014.

Hansen, Niles M. *The Border Economy: Regional Development in the Southwest.* Austin: University of Texas Press, 1981.

Hart, John Mason. *Border Crossings: Mexican and Mexican-American Workers.* Wilmington, DE: SR Books, 1998.

Herzog, Lawrence A. *From Aztec to High Tech: Architecture and Landscape across the Mexico–United States Border.* Baltimore: Johns Hopkins University Press, 1999.

———. *Where North Meets South: Cities, Space, and Politics on the U.S.-Mexico Border.* Austin: Center for Mexican American Studies, University of Texas, 1990.

Heyman, Josiah McC. *Life and Labor on the Border: Working People of Northeastern Sonora, Mexico, 1886–1986.* Tucson: University of Arizona Press, 1991.

Hufbauer, Gary Clyde, and Jeffrey J. Schott. *NAFTA Revisited: Achievements and Challenges.* Washington, D.C.: Institute for International Economics, 2005.

Hundley, Norris, Jr. *The Great Thirst: Californians and Water—a History.* Rev. ed. Berkeley: University of California Press, 2001.

Johnson, Benjamin Heber, and Jeffrey Gusky. *Bordertown: The Odyssey of an American Place.* New Haven, CT: Yale University Press, 2008.

Kingsolver, Barbara. *Holding the Line: Women in the Great Arizona Mine Strike of 1983.* New York: ILR Press, 1996.

López-Hoffman, Laura, Emily D. McGovern, Robert G. Varady, and Karl W. Flessa, eds. *Conservation of Shared Environments: Learning from the United States and Mexico.* Tucson: University of Arizona Press, 2009.

Lowenthal, Abraham F., and Katrina Burgess, eds. *The California-Mexico Connection.* Stanford, CA: Stanford University Press, 1993.

Luna-Firebaugh, Eileen. "The Border Crossed Us: Border Crossing Issues of the Indigenous Peoples of North America." *Wicazo Sa Review* 17, no. 1 (2002): 159–81.

Machado, Manuel A. *The North Mexican Cattle Industry, 1910–1975: Ideology, Conflict, and Change.* College Station: Texas A&M University Press, 1981.

Maril, Robert Lee. *Living on the Edge of America: At Home on the Texas-Mexico Border.* College Station: Texas A&M University Press, 1992.

———. *Patrolling Chaos: The U.S. Border Patrol in Deep South Texas.* Lubbock: Texas Tech University Press, 2004.

Márquez, Raquel R., and Harriett D. Romo, eds. *Transformations of la Familia on the U.S.-Mexico Border.* Notre Dame, IN: University of Notre Dame Press, 2008.

Martínez, Oscar J. *Border People: Life and Society in the U.S.-Mexico Borderlands.* Tucson: University of Arizona Press, 1994.

———. *Troublesome Border.* Rev. ed. Tucson: University of Arizona Press, 2006.

———, ed. *U.S.-Mexico Borderlands: Historical and Contemporary Perspectives.* Wilmington, DE: Scholarly Resources, 1996.

Mattingly, Doreen J., and Ellen R. Hansen, eds. *Women and Change at the U.S.-Mexico Border: Mobility, Labor, and Activism.* Tucson: University of Arizona Press, 2006.

O'Neil, Shannon K. *Two Nations Indivisible: Mexico, the United States, and the Road Ahead.* New York and Oxford: Oxford University Press, 2013.

Papademetriou, Demetrios G., and Deborah Waller Meyers, eds. *Caught in the Middle: Border Communities in the Era of Globalization.* Washington, D.C.: Carnegie Endowment for International Peace, 2001.

Pastor, Robert A. *The North American Idea: A Vision of a Continental Future.* New York: Oxford University Press, 2011.

Payan, Tony. *The Three U.S.-Mexico Border Wars: Drugs, Immigration, and Homeland Security.* Westport, CT: Praeger Security International, 2006.

Pugach, Marleen C. *On the Border of Opportunity: Education, Community, and Language at the U.S.-Mexico Line.* Mahwah, NJ: Lawrence Erlbaum Associates, 1998.

Quintana, Penelope J. E., Paul Ganster, Paula E. Stigler Granados, Gabriela Muñoz-Meléndez, Margarito QuinteroNúñez, and José Guillermo RodríguezVentura, "Risky Borders: Air Pollution and Health Effects at U.S.-Mexican Ports of Entry." *Journal of Borderlands Studies* (forthcoming 2015).

Richardson, Chad. *Batos, Bolillos, Pochos, and Pelados: Class and Culture on the South Texas Border.* Austin: University of Texas Press, 1999.

Ross, Stanley Robert, ed. *Views across the Border: The United States and Mexico.* Albuquerque: University of New Mexico Press, 1978.

Rotella, Sebastian. *Twilight on the Line: Underworlds and Politics at the U.S.-Mexico Border.* New York: W. W. Norton & Company, 1998.

Ruíz, Ramón E. *On the Rim of Mexico: Encounters of the Rich and Poor.* Boulder, CO: Westview Press, 1998.

Ruíz, Vicki L., and Susan Tiano, eds. *Women on the U.S.-Mexico Border: Responses to Change.* Boston: Allen & Unwin, 1987.

Sabet, Daniel M. *Nonprofits and Their Networks: Cleaning the Waters along Mexico's Northern Border.* Tucson: University of Arizona Press, 2008.

Sadowski-Smith, Claudia. *Border Fictions: Globalization, Empire, and Writing at the Boundaries of the United States.* Charlottesville: University of Virginia Press, 2008.

Sánchez Munguía, Vicente, ed., *The U.S.-Mexican Border Environment: Lining the All American Canal: Competition or Cooperation for Water in the U.S.-Mexican Border?* San Diego, CA: San Diego State University Press, 2006.

Schaefer, Agnes. *Security in Mexico: Implications for U.S. Policy Options.* Santa Monica: RAND Corporation, 2009.

Shirk, David A. *The Drug War in Mexico: Confronting a Shared Threat.* New York: Council on Foreign Relations, 2011.

Simon, Joel. *Endangered Mexico: An Environment on the Edge.* San Francisco: Sierra Club Books, 1997.

Spener, David, and Kathleen Staudt, eds. *The U.S.-Mexico Border: Transcending Division, Contesting Identities.* Boulder, CO: Lynne Reinner Publishers, 1998.

Staudt, Kathleen. *Violence and Activism at the Border: Gender, Fear, and Everyday Life in Ciudad Juarez.* Austin: University of Texas Press, 2008.

Staudt, Kathleen, Tony Payan, and Z. Anthony Kruszewski, eds. *Human Rights along the U.S.-Mexico Border: Gendered Violence and Insecurity.* Tucson: University of Arizona Press, 2009.

St. John, Rachel. *Line in the Sand: A History of the Western U.S.-Mexico Border.* Princeton, NJ: Princeton University Press, 2011.

Stoddard, Ellwyn R., and John Hedderson. *Trends and Patterns of Poverty along the U.S.-Mexico Border.* Las Cruces: Joint Border Research Institute, New Mexico State University, 1987.

Toro, María Celia. *Mexico's "War" on Drugs: Causes and Consequences.* Boulder, CO: Lynne Rienner Publishers, 1995.

Truett, Samuel. *Fugitive Landscapes: The Forgotten History of the U.S.-Mexico Borderlands.* New Haven, CT: Yale University Press, 2006.

Tuttle, Carolyn. *Mexican Women in American Factories: Free Trade and Exploitation on the Border.* Austin: University of Texas Press, 2012.

U.S. Bureau of Reclamation (USBR). "Colorado River Basin Water Supply and Demand Study," USBR, 2012, http://www.usbr.gov/lc/region/programs/crbstudy/finalreport/index.html.

Vila, Pablo. *Crossing Borders, Reinforcing Borders: Social Categories, Metaphors, and Narrative Identities on the U.S.-Mexico Border.* Austin: University of Texas Press, 2000.

Vilanova, Núra. *Writing Fiction from Northern Mexico.* San Diego, CA: San Diego State University Press, 2007.

Vulliamy, Ed. *Amexica: War along the Borderline.* New York: Farrar, Straus and Giroux, 2010.

Walker, William O. *Drugs in the Western Hemisphere: An Odyssey of Cultures in Conflict.* Wilmington, DE: Scholarly Resources, 1996.

Walsh, Casey. *Building the Borderlands: A Transnational History of Irrigated Cotton along the Mexico-Texas Border.* College Station: Texas A&M Press, 2008.

Wilder, M., G. Garfin, P. Ganster, H. Eakin, P. Romero-Lankao, F. Lara-Valencia, A. A. Cortez-Lara, S. Mumme, C. Neri, and F. Muñoz-Arriola. "Climate Change and U.S.-Mexico Border Communities." In *Assessment of Climate Change in the Southwest United States: A Report Prepared for the National Climate Assessment,* edited by G. Garfin, A. Jardine, R. Merideth, M. Black, and S. LeRoy, 340–84. A report by the Southwest Climate Alliance. Washington, D.C.: Island Press, 2013.

Wilson, Christopher E., and Erik Lee, eds. *The State of the Border Report: A Comprehensive Analysis of the U.S.-Mexico Border.* Washington, D.C.: Woodrow Wilson International Center for Scholars, 2013.

Wood, Andrew Grant, ed. *On the Border: Society and Culture between the United States and Mexico.* Lanham, MD: SR Books, 2004.

Wright, Richard, and Rafael Vela, eds. *Tijuana River Watershed Atlas/Atlas de la cuenca del Río Tijuana.* San Diego: Institute for Regional Studies of the Californias, San Diego State University, 2005.

REFERENCE

Lorey, David E., ed. *United States–Mexico Border Statistics since 1900.* Los Angeles: University of California, Los Angeles, Latin American Center Publications, 1990.

———, ed. *United States–Mexico Border Statistics since 1900: 1990 Update.* Los Angeles: University of California, Los Angeles, Latin American Center Publications, 1993.

Ochoa, Enrique C. "Constructing *Fronteras*: Teaching the History of the U.S.-Mexico Borderlands in the Age of Proposition 187 and Free Trade." *Radical History Review* 70 (1998): 116–28.

Stoddard, Ellwyn R., Richard L. Nostrand, and Jonathan P. West, eds. *Borderlands Sourcebook: A Guide to the Literature on Northern Mexico and the American Southwest.* Norman: University of Oklahoma Press, 1983.

Wastl-Walter, Doris. *The Ashgate Research Companion to Border Studies.* Burlington, VT: Ashgate, 2011.

INDEX

255

ABOUT THE AUTHORS

Paul Ganster is professor of history, director of the Institute for Regional Studies of the Californias, and director of the biological Field Stations Program at San Diego State University. He received his BA from Yale University and his PhD from the University of California, Los Angeles (UCLA). He is author of more than sixty articles, book chapters, and edited works on policy questions of the U.S.-Mexican border region, border environmental issues, Latin American social history, and comparative border studies. Ganster has been a visiting professor at the School of Economics of the Universidad Autónoma de Baja California in Tijuana. He is chair of the Good Neighbor Environmental Board, a federal panel that advises the president and Congress on U.S.-Mexican border environmental issues.

David E. Lorey received his PhD in Latin American social and cultural history from UCLA in 1990. Between 1989 and 1997 he directed the Program on Mexico and was visiting professor of history at UCLA. From 1997 to 2003 he directed the Latin American program at the William and Flora Hewlett Foundation. Currently, he runs a private consulting practice, working on strategic planning, fund-raising, and marketing with nonprofit organizations in a range of fields. Lorey's many publications include *Global Environmental Challenges for the Twenty-First Century: Resources, Consumption, and Sustainable Solutions* (2003).